Agile Application Security

Enabling Security in a Continuous Delivery Pipeline

Laura Bell, Michael Brunton-Spall,
Rich Smith, and Jim Bird

Beijing · Boston · Farnham · Sebastopol · Tokyo

Agile Application Security

by Laura Bell, Michael Brunton-Spall, Rich Smith, and Jim Bird

Published by O'Reilly Media, Inc., 1005 Gravenstein Highway North, Sebastopol, CA 95472.

O'Reilly books may be purchased for educational, business, or sales promotional use. Online editions are also available for most titles (*http://oreilly.com/safari*). For more information, contact our corporate/institutional sales department: 800-998-9938 or *corporate@oreilly.com*.

Editor: Courtney Allen	**Indexer:** Wendy Catalano
Production Editor: Colleen Cole	**Interior Designer:** David Futato
Copyeditor: Amanda Kersey	**Cover Designer:** Karen Montgomery
Proofreader: Sonia Saruba	**Illustrator:** Rebecca Demarest

September 2017:   First Edition

Revision History for the First Edition
2017-09-08:   First Release

See *http://oreilly.com/catalog/errata.csp?isbn=9781491938843* for release details.

978-1-491-93884-3

[LSI]

Table of Contents

Preface

Software is eating the world. Developers are the new kingmakers. The internet of things means there will be a computer in every light bulb.

These statements indicate the growing dominance of software development, to the point where most people in the world will never be further than a meter away from a computer, and we will expect much of our life to interact with computer assisted objects and environments all the time.

But this world comes with some dangers. In the old world of computing, security was often only considered in earnest for banking and government systems. But the rise of ubiquitous computing means a rise in the value that can be realized from the abuse of systems, which increases incentives for misuse, which in turn increases the risks systems face.

Agile software development techniques are becoming rapidly adopted in most organizations. By being responsive to change and dramatically lowering the cost of development, they provide a standard that we expect will continue to grow until the majority of software is built in an Agile manner.

However, security and Agile have not historically been great bedfellows.

Security professionals have had their hands full with the aforementioned government, ecommerce, and banking systems, trying to architect, test, and secure those systems, all in the face of a constantly evolving set of threats. Furthermore, what is often seen as the most fun and exciting work in security, the things that get covered on the tech blogs and the nightly news, is done by teams of professional hackers focusing on vulnerability research, exploit development, and stunt hacks.

You can probably name a few recent branded vulnerabilities like Heartbleed, Logjam, or Shellshock (or heaven forbid even recognize their logos), or recognize the teams of researchers who have achieved a jailbreak on the latest iPhones and Android devices. But when was the last time a new defensive measure or methodology had a *cool*, media-friendly name, or you picked up the name of a defender and builder?

Security professionals are lagging behind in their understanding and experience of Agile development, and that creates a gap that is scary for our industry.

Equally, Agile teams have rejected and thrown off the shackles of the past. No more detailed requirements specifications, no more system modeling, no more traditional Waterfall handoffs and control gates. The problem with this is that Agile teams have thrown the baby out with the bathwater. Those practices, while sometimes slow and inflexible, have demonstrated value over the years. They were done for a reason, and Agile teams in rejecting them can easily forget and dismiss their value.

This means that Agile teams rarely consider security as much as they should. Some of the Agile practices make a system more secure, but that is often a beneficial side effect rather than the purpose. Very few Agile teams have an understanding of the threats that face their system; they don't understand the risks they are taking; they don't track or do anything to control those risks; and they often have a poor understanding of who it even is that is attacking their creations.

Who Should Read This Book

We don't know if you are an Agile team leader, or a developer who is curious or wants to know more about security. Maybe you are a security practitioner who has just found an entire development team you didn't know existed and you want to know more.

This book was written with three main audiences in mind.

The Agile Practitioner

You live, breathe, and do Agile. You know your Scrum from your Kaizen, your test-driven-development from your feedback loop. Whether you are a Scrum Master, developer, tester, Agile coach, Product Owner, or customer proxy, you understand the Agile practices and values.

This book should help you understand what security is about, what threats exist, and the language that security practitioners use to describe what is going on. We'll help you understand how we model threats, measure risks, build software with security in mind, install software securely, and understand the operational security issues that come with running a service.

The Security Practitioner

Whether you are a risk manager, an information assurance specialist, or a security operations analyst, you understand security. You are probably careful how you use online services, you think about threats and risks and mitigations all of the time, and you may have even found new vulnerabilities and exploited them yourself.

This book should help you understand how software is actually developed in Agile teams, and what on earth those teams are talking about when they talk about sprints and stories. You will learn to see the patterns in the chaos, and that should help you interact with and influence the team. This book should show you where you can intervene or contribute that is most valuable to an Agile team and has the best effect.

The Agile Security Practitioner

From risk to sprints, you know it all. Whether you are a tool builder who is trying to help teams do security well, or a consultant who advises teams, this book is also for you. The main thing to get out of this book is to understand what the authors consider to be the growing measure of good practice. This book should help you be aware of others in your field, and of the ideas and thoughts and concepts that we are seeing pop up in organizations dealing with this problem. It should give you a good, broad understanding of the field and an idea for what to research or learn about next.

Navigating This Book

You could read this book from beginning to end, one chapter at a time. In fact, we recommend it; we worked hard on this book, and we hope that every chapter will contain something valuable to all readers, even if it's just our dry wit and amusing anecdotes!

But actually, we think that some chapters are more useful to some of you than others.

We roughly divided this book into three parts.

Part 1: Fundamentals

Agile and security are very broad fields, and we don't know what you already know. Especially if you come from one field, you might not have much knowledge or experience of the other.

If you are an Agile expert, we recommend first reading Chapter 1, *Getting Started with Security*, to be sure that you have a baseline understanding of security.

If you aren't doing Agile yet, or you are just starting down that road, then before we move on to the introduction to Agile, we recommend that you read Chapter 2, *Agile Enablers*. This represents what we think the basic practices are and what we intend to build upon.

Chapter 3, *Welcome to the Agile Revolution*, covers the history of Agile software development and the different ways that it can be done. This is mostly of interest to security experts or people who don't have that experience yet.

Part 2: Agile and Security

We then recommend that everybody starts with Chapter 4, *Working with Your Existing Agile Life Cycle*.

This chapter attempts to tie together the security practices that we consider, with the actual Agile development life cycle, and explains how to combine the two together.

Chapters 5 through 7 give an understanding of requirements and vulnerability management and risk management, which are more general practices that underpin the product management and general planning side of development.

Chapters 8 through 13 cover the various parts of a secure software development life cycle, from threat assessment, code review, testing, and operational security.

Part 3: Pulling It All Together

Chapter 14 looks at regulatory compliance and how it relates to security, and how to implement compliance in an Agile or DevOps environment.

Chapter 15 covers the cultural aspects of security. Yes, you could implement every one of the practices in this book, and the previous chapters will show you a variety of tools you can use to make those changes stick. Yet Agile is all about people, and the same is true of effective security programs: security is really cultural change at heart, and this chapter will provide examples that we have found to be effective in the real world.

For a company to change how it does security, it takes mutual support and respect between security professionals and developers for them to work closely together to build secure products. That can't be ingrained through a set of tools or practices, but requires a change throughout the organization.

Finally, Chapter 16 looks at what Agile security means to different people, and summarizes what each of us has learned about what works and what doesn't in trying to make teams Agile and secure.

Conventions Used in This Book

The following typographical conventions are used in this book:

Italic
:   Indicates new terms, URLs, email addresses, filenames, and file extensions.

`Constant width`
:   Used for program listings, as well as within paragraphs to refer to program elements such as variable or function names, databases, data types, environment

variables, statements, and keywords. If you see the ↵ at the end of a code line, this indicates the line continues on the next line.

Constant width bold
Shows commands or other text that should be typed literally by the user.

Constant width italic
Shows text that should be replaced with user-supplied values or by values determined by context.

 This element signifies a tip or suggestion.

 This element signifies a general note.

 This element indicates a warning or caution.

O'Reilly Safari

 *Safari* (formerly Safari Books Online) is a membership-based training and reference platform for enterprise, government, educators, and individuals.

Members have access to thousands of books, training videos, Learning Paths, interactive tutorials, and curated playlists from over 250 publishers, including O'Reilly Media, Harvard Business Review, Prentice Hall Professional, Addison-Wesley Professional, Microsoft Press, Sams, Que, Peachpit Press, Adobe, Focal Press, Cisco Press, John Wiley & Sons, Syngress, Morgan Kaufmann, IBM Redbooks, Packt, Adobe Press, FT Press, Apress, Manning, New Riders, McGraw-Hill, Jones & Bartlett, and Course Technology, among others.

For more information, please visit *http://oreilly.com/safari*.

How to Contact Us

Please address comments and questions concerning this book to the publisher:

O'Reilly Media, Inc.
1005 Gravenstein Highway North
Sebastopol, CA 95472
800-998-9938 (in the United States or Canada)
707-829-0515 (international or local)
707-829-0104 (fax)

We have a web page for this book, where we list errata, examples, and any additional information. You can access this page at *http://bit.ly/agile-application-security*.

To comment or ask technical questions about this book, send email to *bookquestions@oreilly.com*.

For more information about our books, courses, conferences, and news, see our website at *http://www.oreilly.com*.

Find us on Facebook: *http://facebook.com/oreilly*

Follow us on Twitter: *http://twitter.com/oreillymedia*

Watch us on YouTube: *http://www.youtube.com/oreillymedia*

Acknowledgments

First, thank you to our wonderful editors: Courtney Allen, Virgnia Wilson, and Nan Barber. We couldn't have got this done without all of you and the rest of the team at O'Reilly.

We also want to thank our technical reviewers for their patience and helpful insights: Ben Allen, Geoff Kratz, Pete McBreen, Kelly Shortridge, and Nenad Stojanovski.

And finally, thank you to our friends and families with putting up with *yet another* crazy project.

CHAPTER 1

Getting Started with Security

So what *is* security?

A deceptively simple question to ask, rather more complex to answer.

When first starting out in the world of security, it can be difficult to understand or to even to know what to look at first. The successful *hacks* you will read about in the news paint a picture of Neo-like adversaries who have a seemingly infinite range of options open to them with which to craft their highly complex attacks. When thought about like this, security can feel like a possibly unwinnable field that almost defies reason.

While it is true that security is a complex and ever-changing field, it is also true that there are some relatively simple first principles that, once understood, will be the undercurrent to all subsequent security knowledge you acquire. Approach security as a journey, not a destination—one that starts with a small number of fundamentals upon which you will continue to build iteratively, relating new developments back to familiar concepts.

With this in mind, and regardless of our backgrounds, it is important that we all understand some key security principles before we begin. We will also take a look at the ways in which security has traditionally been approached, and why that approach is no longer as effective as it once was now that Agile is becoming more ubiquitous.

Security for development teams tends to focus on information security (as compared to physical security like doors and walls, or personnel security like vetting procedures). Information security looks at security practices and procedures during the inception of a project, during the implementation of a system, and on through the operation of the system.

While we will be talking mostly about *information security* in this book, for the sake of brevity we will just use *security* to refer to it. If another part of the security discipline is being referred to, such as physical security, then it will be called out explicitly.

This Isn't Just a Technology Problem

As engineers we often discuss the technology choices of our systems and their environment. Security forces us to expand past the technology. Security can perhaps best be thought of as the overlap between that technology and the people who interact with it day-to-day as shown in Figure 1-1.

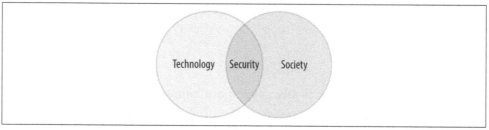

Figure 1-1. When society had less dependence on technology, the need for security was less

So what can this picture tell us? It can be simply viewed as an illustration that security is more than just about the technology and *must*, in its very definition, also include people.

People don't need technology to do bad things or take advantage of each other; such activities happened well before computers entered our lives; and we tend to just refer to this as *crime*. People have evolved for millennia to lie, cheat, and steal items of value to further themselves and their community. When people start interacting with technology, however, this becomes a potent combination of motivations, objectives, and opportunity. In these situations, certain motivated groups of people will use the concerted circumvention of technology to further some very human end goal, and it is this activity that security is tasked with preventing.

However, it should be noted that technological improvements have widened the fraternity of people who can commit such crime, whether that be by providing greater levels of instruction, or widening the reach of motivated criminals to cover worldwide services. With the internet, worldwide telecommunication, and other advances, you are much more easily attacked now than you could have been before, and for the perpetrators there is a far lower risk of getting caught. The internet and related technologies made the world a much smaller place and in doing so have made the asymmetries even starker—the costs have fallen, the paybacks increased, and the chance of being caught drastically reduced. In this new world, geographical distance to the richest targets has essentially been reduced to zero for attackers, while at the same time there is still the old established legal system of treaties and process needed for cross-jurisdictional investigations and extraditions—this aside from the varying definitions of what constitutes a computer crime in different regions. Technology and the internet also help shield perpetrators from identification: no longer do you need to be inside a bank to steal its money—you can be half a world away.

A Note on Terminology

Circumvention is used deliberately to avoid any implicit moral judgments whenever *insecurity* is discussed.

The more technologies we have in our lives, the more opportunities we have to both use and benefit from them. The flip side of this is that society's increasing reliance on technology creates greater opportunities, incentives, and benefits for its misuse. The greater our reliance on technology, the greater our need for that technology to be stable, safe, and available. When this stability and security comes into question, our businesses and communities suffer. The same picture can also help to illustrate this interdependence between the uptake of technology by society and the need for security in order to maintain its stability and safety, as shown in Figure 1-2.

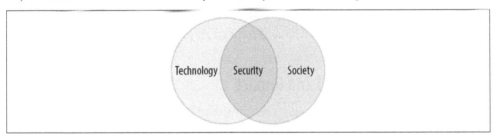

Figure 1-2. As society becomes increasingly dependent on technology, the need for security and impacts of its absence increase significantly

As technology becomes ever more present in the fabric of society, the approaches taken to thinking about its security become increasingly important.

A fundamental shortcoming of classical approaches to information security is failing to recognize that people are just as important as technology. This is an area we hope to provide a fresh perspective to in this book.

Not Just for Geeks

There was a time that security was the exclusive worry of government and geeks. Now, with the internet being an integral part of people's lives the world over, securing the technologies that underlie it is something that is pertinent to a larger part of society than ever before.

If you use technology, security matters because a failure in security can directly harm you and your communities.

If you build technology, you are now the champion of keeping it stable and secure so that we can improve our business and society on top of its foundation. No longer is security an area you can mentally outsource:

- You are responsible for considering the security of the technology.
- You provide for people to embrace security in their everyday lives.

Failure to accept this responsibility means the technology you build will be fundamentally flawed and fail in one of its primary functions.

Security Is About Risk

Security, or securing software more specifically, is about minimizing risk. It is the field in which we attempt to reduce the likelihood that our people, systems, and data will be used in a way that would cause financial or physical harm, or damage to our organization's reputation.

Vulnerability: Likelihood and Impact

Most security practices are about preventing bad things from happening to your information or systems. But risk calculation isn't about stopping things; it's about understanding what could happen, and how, so that you can prioritize your improvements.

To calculate risk you need to know what things are likely to happen to your organization and your system, how likely they are to happen, and the cost of them happening. This allows you to work out how much money and effort to spend on protecting against that stuff.

We Are All Vulnerable

Vulnerability is about exposure. Outside the security field, vulnerability is how we talk about being open to harm either physically or emotionally. In a systems and security sense, we use the word vulnerability to describe any flaw in a system, component, or process that would allow our data, systems, or people to be misused, exposed, or harmed in some way.

You may hear phrases such as, "a new vulnerability has been discovered in…software" or perhaps, "The attacker exploited a vulnerability in…" as you start to read about this area in more depth. In these examples, the vulnerability was a flaw in an application's construction, configuration or business logic that allowed an attacker to do something outside the scope of what was authorized or intended. The exploitation of the vulnerability is the actual act of exercising the flaw itself, or the way in which the problem is taken advantage of.

Not Impossible, Just Improbable

Likelihood is the way we measure how easy (or likely) it is that an attacker would be able (and motivated) to exploit a vulnerability.

Likelihood is a very subjective measurement and has to take into account many different factors. In a simple risk calculation you may see this simplified down to a number, but for clarity, here are the types of things we should consider when calculating likelihood:

Technical skill required to exploit the vulnerability
   Do you need to be a deep technical specialist, or will a passing high-level knowledge be enough?

Reliability
   Does the exploit work reliably? What about over the different versions, platforms, and architectures where the vulnerability may be found? The more reliable the exploit, the less likely attacks are to cause a side effect that is noticeable: this makes it a *safer* exploit for an attacker to use, as it can reduce the chances of detection.

Automation
   Does the exploitation of the vulnerability lend itself well to be automated? This can help its inclusion in things like exploit kits or self-propagating code (worms), which means you are more likely to be subject to indiscriminate exploit attempts.

Access
   Do you need to be have the ability to communicate directly with a particular system on a network or have a particular set of user privileges? Do you need to have already compromised one or more other parts of the system to make use of the vulnerability?

Motivation
   Would the end result of exploiting this vulnerability be enough to motivate someone into spending the time?

Measuring the Cost

Impact is the effect that exploiting a vulnerability or having your systems misused or breached in someway would have on you, your customers, and your organization.

For the majority of businesses, we measure impact in terms of money lost. This could be actual theft of funds (via credit card theft or fraud, for example), or it could be cost of recovering from a breach. Cost of recovery often includes not just addressing the vulnerability, but also:

- Responding to the incident itself
- Repairing other systems or data that may have been damaged or destroyed
- Implementing new approaches to help increase the security of the system in an effort to prevent a repeat
- Increased audit, insurance, and compliance costs
- Marketing costs and public relations
- Increased operating costs or less favorable rates from suppliers

At the more serious end of the scale are those of us who build control systems or applications that have direct impact on human lives. In those circumstances, measuring the impact of a security issue is much more personal, and may include death and injury to individuals or groups of people.

In a world where we are rapidly moving toward automation of driving and many physical roles in society, computerized medical devices, and computers in every device in our homes, the impact of security vulnerabilities will move toward an issue of protecting people rather than just money or reputation.

Risk Can Be Minimized, Not Avoided

We are used to the idea that we can remove the imperfections from our systems. Bugs can be squashed and inefficiencies removed by clever design. In fact, we can perfect the majority of things we build and control ourselves.

Risk is a little different.

Risk is about external influences to our systems, organizations, and people. These influences are mostly outside of our control (economists often refer to such things as *externalities*). They could be groups or individuals with their own motivations and plans, vendors and suppliers with their own approaches and constraints, or environmental factors.

As we don't control risk or its causes, we can never fully avoid it. It would be an impossible and fruitless task to attempt to do so. Instead we must focus on understanding our risks, minimizing them (and their impacts) where we can, and maintaining watch across our domain for new evolving or emerging risks.

The acceptance of risk is also perfectly OK, as long as it is mindful and the risk being accepted is understood. Blindly accepting risks, however, is a recipe for disaster and is something you should be on the lookout for, as it can occur all too easily.

An Imperfect World Means Hard Decisions

While we are on this mission to minimize and mitigate risks, we also have be aware that we live in an environment of limits and finite resources. Whether we like it or not, there are only 24 hours in a day, and we all need to sleep somewhere in that period. Our organizations all have budgets and a limited number of people and resources to throw at problems.

As a result, there are few organizations that can actually address every risk they face. Most will only be able to mitigate or reduce a small number. Once our resources are spent, we can only make a list of the risks that remain, do our best to monitor the situation, and understand the consequence of not addressing them.

The smaller our organizations are, the more acute this can be. Remember though, even the smallest teams with the smallest budget can do something. Being small or resource poor is not an excuse for doing nothing, but an opportunity to do the best you can to secure your systems, using existing technologies and skills in creative ways.

Choosing which risks we address can be hard and isn't a perfect science. Throughout this book, we should give you tools and ideas for understanding and measuring your risks more accurately so that you can make the best use of however much time and however many resources you have.

Threat Actors and Knowing Your Enemy

So who or what are we protecting against?

While we would all love to believe that it would take a comic-book caliber super villain to attack us or our applications, we need to face a few truths.

There is a range of individuals and groups that could or would attempt to exploit vulnerabilities in your applications or processes. Each has their own story, motivations, and resources; and we need to know how these things come together to put our organizations at risk.

There Is an Attacker for Everyone

In recent years we have been caught up with using the word *cyber* to describe any attacker that approaches via our connected technologies or over the internet. This has led to the belief that there is only one kind of attacker and that they probably come from a nation-state actor somewhere "far away."

What Is Cyber?

Cyber is a term that, despite sounding like it originated from a William Gibson novel, actually emanated from the US military.

The military considered there to be four theaters of war where countries can legally fight: land, sea, air, and space. When the internet started being used by nations to interfere and interact with each other, they recognized that there was a new theater of war: cyber, and from there the name has stuck.

Once the government started writing cyber strategies and talking about cyber crime, it was inevitable that large vendors would follow the nomenclature, and from there we have arrived at a place where it is commonplace to hear about the various cybers and their associated threats. Unfortunately cyber has become the all-encompassing marketing term used to both describe threats and brand solutions. This commercialization and over-application has had the effect of diluting the term and making it something that has become an object of derision for many in the security community. In particular, those who are more technically and/or offensively focused often use "cyber" as mockery.

While some of us (including more than one of your authors) might struggle with using the word "cyber," it is undeniable that it is a term well understood by nonsecurity and nontechnical people; alternate terms such as "information security," "infosec," "commsec," or "digital security" are all far more opaque to many. With this in mind, if using "cyber" helps you get bigger and more points across to those who are less familiar with the security space or whose roles are more focused on PR and marketing, then so be it. When in more technical conversations or interacting with people more toward the hacker end of the infosec spectrum, be aware that using the term may devalue your message or render it mute altogether.

That's simply not the case.

There are many types of attackers out there, the young, impetuous, and restless; automated scripts and roaming search engines looking for targets; disgruntled ex-employees; organized crime; and the politically active. The range of attackers is much more complex than our "cyber" wording would allow us to believe.

Motivation, Resources, Access

When you are trying to examine the attackers that might be interested in your organization you must consider both your organization's systems and its people. When you do this, there are three different aspects of the attacker's profile or persona worth considering:

1. Their motivations and objectives (why they want to attack and what they hope to gain)
2. Their resources (what they can do, what they can use to do it, and the time they have available to invest)
3. Their access (what they can get hold of, into, or information from)

When we try to understand which attacker profiles our organization should protect against, how likely each is to attack, and what impact it would have, we have to look at all of these attributes in the context of our organization, its values, practices, and operations.

We will cover this subject in much more detail as we learn to create security personas and integrate them into our requirements capture and testing regimes.

Security Values: Protecting Our Data, Systems, and People

We have a right (and an expectation) that when we go about our days and interact with technologies and systems, we will not come to harm while our data remains intact and private.

Security is how we achieve this and we get it by upholding a set of values.

Know What You Are Trying to Protect

Before anything else, stop for a second and understand *what* it is that you are trying to secure, what are the crown jewels in your world, and where are they kept? It is surprising how many people embark on their security adventure without this understanding, and as such waste a lot of time and money trying to protect the wrong things.

Confidentiality, Integrity, and Availability

Every field has its traditional acronyms, and *confidentiality, integrity, and availability* (CIA) is a treasure in traditional security fields. It is used to describe and remember the three tenets of secure systems—the features that we strive to protect.

Confidentiality: Keep It Secret

There are very few systems now that allow all people to do all things. We separate our application users into roles and responsibilities. We want to ensure that only those people we can trust, who have authenticated and been authorized to act, can access and interact with our data.

Maintaining this control is the essence of confidentiality.

Integrity: Keep It Safe

Our systems and applications are built around data. We store it, process it, and share it in dozens of ways as part of normal operations.

When taking responsibility for this data, we do so under the assumption that we will keep it in a controlled state. That from the moment we are entrusted with data, we understand and can control the ways in which is is modified (who can change it, when it can be changed, and in what ways). Maintaining data integrity is not about keeping data preserved and unchanged; it is about having it subjected to a controlled and predictable set of actions such that we understand and preserve its current state.

Availability: Keeping the Doors Open and the Lights On

A system that can't be accessed or used in the way that it was intended is no use to anyone. Our businesses and lives rely on our ability to interact with and access data and systems on a nearly continuous basis.

The not-so-much witty, as cynical among us will say that to secure a system well, we should power it down, encase it in concrete, and drop it to the bottom of the ocean. This, however, wouldn't really help us maintain the requirement for availability.

Security requires that we keep our data, systems, and people safe without getting in the way of interacting with them.

This means finding a balance between the controls (or measures) we take to restrict access or protect information and the functionality we expose to our users as part of our application. As we will discuss, it is this balance that provides a big challenge in our information sharing and always-connected society.

Nonrepudiation

Nonrepudiation is a proof of both the origin and integrity of data; or put another way, is the assurance that an activity cannot be denied as having been taken. Nonrepudiation is the counterpart to auditability, which taken together provide the foundation upon which every activity in our system—every change and every task—should be traceable to an individual or an authorized action.

This mechanism of linking activity to a usage narrative or an individual's behavior gives us the ability to tell the story of our data. We can recreate and step through the changes and accesses made, and build a timeline. This timeline can help us identify suspicious activity, investigate security incidents or misuse, and even debug functional flaws in our systems.

Compliance, Regulation, and Security Standards

One of the main drivers for security programs in many organizations is compliance with legal or industry-specific regulatory frameworks. These dictate how our businesses are required to operate, and how we need to design, build, and operate our systems.

Love them or hate them, regulations have been—and continue to be—the catalyst for security change, and often provide us with the management buy-in and support that we need to drive security initiatives and changes. Compliance "musts" can sometimes be the only way to convince people to do some of the tough but necessary things required for security and privacy.

Something to be eyes-wide-open about from the outset is that compliance and regulation are related but distinct from security. You can be compliant and insecure, as well as secure and noncompliant. In an ideal world, you will be *both* compliant and secure; however, it is worth noting that one does not necessarily ensure the other.

These concepts are so important, in fact, that Chapter 14, *Compliance* is devoted to them.

Common Security Misconceptions or Mistakes

When learning about something, anti-patterns can be just as useful as patterns; understanding what something *is not* helps you take steps toward understanding what it is.

What follows below is an (almost certainly incomplete) collection of common misconceptions that people have about security. When you start looking for them, you will see them exhibited with an often worrying frequency, not only in the tech industry, but also in the mass media and your workplace in general.

Security Is Absolute

Security is not black and white; however, the concept of something being secure or insecure is one that is chased and stated countless times per day. For any sufficiently complex system, a statement of (in)security in an absolute sense is incredibly difficult, if not impossible, to make, as it all depends on context.

The goal of a *secure* system is to ensure the appropriate level of control is put in place to mitigate the threats you see are relevant to that system's use case. If the use case changes, so do the controls that are needed to render that system secure. Likewise, if the threats the system faces change, the controls must evolve to take into account the changes.

Security from who? Security against what? and *How could that mitigation be circumvented?* are all questions that should be on the tip of your tongue when considering the security of any system.

Security Is a Point That Can Be Reached

No organization or system will ever be "secure." There is no merit badge to earn, and nobody will come and tell you that your security work is done and you can go home now. Security is a culture, a lifestyle choice if you prefer, and a continuous approach to understanding and reacting to the world around us. This world and its influences on us are always changing, and so must we.

It is much more useful to think of security as being a vector to follow rather than a point to be reached. Vectors have a size and a direction, and you should think about the direction you want to go in pursuit of security and how fast you'd like to chase it. However, it's a path you will continue to walk forever.

The classic security focus is summed up by the old joke about two men out hunting when they stumble upon a lion. The first man stops to do up his shoes, and the second turns to him and cries, "Are you crazy? You can't outrun a lion." The first man replies, "I don't have to outrun the lion. I just have to outrun you."

Your systems will be secure if the majority of attackers would get more benefit by attacking somebody else. For most organizations, actually affecting the attackers' motivations or behavior is impossible, so your best defense is to make it so difficult or expensive to attack you that it's not worth it.

Security Is Static

Security tools, threats, and approaches are always evolving. Just look at how software development has changed in the last five years. Think about how many new languages and libraries have been released and how many conferences and papers have been presented with new ideas. Security is no different. Both the offensive (attacker) security worlds and the defensive are continually updating their approaches and developing new techniques. As quickly as the attackers discover a new vulnerability and weaponize it, the defenders spring to action and develop mitigations and patches. It's a field where you can't stop learning or trying, much like software development.

Security Requires Special [Insert Item/Device/Budget]

Despite the rush of vendors and specialists available to bring security to your organization and systems, the real truth is you don't need anything special to get started with security. Very few of the best security specialists have a certificate or special status that says they have passed a test; they just live and breathe their subject every day. Doing security is about attitude, culture, and approach. Don't wait for the perfect time, tool, or training course to get started. Just do something.

As you progress on your security journey, you will inevitably be confronted by vendors who want to sell you all kinds of solutions that will do the security for you. While there are many tools that can make meaningful contributions to your overall security, don't fall into the trap of adding to an ever-growing pile. Complexity is the enemy of security, and more things almost always means more complexity (even if those *things* are security things). A rule of thumb followed by one of the authors of this book is not to add a new solution unless it lets you decommission two, which may be something to keep in mind.

Let's Get Started

If you picked up this book, there is a good chance that you are either a developer who wants to know more about this security thing, or you are a security geek who feels you should learn some more about this Agile thing you hear all the developers rabbiting on about. (If you don't fall into either of these groups, then we'll assume you have your own, damn fine reasons for reading an Agile security book and just leave it at that.)

One of the main motivations for writing this book was that, despite the need for developers and security practitioners to deeply understand each other's rationale, motivations, and goals, the reality we have observed over the years is that such understanding (and dare we say empathy) is rarely the case. What's more, things often go beyond merely just not quite understanding each other and step into the realm of actively trying to minimize interactions; or worse, actively undermining the efforts of their counterparts.

It is our hope that some of the perspectives and experience captured in this book will help remove some of the misunderstandings, and potentially even distrust, that exist between developers and security practitioners, and shine a light into *what the others do and why*.

CHAPTER 2

Agile Enablers

Much of this book is written to help security catch up in an Agile world. We have worked in organizations that are successfully delivering with Agile methodologies, but we also work with companies that are still getting to grips with Agile and DevOps.

Many of the security practices in this book will work regardless of whether or not you are doing Agile development, and no matter how effectively your organization has embraced Agile. However, there are some important precursor behaviors and practices which enable teams to get maximum value from Agile development, as well as from the security techniques that we outline in this book.

All these enabling techniques, tools, and patterns are common in high-functioning, Agile organizations. In this chapter, we will give an overview of each technique and how it builds on the others to enhance Agile development and delivery. You'll find more information on these subjects further on in the book.

Build Pipeline

The first, and probably the most important of these enabling techniques from a development perspective, is the concept of a *build pipeline*. A build pipeline is an automated, reliable, and repeatable way of producing consistent deployable artifacts.

The key feature of a build pipeline is that whenever the source code is changed, it is possible to initiate a build process that is reliably and repeatably consistent.

Some companies invest in repeatable builds to the point where the same build on different machines at different times will produce exactly the same binary output, but many organizations simply instantiate a build machine or build machines that can be used reliably.

The reason this is important is because it gives confidence to the team that all code changes have integrity. We know what it is like to work without build pipelines, where developers create release builds on their own desktops, and mistakes such as forgetting to integrate a coworker's changes frequently cause regression bugs in the system.

If you want to move faster and deploy more often, you must be absolutely confident that you are building the entire project correctly every time.

The build pipeline also acts as a single consistent location for gateway reviews. In many pre-Agile companies, gateway reviews are conducted by installing the software and manually testing it. Once you have a build pipeline, it becomes much easier to automate those processes, using computers to do the checking for you.

Another benefit of build pipelines is that you can go back in time and check out older versions of the product and build them reliably, meaning that you can test a specific version of the system that might exhibit known issues and check patches against it.

Automating and standardizing your build pipeline reduces the risk and cost of making changes to the system, including security patches and upgrades. This means that you can close your window of exposure to vulnerabilities much faster.

However, just because you can compile and build the system fast and repeatedly doesn't mean it will work reliably. For that you will need to use *automated testing*.

Automated Testing

Testing is an important part of most software quality assurance programs. It is also a high source of costs, delays, and wastes in many traditional programs.

Test scripts take time to design and write, and more time to run against your systems. Many organizations need days or weeks of testing time, and more time to fix and retest the bugs that are found in testing before they can finally release.

When testing takes weeks of work, it is impossible to release code into test any faster than the tests take to execute. This means that code changes tend to get batched up, making the releases bigger and more complicated, which necessitates even more testing, which necessitates longer test times, in a negative spiral.

However, much of the testing done by typical user acceptance testers following checklists or scripts adds little value and can be (and should be) automated.

Automated testing generally follows the *test pyramid*, where most tests are low level, cheap, fast to execute, simple to automate, and easy to change. This reduces the team's dependence on end-to-end acceptance tests, which are expensive to set up, slow to run, hard to automate, and even harder to maintain.

As we'll see in Chapter 11, modern development teams can take advantage of a variety of automated testing tools and techniques: unit testing, *test-driven development* (TDD), *behavior-driven design* (BDD), integration testing through service virtualization, and full-on user acceptance testing. Automated test frameworks, many of which are open source, allow your organization to capture directly into code the rules for how the system should behave.

A typical system might execute tens of thousands of automated unit and functional tests in a matter of seconds, and perform more complex integration and acceptance testing in only a few minutes.

Each type of test achieves a different level of confidence:

Unit tests
> These tests use white-box testing techniques to ensure that code modules work as the author intended. They require no running system, and generally test the inputs to expected outputs or expected side effects. Good unit tests will also test boundary conditions and known error conditions.

Functional tests
> These tests test whole suites of functions. They often don't require a running system, but they do require some setup, tying together many of the code modules. In a system comprised of many subsystems, they check a single subsystem, ensuring each subsystem works as expected. These tests try to model real-life case scenarios using known test data and the common actions that system users will perform.

Integration tests
> These tests are the start of standing up an entire system. They check that all the connecting configuration works, and that the subsystems communicate with each other properly. In many organizations, integration testing is performed only on internal services, so external systems are *stubbed* with fake versions that behave in consistent ways. This makes testing more repeatable.

System testing
> This is the standing up of a fully integrated system, with external integrations and accounts. These tests ensure that the whole system runs as expected, and that core functions or features work correctly from end-to-end.

Automation gets harder the further down the table you go, but here are the benefits of testing that way:

Speed

Automated tests (especially unit tests) can be executed often without needing user interfaces or slow network calls. They can also be parallelized, so that thousands of tests can be run in mere seconds.

Consistency

Manual testers, even when following checklists, may miss a test or perform tests incorrectly or inconsistently. Automated tests always perform the same actions in the same way each time. This means that variability is dramatically reduced in testing, far reducing the false positives (and more important, the false negatives) possible in manual testing.

Repeatability

Automated tests, since they are fast and consistent, can be relied on by developers each time that they make changes. Some Agile techniques even prescribe writing a test first, which will fail, and then implementing the function to make the test pass. This helps prevent regressions, and in the case of test-driven development, helps to define the outward behavior as the primary thing under test.

Auditability

Automated tests have to be coded. This code can be kept in version control along with the system under test, and undergoes the same change control mechanisms. This means that you can track a change in system behavior by looking at the history of the tests to see what changed, and what the reason for the change was.

These properties together give a high level of confidence that the system does what its implementers intended (although not necessarily what was asked for or the users wanted, which is why it is so important to get software into production quickly and get real feedback). Furthermore, it gives a level of confidence that whatever changes have been made to the code have not had an unforeseen effect on other parts of the system.

Automated testing is not a replacement for other quality assurance practices, but it does massively increase the confidence of the team to move fast and make changes to the system. It also allows any manual testing and reviews to focus on the high-value acceptance criteria.

Furthermore, the tests, if well written and maintained, are valuable documentation for what the system is intended to do.

Naturally, automated testing combines well with a build pipeline to ensure that every build has been fully tested, automatically, as a result of being built. However, to really get the benefits of these two techniques, you'll want to tie them together to get *continuous integration.*

Automated Security Testing

It's common and easy to assume that you can automate all of your security testing using the same techniques and processes.

While you can—and should—automate security testing in your build pipelines (and we'll explain how to do this in Chapter 12), it's nowhere near as easy as the testing outlined here.

While there are good tools for security testing that can be run as part of the build, most security tools are hard to use effectively, difficult to automate, and tend to run significantly slower than other testing tools.

We recommend against starting with just automated security tests, unless you have already had success automating functional tests and know how to use your security tools well.

Continuous Integration

Once we have a build pipeline, ensuring that all artifacts are created consistently and an automated testing capability that ensures basic quality checks, we can combine those two systems. This is most commonly called *continuous integration* (CI), but there's a bit more to this practice than just that.

The key to continuous integration is the word "continuous." The idea of a CI system is that it constantly monitors the state of the code repository, and if there has been a change, automatically triggers building the artifact and then testing the artifact.

In some organizations, the building and testing of an artifact can be done in seconds, while in larger systems or more complex build-test pipelines, it can take several minutes to perform. Where the times get longer, teams tend to start to separate out tests and steps, and run them in parallel to maintain fast feedback loops.

If the tests and checks all pass, the output of continuous integration is an artifact that could be deployed to your servers after each code commit by a developer. This gives almost instantaneous feedback to the developer that he hasn't made a mistake or broken anybody else's work.

This also provides the capability for the team to maintain a healthy, ready-to-deploy artifact at all times, meaning that emergency patches or security responses can be applied easily and quickly.

However, when you release the artifact, the environment you release it to needs to be consistent and working, which leads us to *infrastructure as code.*

Infrastructure as Code

While the application or product can be built and tested on a regular basis, it is far less common for the systems infrastructure to go through this process—until now.

Traditionally, the infrastructure of a system is purchased months in advance, and is relatively fixed. However the advent of cloud computing and *programmable configuration management* means that it is now possible, and even common, to manage your infrastructure in code repositories.

There are many different ways of doing this, but the common patterns are that you maintain a code repository that defines the desired state for the system. This will include information on operating systems, hostnames, network definitions, firewall rules, installed application sets, and so forth. This code can be executed at any time to put the system into a desired state, and the configuration management system will make the necessary changes to your infrastructure to ensure that this happens.

This means that making a change to a system, whether opening a firewall rule or updating a software version of a piece of infrastructure, will look like a code change. It will be coded, stored in a code repository (which provides change management and tracking), and reliably and repeatably rolled out.

This code is versioned, reviewed, and tested in the same way that your application code is. This gives the same levels of confidence in infrastructure changes that you have over your application changes.

Most configuration management systems regularly inspect the system and infrastructure, and if they notice any differences, are able to either warn or proactively set the system back to the desired state.

Using this approach, you can audit your runtime environment by analyzing the code repository rather than having to manually scan and assess your infrastructure. It also gives confidence of repeatability between environments. How often have you known software to work in the development environment but fail in production because somebody had manually made a change in development and forgotten to promote that change through into production?

By sharing much of the infrastructure code between production and development, we can track and maintain the smallest possible gap between the two environments and ensure that this doesn't happen.

Configuration Management Does Not Replace Security Monitoring!

While configuration management does an excellent job of keeping the operating environment in a consistent and desired state, it is not intended to monitor or alert on changes to the environment that may be associated with the actions of an adversary or an ongoing attack.

Configuration management tools check the actual state of the environment against the desired state on a periodic basis (e.g., every 30 minutes). This leaves a window of exposure for an adversary to operate in, where configurations could be changed, capitalized upon, and reverted, all without the configuration management system noticing the changes.

Security monitoring/alerting and configuration management systems are built to solve different problems, and it's important to not confuse the two.

It is of course possible, and desirable by high-performing teams, to apply build pipelines, automated testing, and continuous integration onto the infrastructure itself, ensuring that you have a high confidence that your infrastructure changes will work as intended.

Once you know you have consistent and stable infrastructure to deploy to, you need to ensure that the act of releasing the software is repeatable, which leads to *release management*.

Release Management

A common issue in projects is that the deployment and release processes for promoting code into production can fill a small book, with long lists of individual steps and checks that must be carried out in a precise order to ensure that the release is smooth.

These runbooks are often the last thing to be updated and so contain errors or omissions; and because they are executed rarely, time spent improving them is not a priority.

To make releases less painful and error prone, Agile teams try to release more often. Procedures that are regularly practiced and executed tend to be well maintained and accurate. They are also obvious candidates to be automated, making deployment and release processes even more consistent, reliable, and efficient.

Releasing small changes more often reduces operational risks as well as security risks. As we'll explain more in this book, small changes are easier to understand, review, and test, reducing the chance of serious security mistakes getting into production.

These processes should be followed in all environments to ensure that they work reliably, and if automated, can be hooked into the continuous integration system. If this is done, we can move toward a continuous delivery or continuous deployment approach, where a change committed to the code repository can pass through the build pipeline and its automated testing stages and be automatically deployed, possibly even into production.

Understanding Continuous Delivery

Continuous delivery and continuous deployment are subtly different.

Continuous delivery ensures that changes are always ready to be deployed to production by automating and auditing build, test, packaging, and deployment steps so that they are executed consistently for every change.

In continuous deployment, changes automatically run through the same build and test stages, and are automatically and immediately promoted to production if all the steps pass. This is how organizations like Amazon and Netflix achieve high rates of change.

If you want to understand the hows and whys of continuous delivery, and get into the details of how to set up your continuous delivery pipeline properly, you need to read Dave Farley and Jezz Humble's book, *Continuous Delivery* (*https://continuousdelivery.com/*) (Addison-Wesley).

One of us worked on a team that deployed changes more than a hundred times each day, where the time between changing code and seeing it in production was under 30 seconds.

However, this is an extreme example from an experienced team that had been working this way for years. Most teams that we come into contact with are content to reach turnaround times of under 30 minutes, and 1 to 5 deploys a day, or even as few as 2 to 3 times a month.

Even if you don't go all the way to continuously deploying each change to production, by automating the release process you take out human mistakes, and you gain repeatability, consistency, speed, and auditability.

This gives you confidence that deploying a new release of software won't cause issues in production, because the build is tested, and the release process is tested, and all the steps have been exercised and proven to work.

Furthermore, built-in auditability means you can see exactly who decided to release something and what was contained in that change, meaning that should an error occur, it is much easier to identify and fix.

It's also much more reliable in an emergency situation. If you urgently need to patch a software security bug, which would you feel more confident about: a patch that had to bypass much of your manual testing and be deployed by someone who hasn't done that in a number of months, or a patch that has been built and tested the same as all your other software and deployed by the same script that does tens of deploys a day?

Moving the concept of a *security fix* to be no different than any other code change is huge in terms of being able to get fixes rapidly applied and deployed, and automation is key to being able to make that mental step forward.

But now we can release easily and often, we need to ensure that teams don't interfere with each other, for that we need *visible tracking*.

Visible Tracking

Given this automated pipeline or pathway to production, it becomes critical to know what is going to go down that path, and for teams to not interfere with each other's work.

Despite all of this testing and automation, there are always possible errors, often caused by dependencies in work units. One piece of work might be reliant on another piece of work being done by another team. In these more complex cases, it's possible that work can be integrated out of order and make its way to production before the supporting work is in place.

Almost every Agile methodology highly prioritizes team communication, and the most common mechanism for this is big *visible tracking* of work. This might be Post-it notes or index cards on a wall, or a Kanban board, or it might be an electronic *story tracker*; but whatever it is, there are common requirements:

Visible
Everybody on the team and related teams should be able to see at a glance what is being worked on and what is in the pathway to production.

Up-to-date and complete
For this information to be useful and reliable, it must be complete and current. Everything about the project—the story backlog, bugs, vulnerabilities, work in progress, schedule milestones and velocity, cycle time, risks, and the current status of the build pipeline—should be available in one place and updated in real-time.

Simple
This is not a system to track all the detailed requirements for each piece of work. Each item should be a placeholder that represents the piece of work, showing a few major things, who owns it, and what state it is in.

Of course having the ability to see what work people are working on is no use if the work itself isn't valuable, which brings us to *centralized feedback*.

Centralized Feedback

Finally, if you have an efficient pipeline to production, and are able to automatically test that your changes haven't broken your product, you need some way to monitor the effectiveness of the changes you make. You need to be able to monitor the system, and in particular how it is working, to understand your changes.

This isn't like system monitoring, where you check whether the machines are working. It is instead *value chain* monitoring: metrics that are important to the team, to the users of the system, and to the business, e.g., checking conversion rate of browsers to buyers, dwell time, or clickthrough rates.

The reason for this is that highly effective Agile teams are constantly changing their product in response to feedback. However, to optimize that cycle time, the organization needs to know what feedback to collect, and more specifically, whether the work actually delivered any value.

Knowing that a team did 10, 100, or 1000 changes is pointless unless you can tie that work back to meaningful work for the organization.

Indicators vary a lot by context and service, but common examples might include value for money, revenue per transaction, conversion rates, dwell time, or mean time to activation. These values should be monitored and displayed on the visible dashboards that enable the team to see historical and current values.

Knowing whether your software actually delivers business value, and makes a visible difference to business metrics, helps you to understand that *the only good code is deployed code*.

The Only Good Code Is Deployed Code

Software engineering and Agile development is not useful in and of itself. It is only valuable if it helps your company achieve its aims, whether that be profit or behavioral change in your users.

A line of code that isn't in production is not only entirely valueless to the organization, but also a net liability, since it slows down development and adds complexity. Both have a negative effect on the security of the overall system.

Agile practices help us shorten the pathway to production, by recognizing that quick turnaround of code is the best way to get value from the code that we write.

This of course all comes together when you consider security in your Agile process. Any security processes that slow down the path to production, without significant business gains, are a net liability for the organization and encourage value-driven teams to route around them.

Security is critically involved in working out what the Definition of *Done* is for an Agile team, ensuring that the team has correctly taken security considerations into account. But security is only one voice in the discussion, responsible for making sure that the team is aware of risks, and enable the business to make informed decisions about these risks.

We hope that the rest of this book will help you understand how and where security can fit into this flow, and give you ideas for doing it well in your organization.

Operating Safely and at Speed

What happens if you can't follow all of these practices?

There are some environments where regulations prevent releasing changes to production without legal sign-off, which your lawyers won't agree to do multiple times per day or even every week. Some systems hold highly confidential data which the developers are not expected or perhaps not even allowed to have access to, which puts constraints on the roles that they can play in supporting and running the system. Or you might be working on legacy enterprise systems that cannot be changed to support continuous delivery or continuous deployment.

None of these techniques are fundamentally required to be Agile, and you don't need to follow all of them to take advantage of the ideas in this book. But if you are aren't following most of these practices to some extent, you need to understand that you will be missing some levels of assurance and safety to operate at speed.

You can still move fast without this high level of confidence, but you are taking on unnecessary risks in the short term, such as releasing software with critical bugs or vulnerabilities, and almost certainly building up technical debt and operational risks over the longer term. You will also lose out on some important advantages, such as being able to minimize your time for resolving problems, and closing your window of security exposure by taking the human element out of the loop as much as possible.

It's also important to understand that you probably can't implement all these practices at once in a team that is already established in a way of working, and you probably shouldn't even try. There are many books that will help you to adopt Agile and explain how to deal with the cultural and organizational changes that are required, but we recommend that you work with the team to help it understand these ideas and practices, how they work, and why they are valuable, and implement them iteratively, continuously reviewing and improving as you go forward.

The techniques described in this chapter build on each other to create fast cycle times and fast feedback loops:

1. By standardizing and automating your build pipeline, you establish a consistent foundation for the other practices.

2. Test automation ensures that each build is correct.

3. Continuous integration automatically builds and tests each change to provide immediate feedback to developers as they make changes.

4. Continuous delivery extends continuous integration to packaging and deployment, which in turn requires that these steps are also standardized and automated.

5. Infrastructure as code applies the same engineering practices and workflows to making infrastructure configuration changes.

6. To close the feedback loop, you need metrics and monitoring at all stages, from development to production, and from production back to development.

As you continue to implement and improve these practices, your team will be able to move faster and with increasing confidence. These practices also provide a control framework that you can leverage for standardizing and automating security and compliance, which is what we will explore in the rest of this book.

CHAPTER 3

Welcome to the Agile Revolution

For a number of years now, startups and web development teams have been following Agile software development methods. More recently, we've seen governments, enterprises, and even organizations in heavily regulated environments transitioning to Agile. But what actually is it? How can you possibly build secure software when you haven't even fleshed out the design or requirements properly?

Reading this book, you may be a long-time security professional who has never worked with an Agile team. You might be a security engineer working with an Agile or DevOps team. Or you may be a developer or team lead in an Agile organization who wants to understand how to deal with security and compliance requirements. No matter what, this chapter should ensure that you have a good grounding in what your authors know about Agile, and that we are all on the same page.

Agile: A Potted Landscape

Agile (whether spelled with a small "a" or a big "A") means different things to different people. Very few Agile teams work in the same way, partly because there is a choice of Agile methodologies, and partly because all Agile methodologies encourage you to adapt and improve the process to better suit your team and your context.

"Agile" is a catch-all term for a variety of different iterative and incremental software development methodologies. It was created as a term when a small group of thought leaders went away on a retreat to a ski lodge in Snowbird, Utah, back in 2001 to discuss issues with modern software development. Large software projects routinely ran over budget and over schedule, and even with extra time and money, most projects still failed to meet business requirements. The people at Snowbird had recognized this and were all successfully experimenting with simpler, faster, and more effective ways to deliver software. The "Agile Manifesto" (*http://agilemanifesto.org/*) is one of the few things that the 17 participants could agree on.

Manifesto for Agile Software Development

We are uncovering better ways of developing software by doing it and helping others do it. Through this work we have come to value:

Individuals and interactions over processes and tools

Working software over comprehensive documentation

Customer collaboration over contract negotiation

Responding to change over following a plan

That is, while there is value in the items on the right, we value the items on the left more.

© 2001, the Agile Manifesto authors
this declaration may be freely copied in any form, but only in its entirety through this notice.

What is critical about the manifesto is that these are simply value statements. The signatories didn't believe that working software was the be-all and end-all of everything, but merely that when adopting a development methodology, any part of the process had to value the first values more than the second ones.

For example, negotiating a contract is important, but only if it helps encourage customer collaboration rather than replace customer collaboration.

Behind the value statements are 12 principles (*https://www.agilealliance.org/agile101/12-principles-behind-the-agile-manifesto/*) which form the backbone of the majority of Agile methodologies.

These principles tell us that Agile methods are about delivering software in regular increments, embracing changes to requirements instead of trying to freeze them up front, and valuing the contributions of a team by enabling decision making within the team, among others.

The Agile Principles

The following principles are based on the Agile Manifesto.

1. Our highest priority is to satisfy the customer through early and continuous delivery of valuable software.

2. Welcome changing requirements, even late in development. Agile processes harness change for the customer's competitive advantage.

3. Deliver working software frequently, from a couple of weeks to a couple of months, with a preference to the shorter timescale.

4. Business people and developers must work together daily throughout the project.

5. Build projects around motivated individuals. Give them the environment and support they need, and trust them to get the job done.

6. The most efficient and effective method of conveying information to and within a development team is face-to-face conversation.

7. Working software is the primary measure of progress.

8. Agile processes promote sustainable development. The sponsors, developers, and users should be able to maintain a constant pace indefinitely.

9. Continuous attention to technical excellence and good design enhances agility.

10. Simplicity—the art of maximizing the amount of work not done— is essential.

11. The best architectures, requirements, and designs emerge from self-organizing teams.

12. At regular intervals, the team reflects on how to become more effective, then tunes and adjusts its behavior accordingly.

So what does "Agile" development look like?

Most people who say they are doing Agile tend to be doing one of Scrum, Extreme Programming, Kanban, or Lean development—or something loosely based on one or more of these well-known methods. Teams often cherry-pick techniques or ideas from various methods (mostly Scrum, with a bit of XP, is a common recipe), and will naturally adjust how they work over time. Normally this is because of context, but also the kind of software we write changes over time, and the methods need to match.

There are a number of other Agile methods and approaches, such as SAFe or LeSS or DAD for larger projects, Cynefin, RUP, Crystal, and DSDM. But looking closer at some of the most popular approaches can help us to understand how to differentiate Agile methodologies and to see what consistencies there actually are.

Scrum, the Most Popular of Agile Methodologies

Scrum is, at the time of writing, by far the most popular Agile methodology, with many Certified Scrum Masters, and training courses continually graduating certified Scrum practitioners and trainers. Scrum is conceptually simple and can integrate into many existing project and program management frameworks. This makes it very popular among managers and senior executives, as they feel they can understand more easily what a team is doing and when the team will be finished doing it.

Scrum projects are delivered by small, multidisciplinary product development teams (generally between 5 and 11 people in total) that work off of a shared requirements backlog. The team usually contains developers, testers, and designers, a product manager or *Product Owner*, and someone playing the *Scrum Master* role, a servant leader and coach for the team.

Sprints and Backlogs

The product backlog or Scrum backlog is a collection of stories, or very high-level requirements for the product. The product manager will continually prioritize work in the backlog and check that stories are still relevant and usable, a process called "backlog grooming."

Scrum teams work in increments called *sprints*, traditionally one month long, although many modern Scrum teams work in shorter sprints that last only one or two weeks. Each sprint is time-boxed: at the end of each sprint, the teams stop work, assess the work that they have done and how well they did it, and reset for the next sprint.

At the beginning of a sprint, the team, including the product manager, will look through the product backlog and select stories to be delivered, based on priority.

The team is asked to estimate the expense of completing each unit of work as a team, and the stories are committed to the sprint backlog in priority order. Scrum teams can use whatever means of estimation they chose. Some use real units of time (that work will take three days), but many teams use relative but abstract sizing (e.g., t-shirt sizes: small, medium, and large; or animals: snail, quail, and whale). Abstract sizing allows for much looser estimates: a team is simply saying that a given story is bigger than another story, and the Scrum Master will monitor the team's ability to deliver on those stories.

Once stories are put into the sprint backlog, the Scrum team agrees to commit to delivering all of this work within the sprint. Often in these cases the team will look at the backlog and may take some stories out, or may select some extra stories. This often happens if there are a lot of large stories: the team has less confidence in completing large stories, and so may swap for a few small stories instead.

The agreement between the team and the product manager is vital here: the product manager gets to prioritize the stories, but the team has to accept the stories into the sprint backlog.

Scrum teams during a sprint generally consider the sprint backlog to be sacrosanct. Stories are never played into the sprint backlog during the sprint. Instead, they are put into the wider product backlog so that they can be prioritized appropriately.

This is part of the contract between the Scrum team and the product manager: the product manager doesn't change the Scrum backlog mid-sprint, and the team can deliver reliably and repeatedly from sprint to sprint. This trades some flexibility to make changes to the product and tune it immediately in response to feedback, for consistency of delivery.

Team members are co-located if possible, sitting next to one another and able to discuss or engage during the day, which helps form team cohesion. If security team members are working with an Agile team, then it is also important for them to sit with the rest of the team. Removing barriers to communication encourages sharing security knowledge, and helps build trusted relationships, preventing an *us versus them* mentality.

Stand-ups

The team's day always starts with a stand-up: a short meeting where everybody addresses a whiteboard or other record of the stories for the sprint and discusses the day's work. Some teams use a physical whiteboard for tracking their stories, with the stories represented as individual cards that move through swimlanes of state change. Others use electronic systems that present stories on a virtual card wall.

Each team organizes its whiteboard differently, but most move from left to right across the board from "Ready to play" through "In development" to "Done." Some teams add extra swimlanes for tasks or states like design, testing, or states to represent stories being queued for the next state.

The Chicken and the Pig

A pig and a chicken are walking down the road.

The chicken says, "Hey, pig, I was thinking we should open a restaurant!"

Pig replies: "Hmm, maybe; what would we call it?"

Chicken responds: "How about *ham-n-eggs*?"

The pig thinks for a moment and says, "No, thanks. I'd be committed, but you'd only be involved."

Each member of the team must attend the daily stand-up. We divide attendance into "chickens" and "pigs," where pigs are delivering team members, and any observers are chickens. Chickens are not allowed to speak or interrupt the stand-up.

Most teams go around the team, one team member at a time, and they answer the following questions:

- What did you do yesterday?
- What are you going to do today?
- What is blocking you?

A team member who completed a story moves the story card to the next column, and can often get a clap or round of applause. The focus for the team is on delivering the stories as agreed, and anything that prevents that is called a *blocker*.

The Scrum Master's principal job day-to-day is to remove blockers from the team. Stories can be blocked because they weren't ready to play, but most often are blocked by a dependency on a third-party resource of some form, something from outside the team. The Scrum Master will chase these problems down and clear them up for the team.

Scrum Feedback Loops

Scrum also depends on strong feedback loops. After each sprint, the team will get together, hold a retrospective on the sprint, and look to see what it can do better in the next sprint.

These feedback loops can be a valuable source of information for security teams to be a part of, to both learn directly from the development teams about a project, as well as to provide continuous security support during the ongoing development process, rather than only at security-specific gating points or reviews.

One of the key questions to work out with Scrum teams is whether security is a chicken (a passive outside observer) or a pig (an active, direct participant in team discussions and problem-solving). Having security expertise as part of the regular life cycle is crucial to building trusted relationships and to open, honest, and effective security-relevant dialog.

This core of Scrum—team communication, ownership, small iterative cycles, and feedback loops—makes Scrum simple for teams (and managers) to understand, and easy to adopt. However, keep in mind that many teams and organizations deviate from pure Scrum, which means that you need to understand and work with their specific interpretation or implementation of Scrum.

You also need to understand the limitations and restrictions that Scrum places on how people work. For example, Scrum prevents or at least severely limits changes during a sprint time-box so that the team can stay committed to meeting its sprint goals, and it tends to discourage engagement with the development team itself by funneling everything through the Product Owner.

Extreme Programming

Extreme Programming (XP) is one of the earliest Agile methodologies, and is one of the most Agile, but it tends to look the most different from traditional software development.

These days, teams using XP are comparatively rare, since it's incredibly disciplined and intense; but because many of the technical practices are in active use by other Agile teams, it's worth understanding where they come from.

The following are the core concepts of Extreme Programming:

- The team has the customer accessible to it at all times.
- It commits to deliver working code in regular, small increments.
- The team follows specific technical practices, using test-driven development, pair programming, refactoring, and continuous integration to build high-quality software.
- The whole team shares the work to be done through collective code ownership, common coding standards, and a shared design metaphor.
- People work at a sustainable pace to prevent team members from burning out.

The Planning Game

An Extreme Programming team, much like a Scrum team, tends to work from a product backlog and plays a *planning game* each iteration to select and prioritize stories.

The team will group-estimate stories, ensuring that everyone agrees on an estimate and commits to it. This is often done through a collaborative game called *planning poker*, where stories are sized using an abstract scheme like story points.

Once the team agrees on the cost of each story and relative prioritization, it starts working in short increments, usually one or two weeks long. Most teams will track and report progress to date using *burn-up* charts, which show the total points completed so far in the project, or *burn-down* charts, which track the points remaining to completion.

The On-Site Customer

XP teams generally sit together with their customer representative, who is responsible for answering their questions and for making day-to-day decisions about the product feature set, and look and feel. A common practice is for teams to agree that the "story card is just a placeholder for a conversation" with the customer. These teams usually do not write down requirements or stories in detail; instead, each person working on a story will demonstrate the work in progress to the on-site customer, potentially multiple times per day.

The customer is encouraged to engage and actively change her mind about the story as she sees work delivered, and the team is responsible for making clear the cost of change as this happens.

XP teams that struggle often do so because the on-site customer is not allowed to make decisions and has to check with other members of the organization, killing the team's velocity.

Pair Programming

Unlike in Scrum, where the team is free to "inspect and adapt" its way to finding technical practices that its feel works best, XP teams commit to a highly disciplined approach to software development. Two of the best known, and most commonly understood, of these practices are *pair programming* and *test-driven development*.

In pair programming, each story is picked up by a pair of developers who most commonly sit at a single computer writing the code. The pair share a single keyboard, and they fall into roles of "Driver" and "Navigator":

Driver
> The "Driver" is the person who has the keyboard, and he is responsible for typing the lines of code himself.

Navigator
> The "Navigator" is responsible for keeping the structure of what to write in her head, and for thinking about the code structure, application contexts, and the other requirements.

Most pairs swap over pretty regularly, from every 15 minutes to every hour, so that they both get to change context.

Pair programming allows the developers to easily keep the context separate from some of the minor implementation details, such as language syntax and details of APIs. It also ensures that two pairs of eyes look at every line of code, and ideally means that one of the pair is thinking about testability, maintainability, or other non-functional qualities of the code, including security. Security engineers can (and should) pair up with developers when they are working on security features, frameworks, and other security-sensitive or high-risk code.

Test-Driven Development

In test-driven development, the key thing is to write an automated test before you start writing the code to implement the test. Developers have long used automated testing, but XP and TDD really push this practice to the extreme, advocating complete testability.

This is commonly done using an approach called *"Red, Green, Refactor."* The developers write a test case to outline what they want the code to do. Once complete, they create any stub methods needed to make the tests compile, and run the tests, which should go red to indicate that they broke the build by adding a failing test.

The developers then write code in such a way as to cause the test to pass. Then they run the test again, creating a green bar, proving that the test is now passing. Next, the developers look at the code they wrote to see if there are opportunities to clean it up, eliminating duplication and simplifying the design.

This is called *refactoring*, changing the internals of the code without changing its behavior. Developers can make structural changes to the code with confidence that it will continue to work as intended, by relying on their test suite to catch any mistakes or incompatibilities.

TDD and pair programming work very well together, as this allows for a ping-pong style of development, where one developer will write the test and pass it over to the other to implement the feature and write the next test before passing it back.

Because the tests should focus on what the code should do, rather than how it does it, they allow conversations around API design, method naming, and method invariants to happen at test creation time, and the tests to drive those aspects of the code.

Shared Design Metaphor

XP includes other practices such as the concept of *Shared Metaphor*, which tells us that we should use a single common language among the team to refer to the system, as that encourages shared code ownership and shared understanding within the team.

Shared Metaphor manifested itself in the first XP project, where a payroll system was implemented as an assembly line process, with various pay fields being stations on the line.

Today this practice is commonly dropped in favor of *domain-driven design*, where the development team is required to use and understand the language of the business to build the software, increasing the understanding of the business domain within the development team.

The big benefit of Extreme Programming is that it is very responsive to change, since the customer gets daily or hourly views of the product as it is built. XP's relentless focus on technical discipline ensures a high level of code quality: it is called *Extreme Programming* for good reason. Many of XP's technical practices (including continuous integration, TDD, refactoring, and even pair programming) have reached the mainstream and are commonly followed by teams who don't use XP, and even by teams who are still working in more traditional development environments.

The big issues with Extreme Programming is that it is hard to predict the efficiency of the team or when a product will be done, and that it has proven very difficult to scale up to large development projects or scale out to multiple locations.

Kanban

Kanban is very different from Scrum or XP in that it is not a methodology for building a software product, but is instead a method for running a high-functioning team. Kanban comes from W. Edwards Deming's work with Toyota and the Toyota Production System, which revolutionized how work would move around a factory floor.

Most of the ongoing work on a manufacturing floor is done at individual stations, and in most manufacturing spaces, each station has an in-queue and an out-queue. Work is processed from the in-queue and results placed into the out-queue.

Deming noted that work was often pushed through the system, so orders for specific parts of systems would be pushed in at the front and make their way through the entire system. Critically, he identified that partially complete work spends the majority of its time in one of the queues at a station or being transferred from one station to another (or even worse, put into storage).

Instead, he proposed a system based on a just-in-time approach to each station, enabling each station to request (or *pull*) work from the preceding station when it was ready for the next piece of work.

This means that work in progress at any given station is highly limited, which creates a more optimal flow through the system. Deming's work was primarily about identifying waste in the system, where work was partially done and turned out not to be needed, or done prematurely.

Kanban systems prioritize *flow*, or *cycle time*, which is a measure of how fast a piece of work can travel from the beginning to the end of the system, and the number of touch points it has as it does so.

In IT processes there may be potentially dozens or even hundreds of touch points between an idea being conceived and getting it into production. Many of these touch points have queues, where work waits until the process can be achieved, each of which creates delays in flow.

A common example is a change control board for reviewing and approving changes to production systems. Because it is inefficient for such a board to meet each day, they often meet only weekly or monthly. Work that needs to be done must sit at the proposal stage waiting for the change control board to approve or process the request.

Because of the number of changes that are queued up for the change control board, sometimes they cannot review each change and have to postpone changes until the next board, which can cause even greater delays. Once a change is approved, it then moves to the implementation team, who may receive many such changes, which means they get queued there, and so on.

Kanban systems are based on three key practices, detailed in the following sections.

Kanban Board: Make Work Visible

Firstly, they use a Kanban board, with a column per "station," which shows the in-queue, the in-process, and the out-queue. In a software development team, you may have stations for analysis, development, test, and deployment, for example. This enables easy visualization of the flow of the team, and ensures that we can see at a glance where the work is clustered and any bottlenecks in the system.

Kanban strictly limits the work in progress at a station. If a station has more work in progress than it can achieve, then it cannot start a new piece of work until it finishes another.

A station which has a full in-queue prevents the previous station from moving work to the out-queue. This causes a ripple effect all the way down the stations. Equally, when the final station clears a piece of work, it can start the next piece of work, and each station pulls a piece of work up to the next one.

Constant Feedback

This might sound horribly inefficient, but actually it means that the process doesn't move any faster than the slowest station in the system. It should be clear that any organization that is trying to move faster than that station is actually just creating waste or delays elsewhere anyway.

This is the second practice of Kanban: constant feedback. By making the work in progress visible, the team gets feedback on its flow and capability.

But Kanban goes further and encourages Kanban teams to rely on each other to give feedback. That radical transparency ensures that sponsors and stakeholders can see the current state of the system and how long it will take for new requests for work to flow through the system, and can prioritize work requests into the system appropriately.

Continuous Improvement

This leads us to the third practice of Kanban: continuous improvement. The entire line, at every station, is encouraged to identify improvements to the system to speed up process flow.

Since it is easy to identify where the bottleneck is in a Kanban process, each improvement should give an immediate boost to the throughput of the entire system. This is obviously more effective than other approaches, where people often attempt to improve the noisiest activities, which may give no real improvement if most of the time is wasted elsewhere.

A significant side effect of Kanban is that most organizations get significantly more predictive processes. A process where requesting a new feature could take anywhere from 7 days to 90 days, depending on how much sponsorship you could get for your feature, becomes a predictive process whereby each feature takes a fairly standard duration.

This means that people requesting features can do much more demand management of the features they request. It enables delivery teams to push prioritization out to the consumers of the delivery function, where we tend to see more horse-trading of features going on.

It is important to note that Kanban doesn't advocate any actual development method itself. Kanban is about team and activity management, and it is most commonly used by teams that look after multiple products, and where the work is significantly less predictable.

This makes Kanban more common in IT support teams and operational teams (and security teams!) than product development teams, but it has been used in full product development by a number of organizations.

Kanban shows that smaller batch sizes tend to increase throughput: any process goes faster with less to process, which means more work can be pushed through faster. It is this understanding that drives DevOps teams to deliver smaller changes, more often.

Lean

Lean development, and more recently Eric Ries's Lean startup model (*http://thelean startup.com/*), are based, again, on Lean manufacturing, which came out of Kanban and the Toyota Production System. However, Lean development has gone a slightly different direction over time.

One of the key differences in Lean is the emphasis on analyzing what you have done and learning from it in order to iterate.

Lean as a methodology prioritizes the principle cycle of *build → measure → learn*.

It suggests that iterative learning is the key to building a successful product, and that to iterate successfully, you need to not just build and build again, but also take the time and effort to measure the impact of each change, and then learn from measurements.

By explicitly calling out the *measure* and *learn* parts of this iteration, the focus for technical teams includes far more emphasis on building measurable systems, and including monitoring and analytics in the design.

Lean teams tend to use *Hypothesis Driven Development* where instead of writing work units in terms of the value it will deliver to the customer (like user stories), they state a hypothesis on how the change will affect a business value measure.

Stories are not *done* simply when they are coded and deployed to production, but are instead only considered done when the data has been gathered and analyzed to find out if the feature actually delivers the value hypothesized.

Secondly, Lean teams tend to encourage the use of experimental models that can be statistically compared, such as A/B testing frameworks, which allow multiple implementations of a feature to be put in front of customers for evaluation.

An example of a Lean story might be "Providing customers a buy button on every page instead of once added to the cart will encourage customers to make more purchases." The story might be implemented by showing the buy button on every page to just 20% of customers, with the other 80% seeing the current behavior in an A/B test. Results will be gathered and compared to see if the work was worthwhile.

Lean also emphasizes early delivery of a Minimum Viable Product (MVP). The team starts by designing and delivering only the minimum feature set necessary to start gathering data on what users want and are willing to pay for, and then rapidly iterates and evolves the product based on real user feedback.

Agile Methods in General

Regardless of which Agile methodology your development team is using—and many teams are using hybrid methodologies, where they started with a well-known methodology but have adjusted it to fit their needs—we tend to find that all Agile teams value and practice the following:

Prioritizing feedback
> Agile teams place a massive value on getting feedback on their products as soon as possible. This generally means increasing the speed at which software is in a

demonstrable state, as well as decreasing the barriers to communication that prevent real decision makers from seeing the results of their decisions.

Agile teams also value feedback loops within their development methods, encouraging retrospectives each iteration or continuous improvement capabilities that ensure that the process itself is adaptive and delivering value.

Any mechanism to speed up feedback is the hallmark of Agile software. That can include practices such as continuous integration, rapid deployment systems, and production testing facilities.

Minimizing the pathway to production is key to getting feedback as fast as possible.

Speedy delivery of small batches

Most Agile methods have some basis in the Lean manufacturing industry, or awareness of it, and the key learning is about reducing batch size. Almost all Agile teams prefer to deliver software in small iterative chunks rather than in single large batches of features.

In some cases, delivery may be into a pre-production or staging environment rather than directly to production, but the team is able to concentrate on small numbers of features at a time, and to iterate on the feedback given on the completed work.

Agile teams measure their effectiveness in terms of *velocity*, the number of features delivered to production. Teams will invest time in automating their systems and tools if that will improve the team's velocity.

Iterative development

Agile methods all aim to allow some form of iteration—the feedback gained from delivering features early is only useful if it can be acted upon quickly. Most Agile methods have facilities to reduce the impact of rework, and also give strong feedback to the decision makers as to the cost of the rework. For example, in a Scrum team, rework is added to the product backlog, and the team then needs to estimate and prioritize this work against other features.

Team ownership

Agile methods empower development teams, pushing decision making down to the team level, making the team responsible and accountable for how to do its own work, and for its own success or failure. Teams are also free—and expected—to find ways to improve their processes and practices on their own.

Many Agile teams have a coach, an experienced person who can help them to understand the practice framework and guide them through the rituals and retrospectives. Coaches are there to help the team self-direct and orient toward high-functioning capability, not force people to work a specific way.

If it hurts, do it more often

Agile tends to force us to find the pain points in development processes; and where we find difficult or painful areas, we encourage doing it more often.

While this may sound ridiculous and not at all sensible, we recognize that many actions that we find awkward or difficult are often because of unfamiliarity. Deployment is the classic case. When a team deploys its system only once every six months, we find processes that don't match the reality, and staff members who may have done one or two deploys in their working lifetime. When teams deploy multiple times per day, we find team members who are intimately familiar with the process and the context.

A process that is done rarely tends to be manual because the cost of automating it and maintaining the automation is high compared to the number of executions. But once you start doing a process an order of magnitude more often, automation can start to reduce the pain and can earn huge dividends in terms of effort expended. Furthermore, automation increases repeatability and quality, giving further benefits to the team that uses it.

Inspect and adapt

Agile methods require teams to iterate not only on the product or service that they are building, but also on their methodology and internal processes. In order to do that, just as we monitor the effectiveness of the product or service, we need to inspect our own processes and identify the value delivered.

Teams use concepts such as value stream mapping, time logs, velocity, and retrospectives to examine and adjust the process. This continual learning culture and openness to changing the process enables teams to adapt effectively to changing contexts of an organization.

What About DevOps?

DevSecOps, or This Might Sound Familiar

If you are from security, a lot of what you will hear about the drivers behind DevOps might sound awfully familiar. We recognize that the state of security today is very similar to the state of operations back in 2009 when DevOps started.

We are starting to see a serious increase in interest in DevSecOps, DevOpsSec, or other monikers that combine Agile, operations, and security. In the meantime, we think there is a lot that security teams can learn from the history of DevOps and where it is going.

This Agile stuff is all well and good, providing it actually results in working software. As more and more development teams across the world moved to this way of working, they started to encounter problems in operations.

Agile teams are almost exclusively measured by the amount of working software delivered, the "velocity" of the development team. However, most operations teams are valued and rewarded on the basis of system stability. This can be measures of uptime or incidents.

Development and operations teams can end up almost at war with each other because of their opposing priorities.

Developers often have to make decisions that trade off time to delivery, and cost of delivery against long-term operability concerns. If developers don't share some accountability for operations and support, this creates an externality, rewarding short-term thinking and encouraging developers to cut corners. While taking extra time to think about improving operability means that stories are delivered slower, penalizing the development team.

The DevOps movement came from the recognition of this as a problem, combined with a massive structural shift in automation of large operations platforms, such as the move to cloud computing, virtualization, and programmable automated tooling for operations teams.

Operations teams began to recognize that they were seen as a blocker to Agile development teams, and that in many cases their jobs had to change from being the doers to being the enablers in the organization.

Organizations that practice DevOps tend to organize their infrastructure and operations teams into different focus areas:

- Infrastructure teams that buy and manage infrastructure
- Tooling teams that build automated tooling for self-provisioning and management of said infrastructure
- Support teams that respond to incidents

Some companies have moved their infrastructure wholesale to large cloud providers, essentially outsourcing the infrastructure teams, and putting most of their operations work into tooling teams that enable developers to self-service in the provision, operation, and maintenance of the infrastructure.

Things like logging, monitoring, alerting, patching, and so forth tend to be problems that most organizations should only need to solve once (per infrastructure provider), and then developers can be provided with the APIs and tools to manage themselves.

Support is a much bigger problem, but some DevOps organizations moved quickly toward requiring development teams to support their own applications. This de-siloization caused development teams to in-source the operational pain that their decisions could cause, and removed the externalities, creating more robust services as a result.

Enabling development teams to maintain and operate their own services requires a level of organizational maturity that not all organizations are capable of. But organizations that succeed at this can reach incredible levels of speed and efficiency.

Many DevOps teams are releasing code to production multiple times per day, with some organizations reaching levels of hundreds or even thousands of deploys per day.

Looking back at Lean and Kanban, we can see that if the largest queue in your system is around waiting to get the code into production to get feedback, eliminating this bottleneck can be a huge business enabler.

Improving feedback and reducing time to market aren't the only benefits of this approach. We also see that organizations that are capable of releasing more often are significantly more reliable.

Organizations that deploy infrequently tend to focus on *mean time between failures* (MTBF), which is a risk-averse strategy, but means that they are much less prepared to deal with failures when they do happen. Instead, the key metric that we start to look at is the *mean time to recovery* (MTTR) from operational failures. Organizations that release smaller changes more often can identify the cause of problems much faster and are significantly more capable of getting fixes out, which reduces their MTTR.

But the extreme velocity of change in DevOps does create major challenges for security and requires a new way of thinking about security. This is something that we will look at throughout this book, especially in the chapters on operations, risk management, compliance, and testing.

Agile and Security

Getting Agile teams to work well with security people has historically been quite difficult. Part of the problem is that most security processes and practices have been built for large Waterfall projects with requirements set up front, instead of for small teams working quickly and iteratively.

Many security professionals have a hard time adapting their existing practices to a world where requirements can change every few weeks, or where they are never written down at all. Where design and risk-management decisions are made by the team just in time, instead of being planned out and directed from top down. And where manual testing and compliance checking cannot possibly keep up with the speed of delivery.

Worse still, too many security teams work with a worldview where their goal is to inhibit change as much as possible, in an effort to minimize the change in risk profile of the application or environment: if there is no change in risk, then the security team cannot be *blamed* for new security issues that may arise.

Security teams that try to reduce risk by minimizing change, rather than supporting development teams to realize their ideas in a secure way, are doomed to be increasingly irrelevant in an Agile world, and will therefore be bypassed. The result will be systems that are not secure, safe, or compliant, because security becomes removed from the development process.

Despite all this, there are teams that are successfully following Agile methods to deliver secure software, and the rest of this book is going to show you techniques and tools that can work well with Agile teams and practices that we think can improve the entire process.

For this to work, everyone needs to do their part.

Agile teams need to understand and choose to adopt security practices, and take more responsibility for the security of their systems.

Product Owners for these teams need to give the teams enough time to do this properly, and they need to understand and prioritize security and compliance requirements.

Security professionals have to learn to accept change, to work faster and more iteratively, and be able to think about security risks, and how to manage risks, in incremental terms. And most important, security needs to become an enabler, instead of a blocker.

Agile and DevOps are not fads. The future of IT is going to be faster, more responsive, more collaborative, and more automated.

Security has to face these challenges and ensure that the future is not only fast, but safe, too. In the next chapter, we'll start by looking at how and where security can be added into the Agile development life cycle.

CHAPTER 4

Working with Your Existing Agile Life Cycle

So you want to start building more secure software, but your security and compliance checklists require you to have design review gates and penetration testing, and you can't work out where these fit in an Agile life cycle.

Traditional Application Security Models

In a traditional application security model, the security touchpoints during software development are mostly gates that the product must stop at and pass. Some security work is done in parallel with development, and the gates are a chance to verify that the security work and development work haven't diverged. The following are common security gates:

Design or requirements review
> The security team looks at the requirements list or early designs and adds any security requirements based on threat models and attack trees.

Architecture review
> The security team reviews the proposed architecture, such as infrastructure or information flows, and proposes a set of security controls in order to minimize risk.

Code review
> The security team reviews sensitive areas of code and confirms that the security requirements are met, and that the code matches the architecture.

Security testing
> The security team or an external team checks the test version of the product against a set of security requirements to see if the system is safe and secure.

The idea behind these gates is that work is delivered in large batches. It is predicated on the old rule that the earlier a defect is caught, the cheaper it is to fix; therefore we need to do a security review as early as possible to catch security defects before they get too far.

Agile practitioners argue that while this rule is broadly speaking true—catching a defect later *is* more expensive than catching one earlier—the solution is not to attempt the impossible task of catching all defects earlier, but instead to focus on reducing the cost of fixing defects by making change safer and easier.

The same is true of security features and controls. We want to reach a fine balance between finding and fixing (or better, preventing) security problems up front where it makes sense to do so, and making sure that we can fix them quickly and cheaply later if something gets by.

Some security defects fall into a special category of defects: design flaws that are critical showstoppers or fundamental issues with the way a system works. While many bugs are relatively easy to fix at a later date and may not drastically increase the risk to the system, correcting a fundamental security design flaw may require you to start again from scratch, or force people to fix an endless stream of security bugs one-by-one.

For example, choosing the wrong language or framework, or relying too much on features of a PaaS platform or on an infrastructure black box to take care of problems for you, can lead to serious security risks, as well as fundamental run time reliability and scalability problems.

Therefore, even in an Agile environment, security needs to be involved at the early product direction stages and in architecture discussions, not just in later parts of the development life cycle.

What's the Difference Between a Bug and a Flaw?

While in common speech, the terms "bug" and "flaw" can be used interchangeably, in security, each term is used to describe very different types of security issues.

A *bug* is a low-level implementation failure that results in a system operating in an unintended manner that gives rise to a security issue. A generic example of a bug would be failing to sanitize user-supplied input that gets used in a database call, leading to SQL injection.

A famous example of a security bug would be the Heartbleed vulnerability in OpenSSL (CVE-2014-0160), where the server failed to check if the stated length of data sent in a heartbeat message was actually the length of the data sent. This mistake allowed an attacker to cause a vulnerable server to send him excess data, which leaked secrets.

A *flaw* is a design failure where a system operates exactly as intended but inherently causes a security issue to arise. Flaws often come from systems that have been designed without security needs in mind. A generic example of a flaw would be a client-server system that is designed to perform the authentication of a user on the client side and to send the server the result of the authentication check, making the system vulnerable to man-in-the-middle attacks.

A famous example of a security flaw would Dirty Cow (CVE-2016-5195), an issue that affected the GNU/Linux kernel. The design of the copy-on-write (COW) and memory management systems had a race condition which when triggered would allow an unprivileged user to write to a file owned by the root user, allowing that user to escalate her privileges to those of root.

Why are these distinctions important? In general, fixing a bug is cheaper and easier than fixing a flaw, as a bug usually only requires correcting a developer's specific mistake, whereas a flaw can require a significant restructuring of both the problematic code as well as code that is reliant on that code. Restructuring code within an already implemented system can be highly complex and runs the risk of introducing new bugs and flaws.

In certain situations flaws are not fixable at all, and the system will remain vulnerable to security issues for the rest of its life. The best way to prevent security flaws from being introduced into an application is to ensure security is considered during its design. The earlier security architecture is included in the development life cycle, the fewer security flaws are likely to be designed in.

Let's work backward from coding and testing (which are done simultaneously in Agile) to planning and design, and discuss what security activities should happen at each stage.

Per-Iteration Rituals

During a product development iteration, there are a number of rituals where security should be involved.

Who Is Security?

In an organization embracing Agile development, who exactly do we mean when we say "security"?

The answer is going to depend on the size of your company and the focus of your team. If you are a startup or small company, you may not have a dedicated security specialist available. Instead, someone on the team may have to own that role, with occasional guidance and checkups from an outside expert (however, see Chapter 14 for issues and risks with this model).

In a larger organization, you may have a dedicated specialist or team that owns security for the company. However, most security teams cover physical security, network security, and compliance and audit responsibilities, not necessarily application security advice and support.

Some organizations that take security and compliance seriously have a person on each Agile team who is dedicated to the security role for that team. This might be a job share, 20% of the time for example; or it might be a dedicated security person shared across multiple teams; or in some cases teams may have their own full-time security specialist.

The key thing is that somebody on the team needs to be able to take on the role of "security" during each iteration and ensure that security concepts and risks, and the perspectives of an attacker, are included in requirements, design, coding, testing, and implementation. Whoever takes on this responsibility, as well as the other members of the team, have to approach security as an enabler, and understand and agree that considering security early on and throughout the process contributes to a more successful end product.

At the daily stand-up meeting, where the state of stories is reviewed, the team should be listening for any issues raised that may affect security and privacy. If there are stories of security importance, then progress on those stories needs to be monitored.

During development, having someone with a strong security background available to pair on security-sensitive code can be worthwhile, especially on teams that follow pair programming as a general practice.

If your team does team code reviews (and it should) through pull requests or collaborative review platforms, then having a security person reviewing code changes can help identify areas of the code base that need careful attention and additional testing.

At the beginning of each iteration, at the kick-off or planning meeting, most teams walk through all the potential stories for the iteration together. Somebody representing security should be present to ensure that security requirements are understood and applicable to each story. This helps ensure that the team owns and understands the security implications of each story.

At the end of each iteration, there are times when security should also be involved in the reviews and retrospective meetings to help understand what the team has done and any challenges that it faced.

All of these points provide opportunities for security to engage with the development team, to help each other and learn from each other, and to build valuable personal connections.

Making the barrier to interacting with the security team as low as possible is key to ensuring that security does not get in the way of delivery. Security needs to provide quick and informal guidance, and answers to questions through instant messaging or chat platforms, email, and wherever possible in person so that security is not seen as a blocker. If those responsible for security are not reachable in an easy and timely manner, then it is almost certain that security considerations will be relegated to the sidelines as development charges ahead.

Tools Embedded in the Life Cycle

The best way to assure yourself of the security of the system you are building is to perform an exhaustive set of checks before it is allowed out.

Advances in security technology allow us to use tools such as the following:

- Gauntlt
- BDD-Security
- Snyk
- InSpec
- Brakeman
- ZAP
- OSQuery
- TruffleHog
- Dependency-Check
- Error-Prone

These tools and others that we will look at in this book automate many of the assurance processes that manual testers are traditionally responsible for. They don't obviate the need for any manual testing, but they can help to prioritize time and effort in testing by removing the need to do detailed, routine, and time-consuming work, and ensuring that testing is more repeatable and reliable.

The security team needs to own these tools, while the development team owns the implementation of the tools in its pipeline.

This means that the development team cares about ensuring that the tool is in its pipeline, that it is correctly configured for the project, and that the team can act on the results.

The security team is responsible for deciding what features the tool should have, for making it easy to embed in the pipeline, and for ensuring that the tool or tools cover the areas that the team is most concerned about.

Pre-Iteration Involvement

Most Agile teams not only have a product development team working in iterations, but a product designer or design team working in advance of the development team, working on design problems, prototypes, and architectural discussions. The output of this team feeds directly into the product backlog, ensuring that the development team is primed with stories ready for the forthcoming iteration.

We've seen several ways this can work, from a separate design team working just one iteration ahead, to monthly product design meetings that produce several sprints' worth of backlog in batches.

Security is critical in the design and architecture phase. It is at this point that instead of worrying about software library patch levels or secure coding guidelines, you need to be thinking about secure service design, trust modeling, and secure architecture patterns.

It's important to note that design in this case is not about the look of the system—we aren't talking about Photoshop jockeys here. Design is about how the system works, the principal user interactions, APIs, and the flow of data through the system.

The design team should have access to security training or security expertise to ensure that the service the team is designing enables security through the user experience. Examples of this work may include understanding how or whether to obfuscate user details when displayed, how changes to information are gathered, and what identification requirements are needed for specific actions.

The architecture team may also need access to a security architect for any complex architecture. Building an architecture to be secure by design is very different than writing code that is secure or ensuring that there are no defects in the product.

Architects need to think carefully about threat models (or *threat reckons* for teams that don't do formal modeling) and about trust boundaries in their systems (something that we'll explain later in Chapter 8, *Threat Assessments and Understanding Attacks*).

Tooling for Planning and Discovery

Security teams should be providing tooling, processes, and guidance that help product managers, architects, and developers follow good security practice while designing a new system.

This might be as simple as a wiki with common security patterns already in use in the organization, or it might be threat modeling tools, or technical risk assessment checklists or questionnaires that make it easy for architects to understand security problems and how to deal with them up front.

Post-Iteration Involvement

Agile teams that are adopting a DevOps culture need automated fast systems for building and deploying their work into production reliably and repeatably.

Security matters during the build and deployment process for several different reasons:

1. Providing assurance that the correct thing was built and deployed
2. Assuring that the thing that was built and deployed is secure
3. Ensuring that the thing will be built and deployed in a secure way every time

Security checks that happen at this stage need to be automatable, reliable, repeatable, and understandable for a team to adopt them.

Manual processes are the opposite of this: most are not reliable (in terms of consistently catching the same errors), repeatable (in terms of repeating a finding), or understandable to the team.

Ideally the security team is already heavily involved in operations: it has to help define business continuity plans, incident response plans, as well as monitor and audit suspicious activity on the systems.

But is that an effective use of the team's time? The security team should know what features have been released in the last iteration and ensure that those new features are added to the logging, fraud detection, analysis, and other security systems.

It should be clear that high-risk features need to be monitored more closely. One possible action during iteration is to accept the risk temporarily, essentially assuming that the likelihood of the risk happening before a control can be put in place in a few itera-tions time is very low.

But the security team needs to be aware of these risks and monitor them until they are mitigated. This means that early on in system development, effective logging and auditing controls need to be put in place to ensure that we can see this kind of thing.

We'll cover a lot more on this in Chapter 12 under security in operations.

Tools to Enable the Team

As well as automated security testing tools that can be easily plugged into developer workflows, the security team should look for ways to make the development team's job easier, that help the team develop and deliver software faster—and at the same time, more securely.

For example, the security team can help development create effective build and deployment pipelines, and come up with a simple process and tools to compile, build, test, and automatically deploy the system in ways that also include security checks all along the path.

The security team may also want to provide tools for internal training, such as OWASP's WebGoat Project (*https://www.owasp.org/index.php/Cate gory:OWASP_WebGoat_Project*), the Damn Vulnerable Web Services (*https:// github.com/snoopysecurity/dvws*) project, or other intentionally vulnerable applica-tions that developers can explore and test, so that they can learn about how to find and remediate security issues safely.

The security team should do everything that it can to ensure that the easiest way to build something inside the organization is the safe and secure way, by providing teams with secure headers, hardened runtime configuration recipes and playbooks, and vetted third-party libraries and images that are free from vulnerabilities, which teams can grab and use right away. We'll look at how to do this in later chapters of this book.

When security stops being the team that says no, and becomes the team that enables reliable code to ship, then that's true Agile security.

Compliance and Audit Tools

How about once the system is in production? As well as tooling that does simple vul-nerability testing, good security teams know that they need to enforce compliance and do audits. Why not automate as much of the process and give the development teams access to the same tooling?

Build a tool that checks the list of users authorized in a system against the company HR database to ensure that leavers have had their credentials revoked.

How about a tool that confirms via APIs that all nodes in the cloud infrastructure are built from a secure base image, have been patched within the current patch window, and are placed in security groups appropriately?

These audit and compliance tools help the security team as well as operations to detect mistakes when they happen and ensure that a strong security person can focus her energy and time on actually auditing the really interesting or tough problems.

Setting Secure Baselines

How do you know whether your tools are doing the right job? How can you tell if your product is actually secure?

The real answer is that you can't ever be certain that your product is really secure, but you can have confidence that your product meets a baseline of security.

By adding security touchpoints into your team's Agile life cycle, and using your tools and templates, it should be possible to assert what baseline of security you want your product to meet and to be assured that each build coming out of the team meets that level.

This should enable you to have confidence in writing a statement of assurance about your product and to know not only that the build meets that level of assurance, but also that any future builds will continue to meet that level.

What About When You Scale?

The model that we have outlined works well when you have a small number of development teams and a small team of security engineers who can divide the work among themselves equally. This will work for most of the readers of this book. For example, if you have six development teams and two security engineers, then you should be able to scale your security team's time to handle most of the issues that will come up.

But what if the number of products or services continues to grow?

If you follow Amazon's two-pizza model,[1] then a development organization of 200 might be made up of 30 or more teams, which means you need at least 10 security engineers to support them. If you follow Netflix's model of two-person engineering teams, then this model of security won't scale for you at all. The more development teams you have, the less likely that you can afford to dedicate a security specialist to work with them.

---

1 No team should be bigger than you can afford to feed with two pizzas, so between five and seven people, depending on how hungry they are.

In large organizations, you need to look at application security as a pipeline problem. Instead of trying to solve the problem at the point where it's no longer possible to cope with the amount of work, your security engineers need to work further up the pipeline, ensuring that development teams are enabled to make security decisions by themselves.

Building Security Teams That Enable

Instead of security teams that *do security*, you could envision a team that *enables security*. By this we mean that the team's primary purpose is to build tools, document techniques, and build capability to develop and deploy secure services. Truly Agile security teams measure themselves on what they can enable to happen, rather than the security issues they have blocked from going out the door.

Creating an environment where the secure thing to do is the easiest thing to do is a great goal for any security team to keep front of mind. It also has the additional positive impact whereby everyone involved is now directly contributing to the security of the development process. This is the only scalable way in which a security team can sustain, if not increase, its impact in a growing organization facing the unfortunate reality that there are never enough funds or qualified practitioners to do all the security work that needs to be done.

Building Tools That People Will Use

By building tools, we mean developing security tooling that can be used by development teams to assure themselves of the security of their products. This might mean looking at the risk management tooling, attack tree analysis, and Agile story tracking tools. Or it might mean automating testing tools to fit into your build pipeline, and automatic dependency inspection tools. Or security libraries or microservices that teams can take advantage of to solve specific problems such as crypto, multifactor authentication, and auditing. It could also be tooling that can safely audit and correct the configurations of your primary security systems, such as your firewalls, or of third-party services, such as those provided by AWS or GCP.

It's our experience that forcing a team to use a specific tool will produce a compliance or checklist culture, where the tool is an alien artifact that is ill understood and used reluctantly. Development teams should be free to choose appropriate tools based on their needs, and on the risk profile of the system that they are working on. Tools that they understand, that fit into their workflows, and that they will take ownership of.

It's important to note that these tools should not just identify security defects, but also enable teams to fix problems easily. So a tool that simply does a security scan and dumps the output for someone to review won't help the average team unless you can link the results to common remediations that are known to work and demonstrate that the tool adds value.

Tools that require significant effort on the part of developers will inevitably end up not being used. Examples of such high user cost are things such as noisy output that requires a developer to actively tease out the parts she cares about from a larger body of superfluous data, or where the actual determination of whether something is important or not requires a developer to take a series of additional and external steps.

When building security tooling, it cannot be stressed enough how important it is to make it easily extensible either through APIs or through the Unix principle of solving a single task and allowing the output to be passed into another tool. View your security toolset as an extensible toolkit that you will continue to add to over time, and where you can combine tools together in complimentary ways without having to rewrite them from scratch every time.

Documenting Security Techniques

There isn't a great deal written about good application security practices. Security is still viewed as a dark art, practiced only furtively in shadowy corners by learned masters. For many developers, security is mostly about obscure bugs and defensive coding techniques that they think are only needed in special cases.

Security engineers need to teach developers good techniques that are appropriate for your organization. These could cover the steps to safely configure a base web application, usage guidance for working with your cloud service provider in an effective and secure manner, secure coding guidelines and code review checklists for their languages and frameworks, and common risk lists for the kind of application that they are working on.

The key thing is that these techniques need to be applicable, timely, and relevant. NIST guidelines (*http://csrc.nist.gov/publications/PubsSPs.html*) or the UK government's good practice guide (*http://bit.ly/uk-gov-guidance*) and other common guidance from governments and regulators tend to be so generic and bureaucratic as to be useless to most teams.

Because Agile development teams value working software over documentation, code always trumps paper. Wherever possible, get security guidelines and checklists directly into code: secure headers, secure configuration recipes and playbooks and cloud templates, frameworks with security features enabled by default, and automated security tests and compliance checks that can be plugged into build pipelines and run in production. Code that developers can pick up and use easily, without slowing down.

Key Takeaways

Agile development creates new challenges for security teams. The keys for a successful agile security program are:

Involvement

There are frequent opportunities in an agile life cycle for security and developers to work together, learn from each other, and help each other. Someone playing the role of security on the team (a security engineer assigned to the team or a developer taking on security responsibilities) can be and should be involved in planning sessions, stand-ups, retrospectives, and walkthroughs.

Enablement

Agile teams move fast and are continuously learning and improving, and security needs to help them keep moving and learning and improving instead of blocking them from moving forward.

Automation

Security checks and tests must be automated in ways that they can be easily and transparently plugged into developer workflows and build pipelines.

Agility

Security has to be Agile to keep up with Agile teams. Security has to think and act quickly and iteratively, respond quickly, and keep learning and improving along with developers.

CHAPTER 5

Security and Requirements

All systems start with requirements. And so does security.

In this chapter we'll look at community-built tools such as the OWASP Application Security Verification Standard (ASVS), which lists standard security mechanisms and controls for designing and reviewing applications; and the SAFECode group's list of security stories, which you can use to help make sure that security is taken into account when the team is thinking about requirements or filling requirements in.

We'll also look at some simple techniques for defining security requirements in an Agile way, and at how and where the security team needs to be engaged in building and managing requirements.

Dealing with Security in Requirements

Traditional Waterfall or V-model software development assumes that all the requirements for a system can be captured, analyzed, and exhaustively defined up front, then handed off to the development team to design, build, and test. Any changes would be handled as exceptions.

Agile software development assumes that requirements or needs can only be understood in person, because many functional requirements are like art: "I'll know it when I see it."

Specifically, Agile software practitioners believe that requirements are difficult for users or customers to accurately specify, because language is a lossy communication mechanism, and because often what the users say they want is not what they actually want.

Agile requirements are therefore done iteratively and concretely, relying heavily on personas and prototypes, then delivered in small, frequent steps for demos and feedback.

Regardless of how you are specifying requirements, it is often hard to define the security attributes of the software that you are designing and building.

Users are able to explain their needs for software to act in certain ways, but no user is ever going to know that she needs secure tokens at the session layer for CSRF protection—nor should the user be expected to know this kind of thing.

Software development methodologies group requirements like this into sets of cross-functional or nonfunctional requirements, taking into account security, maintainability, performance, stability, and other aspects of a system that need to be accounted for as teams design, code, and test software.

But Agile methods have a difficult time dealing with nonfunctional and cross-functional requirements, but they are difficult to associate with concrete user needs, and difficult for a customer or customer representative to prioritize against delivering customer-facing features.

The security and reliability of a system often depends on fundamental, early decisions made in architecture and design, because security and reliability can't be added later without having to throw away code and start over, which nobody wants to do.

People who object to the Agile way of working point to this as where Agile falls down. A lack of forward planning, up front requirements definition and design, and an emphasis on delivering features quickly can leave teams with important nonfunctional gaps in the system that might not be found until it's too late.

In our experience, Agile doesn't mean unplanned or unsafe. Agile means open to change and improvement, and as such we believe that it is possible to build software with intrinsic security requirements in an Agile manner.

Let's start with explaining a bit about how requirements are done in Agile development—and why.

Agile Requirements: Telling Stories

Most requirements in Agile projects are captured as *user stories*: informal statements that describe what a user needs and why. Stories are concrete descriptions of a need, or a specific solution to a problem, stating clearly what the user needs to do and the goal the user wants to achieve, usually from the point of view of a user or type of user in the system. They are written in simple language that the team and users can all understand and share.

Most stories start off as an "epic": a large, vague statement of a need for the system, which will be progressively elaborated into concrete stories, until the team members clearly understand what they actually need to build, closer to when they need to build it.

Stories are short and simple, providing just enough information for the team to start working, and encouraging the team to ask questions and engage the users of the system for details. This forces team members to work to understand what the user wants and why, and allows them to fill in blanks and make adjustments as they work on implementing the solution.

Unlike Waterfall projects, where the project manager tries to get the scope defined completely and exhaustively up front and deal with changes as exceptions, Agile teams recognize that change is inevitable and expect requirements to change in response to new information. They want to deliver working software quickly and often so that they can get useful feedback and respond to it.

This is critical, since it means that unlike planned Waterfall projects, Agile teams tend not to create interconnected requirements. Each user story or piece of functionality should stand on its own if the team decides to stop delivering at any point. This fixed-time-and-budget, variable-scope approach is common in Agile projects.

What Do Stories Look Like?

Most Agile teams follow a simple user story template popularized by Mike Cohn (*https://www.mountaingoatsoftware.com/books/user-stories-applied*) and others:

> As a {type of user}
>
> I want to {do something}
>
> so that {I can achieve a goal}

Each story is written on a story card, an index card, or sticky note, or as an electronic representation of this.

Conditions of Satisfaction

For each story, the team works with the Product Owner to fill in details about the feature or change, and writes up conditions of satisfaction (*https://www.mountaingoat software.com/blog/clarifying-the-relationship-between-definition-of-done-and-conditions-of-sa*), or acceptance criteria. If you are using written story cards, these details would be recorded on the back of the card. The *conditions of satisfaction* are a list of specific functionality that the team needs to demonstrate to prove that the story is done.

Conditions of satisfaction guide the team on designing a feature and make up the list of test cases that must pass for a specific story. These criteria are statements of what the system must do under different circumstances: what the user's choices will be, how the system should respond to the user, and any constraints on the user's actions.

Most of these statements will be positive, focused on the main success scenarios of a feature or interaction. Which means that most of the tests that the team writes will be positive tests, intended to prove that these scenarios pass.

When writing conditions of satisfaction, there is usually little attention paid to what should happen if an action fails, or on exceptions or other negative scenarios. As we'll see in Chapter 11, *Agile Security Testing*, this is a serious problem when it comes to security, because attackers don't stay on the main success paths through the system. They don't behave like normal users. They try to abuse the capabilities of the system, looking for weaknesses and oversights that will give them access to features and information that they shouldn't have.

Tracking and Managing Stories: The Backlog

As stories are written, they are added to a product or project backlog. The *backlog* is a list of stories in prioritized order that defines all the features that need to be delivered, and changes or fixes that need to be made to the system at that point in time. Teams pull stories from the backlog based on priority, and schedule them to be worked on.

In Kanban or other *continuous flow* models, individual team members pull the highest priority story from the top of the backlog queue. In Scrum and XP, stories are selected from the overall product backlog based on priority and broken down into more detailed tasks for the team in its sprint backlog, which defines the set of work that the team will deliver in its next time box.

In some Agile environments, each story is written up on an index card or a sticky note. The backlog of stories is put up on a wall so that the work to be done is visible to everyone on the team.

Other teams, especially in larger shops, track stories electronically, using a system like Jira, Pivotal Tracker, Rally, or VersionOne. Using an electronic story tracking system offers a few advantages, especially from a compliance perspective:

1. An electronic backlog automatically records history on changes to requirements and design, providing an audit trail of when changes were made, who approved them, and when they were done.

2. Other workflows can automatically tie back into stories. For example, code check-ins can be tagged with the story ID, allowing you to easily trace all the work done on a story, including coding changes, reviews, automated testing, and even deployment of the feature through build pipelines.

3. You can easily search for security stories, compliance requirements, stories that deal with private information, or critical bug fixes, and tag them for review.

4. You can also tag security and compliance issues for bigger-picture analysis to understand what kinds of issues come up and how often across projects, and use this information to target security education or other proactive investments by your security team.

5. Information in online systems can be more easily shared across teams, especially in distributed work environments.

Stories in the product backlog are continuously reviewed, updated, elaborated on, re-prioritized, or sometimes deleted by the Product Owner or other members of the team, as part of what is called "grooming the backlog."

Dealing with Bugs

Are bugs stories? How are bugs tracked? Some teams don't track bugs at all. They fix them right away, or they don't fix them at all. Some teams only track the bugs that they weren't able to fix right away, adding them to the backlog as technical debt.

But what about security vulnerabilities? Are they tracked by the team as bugs? Or are they tracked by the security team separately, as part of its vulnerability management program? We'll look at this in more detail in Chapter 6, *Agile Vulnerability Management*.

Getting Security into Requirements

For security teams, the speed that decisions are made in Agile development environments and the emphasis on "working software over documentation" means that they need to stay close to development teams to understand what the team is working on and recognize when requirements and priorities are changing.

As we discussed earlier in how to scale security across teams, you will need to work out how and when you can afford to get the security team involved—and when you can't afford not to.

The security team should participate in release planning, sprint planning, and other planning meetings to help review and fill in security-related and compliance-related stories, and other high-risk stories, as they come up. Being part of the planning team gives security a better understanding of what is important to the organization, and a chance to help the Product Owner and the rest of the team understand and correctly prioritize security and compliance issues.

If possible, they also should participate in the development team's daily stand-ups to help with blockers and to watch out for sudden changes in direction.

Security should also be involved in backlog reviews and updates (*backlog grooming*), and stay on the lookout for stories that have security, privacy, or compliance risks.

Security doesn't always have to wait for the development team. They can write stories for security, privacy, and compliance requirements on their own and submit them to the backlog.

But the best way to scale your security capability is to train the team members on the ideas and techniques in this chapter and help them to create security personas and attack trees so that they can understand and deal with security risks and requirements on their own.

Security Stories

How do security requirements fit into stories?

Stories for security features (user/account setup, password change/forgot password, etc.) are mostly straightforward:

> As a {registered user}
>
> I want to {log on to the system}
>
> so that {I can see and do only the things that I am authorized to see and do}

Stories for security features work like any other story. But, because of risks associated with making a mistake in implementing these features, you need to pay extra attention to the acceptance criteria, such as the following examples and test scenarios:

User logs on successfully
What should the user be able to see and do? What information should be recorded and where?

User fails to log on because of invalid credentials
What error(s) should the user see? How many times can the users try to log on before access is disabled, and for how long? What information should be recorded and where?

User forgets credentials
This should lead to another story to help the user in resetting a password.

User is not registered
This should lead to another story to help the user get signed up and issued with credentials.

Using OWASP ASVS to Define Acceptance Criteria

OWASP's Application Security Verification Standard (ASVS) (*https://www.owasp.org/ index.php/Category:OWASP_Application_Security_Verification_Standard_Project*) project is a valuable resource to help in writing security stories, especially for web and mobile projects.

The ASVS is an open source resource designed for security auditors, but it can also be used by developers and testers when defining requirements, and especially acceptance criteria—just skip the up-front stuff about auditing and go straight to the checklists.

ASVS checklists include information on how to make sure that you are doing user management correctly, and what you need to check for when implementing access controls, auditing, logging, crypto, and other security controls. We recommend that someone with good security knowledge reviews the checklists and selects acceptance criteria that are appropriate for your project.

For the preceding user logon story, ASVS 3.0 lists 28 things that you should check to make sure that the story is implemented correctly:

1. Verify all pages and resources by default require authentication except those specifically intended to be public.

2. Verify that forms containing credentials are not filled in by the application. Pre-filling by the application implies that credentials are stored in plain text or a reversible format, which is explicitly prohibited.

3. Verify all authentication controls are enforced on the server side.

4. Verify all authentication controls fail securely to ensure attackers cannot log in.

5. Verify password entry fields allow, or encourage, the use of passphrases, and do not prevent password managers, long passphrases, or highly complex passwords from being entered.

6. Verify all account identity authentication functions (such as update profile, forgot password, disabled or lost token, help desk, and IVR) that might regain access to the account are at least as resistant to attack as the primary authentication mechanism.

7. Verify that the changing password functionality includes the old password, the new password, and a password confirmation.

8. Verify that all authentication decisions can be logged, without storing sensitive session identifiers or passwords. This should include requests with relevant metadata needed for security investigations.

9. Verify that account passwords are one-way hashed with a salt, and that there is sufficient work factor to defeat brute-force and password hash recovery attacks.

10. Verify that credentials are transported using a suitable encrypted link, and that all pages/functions that require a user to enter credentials are done so using an encrypted link.

11. Verify that the forgotten password function and other recovery paths do not reveal the current password, and that the new password is not sent in clear text to the user.

12. Verify that information enumeration is not possible via login, password reset, or forgot account functionality.

13. Verify there are no default passwords (such as "password") in use for the application framework or any components used by the application.

14. Verify that anti-automation is in place to prevent breached credential testing, brute forcing, and account lockout attacks.

15. Verify that all authentication credentials for accessing services external to the application are encrypted and stored in a protected location.

16. Verify that forgotten password and other recovery paths use a TOTP or soft token, mobile push, or other offline recovery mechanism. Use of a random value in an email or SMS should be a last resort and is known to be weak.

17. Verify that account lockout is divided into soft and hard lock status, and these are not mutually exclusive. If an account is temporarily soft locked out due to a brute-force attack, this should not reset the hard lock status.

18. Verify that if shared knowledge-based questions (also known as "secret questions") are required, the questions do not violate privacy laws and are sufficiently strong to protect accounts from malicious recovery.

19. Verify that the system can be configured to disallow the use of a configurable number of previous passwords.

20. Verify that risk-based reauthentication, two-factor or transaction signing is in place for high-value transactions.

21. Verify that measures are in place to block the use of commonly chosen passwords and weak passphrases.

22. Verify that all authentication challenges, whether successful or failed, should respond in the same average response time.

23. Verify that secrets, API keys, and passwords are not included in the source code or online source code repositories.

24. Verify that if an application allows users to authenticate, they can authenticate using two-factor authentication or other strong authentication, or any similar scheme that provides protection against username + password disclosure.

25. Verify that administrative interfaces are not accessible to untrusted parties.

26. Browser autocomplete and integration with password managers are permitted unless prohibited by risk-based policy.

That's a lot of things to check for in what looked like a simple story! How many of these would you have come up with on your own?

OWASP's ASVS has been built up over time by some of the smartest security people around. Make sure to take advantage of it. We'll look at how to use it to help in code reviews in a later chapter.

Privacy, Fraud, Compliance, and Encryption

Besides security features, the following are other security requirements that may need to be considered:

Privacy
Identifying information that is private or sensitive, and that needs to be protected through encryption or tokenization, access control, and auditing.

Fraud protection
Identity management, enforcing separation of duties, verification and approval steps in key workflows, auditing and logging, identifying patterns of behavior, and thresholds and alerting on exceptions.

Regulatory compliance
What do you need to include in implementing controls (authentication, access control, auditing, encryption), and what do you need to prove in development and operations for assurance purposes?

Compliance requirements will constrain how the team works, what reviews or testing it needs to do, and what approvals or oversight it requires, as well as what evidence the team needs to keep of all these steps in developing and delivering the system. We will look more into how compliance is handled in Agile and DevOps environments in a separate chapter.

Encryption
There are two parts to encryption requirements:

1. Understanding what information needs to be encrypted

2. How encryption must be done: permitted algorithms and key management techniques

Crypto Requirements: Here Be Dragons

Encryption is an area where you need to be especially careful with requirements and implementation. Some of this guidance may come from regulators. For example, the Payment Card Industry Data Security Standard (PCI DSS) for systems that handle credit card data lays out explicit cryptographic requirements:

1. In Section 3, PCI DSS lists the information that needs to be tokenized, one-way hashed, or encrypted; and requirements for strong cryptography and key management (generating and storing keys, distributing keys, rotating and expiring them).

2. In the glossary, of all places, PCI DSS defines "strong cryptography" and lists examples of standards and algorithms that are acceptable. It then points to "the current version of NIST Special Publication 800-57 Part 1 (*http://csrc.nist.gov/publica tions/*) for more guidance on cryptographic key strengths and algorithms." In the glossary under "Cryptographic Key Generation," it refers to other guides that lay out how key management should be done.

This isn't clear or simple—but crypto is not clear or simple. Crypto is one area where if you don't know what you are doing, you need to get help from an expert. And if you do know what you are doing, then you should probably still get help from an expert.

Whatever you do when it comes to crypto: *do not try to invent your own crypto algorithm or try to modify somebody else's published algorithm, ever.*

We'll look at compliance and privacy requirements (and at encryption again) in Chapter 14, *Compliance*.

The team needs to find some way to track these requirements and constraints, either as part of the team's guidelines for development or checklists in story writing or their *Definition of Done*: the team's contract with one another and with the rest of the organization on what is needed before a story is complete and ready to be delivered, and before the team can move on to other work.

Tracking and dealing with nonfunctional requirements like security and reliability is an unsolved problem in Agile development. Experts disagree on "the right way" to do this. But they do agree that it needs to be done. The important thing is to make sure that the team comes up with a way to recognize and track these requirements, and that the team sticks with it.

SAFECode Security Stories

SAFECode (*https://www.safecode.org*), the Software Assurance Forum for Excellence in Code, is an industry group made up of vendors like Adobe, Oracle, and Microsoft which provides guidance on software security and assurance. In 2012, it published a free list of "Practical Security Stories and Security Tasks for Agile Development Environments" (*http://safecode.org/publication/SAFECode_Agile_Dev_Security0712.pdf*), sharing some of their ideas on how to include security in Agile requirements planning and implementation.

There are SAFECode stories to prevent common security vulnerabilities in applications: XSS, path traversal, remote execution, CSRF, OS command injection, SQL injection, and password brute forcing. Other stories cover checks for information exposure through error messages, proper use of encryption, authentication and session management, transport layer security, restricted uploads, and URL redirection to untrusted sites.

There are also stories that go into detailed coding issues, such as NULL pointer checking, boundary checking, numeric conversion, initialization, thread/process synchronization, exception handling, and use of unsafe/restricted functions. And there are stories which describe secure development practices and operational tasks for the team: making sure that you're using the latest compiler; patching the runtime and libraries; using static analysis, vulnerability scanning, and code reviews of high-risk code; tracking and fixing security bugs; and more advanced practices that require help from security experts, like fuzzing, threat modeling, pen tests, and environmental hardening.

Altogether this is a comprehensive list of security risks that need to be managed, and secure development practices that should be followed on most projects. While the content is good, there are problems with the format.

To understand why, let's take a look at a couple of SAFECode security stories:

> As a(an) architect/developer, I want to ensure,
> AND as QA I want to verify that
> the same steps are followed in the same order to
> perform an action, without possible deviation on purpose or not

> As a(an) architect/developer, I want to ensure,
> AND as QA I want to verify that
> the damage incurred to the system and its data
> is limited if an unauthorized actor is able to take control of a process or
> otherwise influence its behavior in unpredicted ways

As you can see, SAFECode's security stories are a well-intentioned, but *a-w-k-w-a-r-d* attempt to reframe nonfunctional requirements in Agile user story format. Many teams will be put off by how artificial and forced this approach is, and how alien it is to how they actually think and work.

Although SAFECode's stories look like stories, they can't be pulled from the backlog and delivered like other stories, and they can't be removed from the backlog when they are done, because they are never "done." The team has to keep worrying about these issues throughout the project and the life of the system.

Each SAFECode security story has a list of detailed backlog tasks that need to be considered by the team as it moves into sprint planning or as it works on individual user stories. But most of these tasks amount to reminding developers to follow guidelines for secure coding and to do scanning or other security testing.

Teams may decide that it is not practical or even necessary to track all these recurring tasks in the backlog. Some of the checks should be made part of the team's Definition of Done for stories or for the sprint. Others should be part of the team's coding guidelines and review checklists, or added into the automated build pipeline, or they could be taken care of by training the team in secure coding so that the team members know know how to do things properly from the start.

Free Security Guide and Training from SAFECode

SAFECode also provides free training and secure coding guidelines that teams can follow to build secure systems.

This includes a free guide for secure development (*https://www.safe code.org/publication/SAFECode_Dev_Practices0211.pdf*) which is especially valuable for C/C++ developers, covering common security problems and providing extensive links to tools, articles, and other guidance.

If you can't afford more comprehensive secure development training for your team, SAFECode offers a set of introductory online training courses (*https://training.safecode.org/courses*) in secure coding for C/C++ and Java, crypto, threat modeling, security in cloud computing, penetration testing, and how to defend against specific attacks like SQL injection.

SAFECode's Security Stories are not a tool that you should try to force onto an Agile team. But they are a way to get security requirements on the table. Reviewing and discussing these stories will create a conversation about security practices and controls with the team and encourage the team members to respond with ideas of their own.

Security Personas and Anti-Personas

Personas are another tool that many Agile teams use when defining requirements and designing features. Personas are fictional descriptions of different types of people who will use the system. For each persona, the team writes a fictional biography, describing their background and experience, technical ability, goals, and preferences. These profiles could be built up from interviews, market research, or in brainstorming sessions.

Personas help the team to get into the mindset of users in concrete ways, to understand how someone would want to use a feature and why. They can be helpful in working out user experience models. Personas are also used in testing to come up with different kinds of test scenarios.

For teams that are already using personas, it can be useful to ask the team to also consider *anti-personas*: users of the system that won't follow the normal rules.

Designers and teams look for ways to make system features as simple and intuitive to use as possible. However, security can require that a system put deliberate speed bumps or other design anti-patterns in place, because we recognize that adversaries are also going to use our system, and we need to make it difficult for them to achieve their goals.

When defining personas, the recommendation is to create a single persona for each "category" or "class" of user. There is very little to gain from creating too many or complex personas when a few simple ones will do.

For example, one system that an author worked on had 11 user personas, and only 5 anti-personas: Hacking Group Member, Fraudulent User, Organized Criminal Gang, Malware Author, and Compromised Sysadmin.

When detailing an anti-persona, the key things to consider are the motivations of the adversary, their capability, and their cutoff points. It's important to remember that adversaries can include legitimate users who have an incentive to break the system. For example, an online insurance claim system might have to consider users who are encouraged to lie to claim more money.

Personas are used by the entire team to help design the entire system. They shouldn't be constrained to the application, so understanding how those users might attack business processes, third parties, and physical premises can be important. It's possible that the team is building a computer solution that is simply one component of a large business process, and the personas represent people who want to attack the process through the application.

Here are some examples of simple anti-personas:

- Brian is a semiprofessional fraudster
  - He looks for a return on investment of attacks of at least £10k
  - Brian doesn't want to get caught, and won't do anything that he believes will leave a trail
  - Brian has access to simple hacking tools but has little computer experience and cannot write code on his own
- Laura is a low-income claimant
  - Laura doesn't consider lying to the welfare system immoral and wants to claim the maximum she can get away with
  - Laura has friends who are experts in the benefits system
  - Laura has no technical competence
- Greg is an amateur hacker in an online hacking group
  - Greg wants to deface the site or otherwise leave a calling card
  - Greg is after defacing as many sites as possible and seeks the easiest challenges
  - Greg has no financial acumen and is unaware of how to exploit security holes for profit
  - Greg is a reasonable programmer and is able to script and modify off-the-shelf tools

For more examples of anti-personas, and more on how to use attacker personas or anti-personas in security requirements and threat modeling, check out Appendix C of Adam Shostack's book *Threat Modeling: Designing for Security* (Wiley) (*https://threat modelingbook.com*).

Attacker Stories: Put Your Black Hat On

Another way to include security in requirements is through attacker stories or misuse cases (instead of use cases). In these stories the team spends some time thinking through how a feature could be misused by an attacker or by another malicious, or even careless, user. This forces the team to think about what specific actions it needs to defend against, as the following example shows:

As {some kind of adversary}

I want to {try to do something bad}

so that {I can steal or damage sensitive information
or get something without paying for it

or disable a key function of the system
or some other bad thing...}

These stories are more concrete, and more testable, than SAFECode's security stories. Instead of acceptance criteria which prove out success scenarios, each attacker story has a list of specific "negation criteria" or "refutation criteria": conditions or scenarios that you need to disprove for the story to be considered done.

Take a user story, and as part of elaborating the story and listing the scenarios, step back and look at the story through a security lens. Don't just think of what the user wants to do and can do. Think about what you don't want them to do. Get the same people who are working on the story to "put their black hats on" and think evil for a little while, to brainstorm and come up with negative cases.

Thinking like an attacker isn't easy or natural for most developers, as we discuss in Chapter 8, *Threat Assessments and Understanding Attacks*. But it will get easier with practice. A good tester on your team should be able to come up with ideas and test cases, especially if he has experience in exploratory testing; or you could bring in a security expert to help the team to develop scenarios, especially for security features. You can also look at common attacks and requirements checklists like SAFECode's security stories or the OWASP ASVS, which we will look at later in this chapter.

Anti-personas can come in very useful for misuse cases. The *As A* can be the name or anti-persona in question, and this can also help developers to build the *so that*.

Attacker Stories Versus Threat Modeling

Writing attacker stories or misuse cases overlaps in some ways with threat modeling. Both of these techniques are about looking at the system from the point of view of an attacker or other threat actor. Both of these techniques help you to plug security holes up front, but they are done at different levels:

- Attacker stories are done from the point of view of the user, as you define feature workflows and user interactions, treating the system as a black box.

- Threat modeling is a white-box approach, done from the point of view of the developer or designer, reviewing controls and trust assumptions from an insider's perspective.

Attacker stories can be tested in an automated fashion. This is particularly useful to teams that follow test-driven development (TDD) or behavior-driven development (BDD) practices, where developers write automated tests for each story before they write the code, and use these tests to drive their design thinking. By including tests for attacker stories, they can ensure that security features and controls cannot be disabled or bypassed.

Writing Attacker Stories

Attacker stories act as a mirror to user stories. You don't need to write attacker stories for every user story in the system. But you should at least write them in the following scenarios:

- You write stories for security features, like the logon story.
- You write or change stories that deal with money, private data, or important admin functions in the system.
- You find that a story calls into other services that deal with money, private data, or important admin functions so that your feature doesn't become a back door.

These are the kinds of user stories that are most interesting to attackers or fraudsters. This is when you need to take on the persona of an attacker and look at features in the system from an adversarial point of view.

As we've seen, the adversary doesn't have to be a hacker or a cyber criminal. The adversary could be an insider with a grudge, a selfish user who is willing to take advantage of others, or a competitor trying to steal information about your customers or your intellectual property. Or the *adversary* could just be an admin user who needs to be protected from making expensive mistakes, or an external system that may not always behave correctly.

Challenge the scenarios in the user story, and ask some basic questions:

1. What could go wrong? What would happen if the user doesn't follow the main success scenarios through a feature? What checks do you need to add, and what could happen if a check fails? Look carefully at limits, data edits, error handling, and what kind of testing you need to do.

2. Ask questions about the user's identity and the data that is provided in the scenario. Can you trust them? How can you be sure?

3. What information could an adversary be looking for? What information can she already see, and what could he do with this information?

4. Are you logging or auditing everything that you need to? When should you create an alert or other notification?

Use this exercise to come up with refutation criteria (the user can do this, but can't do that; the user can see this, but can't see that), instead of, or as part of, the conditions of satisfaction for the story. Prioritize these cases based on risk, and add the cases that you agree need to be taken care of as scenarios to the current story or as new stories to the backlog if they are big enough.[1]

As an Attacker, I MUST NOT Be Able To…

Another way of writing attacker stories is to describe in the story what you don't want the attacker to be able to do:

> As {some kind of adversary}
>
> I MUST NOT be able to {do something bad}
>
> so that….

This can be easier than trying to write a story from the attacker's point of view, because you don't have to understand or describe the specific attack steps that the adversary might try. You can simply focus on what you don't want him to be able to do: you don't want him to see or change another user's information, enter a high-value transaction without authorization, bypass credit limit checks, and so on.

The team will have to fill in acceptance criteria later, listing specific actions to check for and test, but this makes the requirements visible, something that needs to be prioritized and scheduled.

Attacker stories or misuse cases are good for identifying business logic vulnerabilities, reviewing security features (e.g., authentication, access control, auditing, password management, and licensing) and anti-fraud controls, tightening up error handling and basic validation, and keeping onside of privacy regulations. And they can help the team come up with more and better test cases.

Writing these stories fits well into how Agile teams think and work. They are done at the same level as user stories, using the same language and the same approach. It's a more concrete way of thinking about and dealing with threats than a threat modeling exercise, and it's more useful than trying to track a long list of things to do or not to do.

You end up with specific, actionable test cases that are easy for the team, including the Product Owner, to understand and appreciate. This is critically important in Scrum, because the Product Owner decides what work gets done and in what priority. And because attacker stories are done in-phase, by the people who are working on the stories as they are working on the stories (rather than a separate review activity that needs to coordinated and scheduled), they are more likely to get done.

---

1 This description of attacker stories is based on work done by Judy Neher, an independent Agile security consultant. Watch "Abuser Stories - Think Like the Bad Guy with Judy Neher - at Agile 2015" (*https://www.youtube.com/watch?v=hxQ1j_HQhGw*).

Spending a half hour or so together thinking through a piece of the system from this perspective should help the team find and prevent weaknesses up front. As new threats and risks come up, and as you learn about new attacks or exploits, it's important to go back and revisit your existing stories and write new attacker stories to fill in gaps.

Attack Trees

A relatively new methodology for understanding the ways that systems can be attacked is to use an *attack tree*.

This approach was first described by Bruce Schneier in 1999, where he proposed a structured method of outlining growing chains of attack (*https://www.schneier.com/ academic/archives/1999/12/attack_trees.html*).

To build an attack tree, you start by outlining the goals of an attacker. This might be to decrypt secrets, gain root access, or make a fraudulent claim.

We then map all the possible ways that someone can achieve the action. The canonical example from Schneier says that to open a safe, you might pick the lock, learn the combination, cut open the safe, or install it improperly.

We then iterate on the attack tree, covering any points where we think that we are involved; so for example, to learn the combination, one could find the combination written down, or one could get the combination from a target.

Modern usage of these attack trees can result in very broad trees and very deep trees at times. Once we have this tree, we can start looking at each node and determining properties such as likelihood, cost, ease of attack, repeatability, chance of being caught, and total reward to the attacker. The properties you will use will depend on your understanding of your adversaries and the amount of time and effort you want to go to.

For each node in the tree, you can easily identify which nodes are higher risk by calculating the cost-benefit ratio for the attacker.

Once we have identified the highest risk areas, we can consider countermeasures, such as staff training, patrolling guards, and alarms.

If done well, this can enable security to trace back controls and identify why they put a control in place, and justify its value. If you get extra investment, would you be better off with a more expensive firewall or installing a secrets management system? It can also help you identify replacement controls. So if a security control is unacceptable to the use of the system, you can understand what the impact is to removing it and what risks it opens up.

Advanced users of this attack tree method are able to build per-system attack trees as well as departmental, unit, and even organization-wide attack trees. One of us used this method to completely change the security spending of the organization toward real risks rather than the traditional security views of where to spend money (hint: it meant spending a lot less on fancy firewalls than before).

Building an Attack Tree

Building an attack tree is an interesting experience. This technique is very powerful, but also very subjective.

We've found that it is best to build the trees over a series of workshops, each workshop containing a mix of security specialists, technical specialists, and business specialists.

An initial workshop with a security specialist should be used to outline the primary goals of the trees that you want to consider. For example, in one recent session looking at a federated login system, we determined that there were only three goals that we cared about: logging in, stealing credentials, and denial of service.

Use the STRIDE acronym to review common threats:

- Spoofing user identity
- Tampering
- Repudiation
- Information disclosure
- Denial of service
- Elevation of privilege

Consider your system in the face of these threats, and come up with a set of goals.

Then call together workshops with a mix of security professionals, technical specialists, and business specialists. We've found that the business specialists are the most valuable here. While the security and technical professionals are good at creatively coming up with how to achieve a goal, the business professionals tend to be much better at coming up with the goals themselves, and they tend to know the limits of the system (somehow security and technical professionals seem to view computer systems as perfect and inviolate). Business professionals tend to be far more realistic about the flaws and the manual workarounds in place that make the systems work.

Once the trees are complete, security professionals can do a lot of the work gauging the properties, such as cost and so forth.

Maintaining and Using Attack Trees

Once the trees are written and available to the teams, they will of course slowly become out of date and incorrect as the context and situation change.

Attack trees can be stored in digital form, either in spreadsheets, or we've found the *mind map* format to work effectively.

They should be reviewed on a regular basis; and in particular, changes in security controls should be checked with the attack trees to ensure that the risk profile hasn't changed significantly.

We've had experience in at least one company where the attack trees are stored electronically in a wiki, and all the controls are linked to the digital story cards, so the status of each story is recorded in a live view. This shows the security team the current state of the threat tree, any planned work that might affect it, and allows compliance officers to trace back from a work order to find out why it was requested and when it was completed.

You should see what works for your teams and your security and compliance officers, but this kind of interlinking is very valuable for high-performing and fast-moving teams to give them situational awareness to help in making decisions.

Infrastructure and Operations Requirements

Because of the speed at which today's Agile—and especially DevOps—teams deliver systems to production, and the rate that they make changes to systems once they are being used, developers have to be much closer to operations and the infrastructure. There are no Waterfall handoffs to separate operations and maintenance as developers move on to the next project. Instead, these teams work in a service-based model, where they share or sometimes own the responsibility of running and supporting the system. They are in it for the life of the system.

NoOps and "You Build It, You Run It"

Netflix made the decision several years ago to outsource its IT operations and infrastructure to Amazon. Today Netflix is one of the biggest users of cloud services and internet bandwidth. Netflix's position is that data center management and infrastructure provisioning and network engineering are "undifferentiated heavy lifting": work that it is important and expensive to do properly (the "heavy lifting" part) but that can be better done by somebody else so that Netflix can focus on product and service design and delivery.

Netflix has no operations engineering organization: it does all its operations through Amazon's AWS API. Netflix has some platform engineering teams that build common services shared by the other engineering teams. But each engineering team is respon-

---

sible for designing, building, delivering, and supporting the code that it writes. Netflix calls this "NoOps."

At Amazon, like Netflix, systems are broken down into microservices that are designed and delivered by small teams. This includes the Amazon AWS services that Netflix and other AWS customers use. And like Netflix, Amazon teams are responsible for delivering, supporting, and operating their piece of the system. At Amazon, they call this "You build it, you run it."

These are extreme examples of how the roles of operations and development are changing as organizations adopt new technology architectures and new ways of delivering systems faster and cheaper.

The DevOps and NoOps movements are gaining speed and traction, and we expect that many more traditional teams will start moving this way over time.

This means that they need to think not just about the people who will use the system, but also the people who will run it and support it: the infrastructure and network engineers, operations, and customer service. All of them become customers and partners in deciding how the system will be designed and implemented.

For example, while working on auditing and logging in the system, the team must meet the needs of the following teams and requirements:

Business analytics
Tracking details on users and their activity to understand which features users find valuable, which features they don't, how they are using the system, and where and how they spend their time. This information is used in A/B testing to drive future product design decisions and mined using big data systems to find trends and patterns in the business itself.

Compliance
Requirements for activity auditing to meet regulatory requirements, what information needs to be recorded, for how long, and who needs to see this information.

Infosec
What information is needed for attack monitoring and forensic analysis.

Ops
System monitoring and operational metrics needed for service-level management and planning.

Development
The development team's own information needs for troubleshooting and debugging.

Teams need to understand and deal with operational requirements for confidentiality, integrity, and availability, whether these requirements come from the engineering teams, operations, or compliance. They need to understand the existing infrastructure and operations constraints, especially in enterprise environments, where the system needs to work as part of a much larger whole. They need answers to a lot of important questions:

- What will the runtime be: cloud or on-premises or hybrid, VMs or containers or bare metal servers?
- What OS?
- What database or backend data storage?
- How much storage and CPU and memory capacity?

How will the infrastructure be secured? What compliance constraints do we have to deal with?

Packaging and deployment
How will the application and its dependencies be packaged and built? How will you manage the build and deployment artifacts? What tools and procedures will be used to deploy the system? What operational windows do you have to make updates– when can you take the system down, and for how long?

Monitoring
What information (alerts, errors, metrics) does ops need for monitoring and troubleshooting? What are the logging requirements (format, time synchronization, rotation)? How will errors and failures be escalated?

Secrets management
What keys, passwords, and other credentials are needed for the system? Where will they be stored? Who needs to have access to them? How often do they need to be rotated, and how is this done?

Data archival
What information needs to be backed up and kept and for how long to meet compliance, business continuity or other requirements? Where do logs need to be stored, and for how long?

Availability
How is clustering handled -at the network, OS, database and application level? What are the Recovery Time and Recovery Point Objectives (RTO/RPO) for serious failures? How will DDOS attacks be defended against?

Separation of duties

Are developers permitted access to production for support purposes? Is testing in production allowed? What can developers see or do, what can't they see or do? What changes (if any) are they allowed to make without explicit approval? What auditing needs to be done to prove all of this?

Logging

As we've already seen, logging needs to be done for many different purposes: for support and troubleshooting, for monitoring, for forensics, for analytics. What header information needs to be recorded to serve all of these purposes: date and timestamp (to what precision?), user ID, source IP, node, service identifier, what else? What type of information should be recorded at each level (DEBUG, INFO, WARN, ERROR)?

Should log messages be written for human readers, or be parsed by tools? How do you protect against tampering and poisoning of logs? How do you detect gaps in logging? What sensitive information needs to be masked or omitted in logs?

What system events and security events need to be logged? PCI DSS provides some good guidance for logging and auditing. To comply with PCI DSS, you need to record the following information:

- All access to critical or sensitive data
- All access by root/admin users
- All access to audit trails (audit the auditing system)
- Access control violations
- Authentication events and changes (logons, new users, password changes, etc.)
- Auditing and logging system events: start, shutdown, suspend, restart, and errors

Security and the CIA

All operational requirements for security are mapped to one or more elements of the CIA (C: Confidentiality, I: Integrity, A: Availability) triad:

Confidentiality
> Ensuring that the information can only be read, consumed, or used by system users who are the appropriate people.

Integrity
> Ensuring that the information can only be modified or changed by system users who are supposed to change it. That it is only changed in the appropriate way and that the changes are correctly logged.

Availability
> Ensuring that the information is accessible to users who need it at the time when they need it.

Key Takeaways

Here are the key things that you need to think about to get security onto the backlog:

- Security happens in the thought processes and design of stories, not just during coding. Be involved early and educate everyone to think about security.
- Pay attention to user stories as they are being written and elaborated. Look for security risks and concerns.
- Consider building attack trees to help your team understand the ways that adversaries could attack your system, and what protections you need to put in place.
- Write attacker stories for high-risk user stories: a mirror of the story, written from an adversary's point of view.
- Use OWASP's ASVS and SAFECode's Security Stories as resources to help in writing stories, and for writing conditions of satisfaction for security stories.
- If the team is modeling user personas, help them to create anti-personas to keep adversaries in mind when filling out requirements and test conditions.
- Think about operations and infrastructure, not just functional needs, when writing requirements, including security requirements.

CHAPTER 6

Agile Vulnerability Management

New vulnerabilities in software are found every day. Many organizations are not aware of vulnerabilities in their systems until it is too late. What's worse is that developers and their managers often ignore vulnerabilities that they do know about. This means that attackers can continue to exploit software vulnerabilities months or years after they were first reported, using automated scanners and exploit kits.

One of the most important responsibilities of a security team is vulnerability management: ensuring that people in your organization continuously check for known vulnerabilities, assess and understand the risks that these vulnerabilities pose to the organization, and take appropriate steps to remediate them.

Security teams need to work with developers, operations, compliance, and management in order to get all of this done, making vulnerability management an important touch point.

In this chapter, we'll look at how to manage vulnerabilities and how to align vulnerability management with Agile approaches to getting work done. We'll also look at how to fulfill the CYA paperwork aspect of vulnerability management required for compliance, in a lightweight, efficient way.

Vulnerability Scanning and Patching

Setting up and scheduling vulnerability scans properly, making sure that scanning policies are configured correctly and consistently enforced, reviewing and triaging the results based on risk, packaging up patches and testing to make sure that patches don't introduce new problems, scheduling and deploying updates, and keeping track of all of this work so that you can prove that it has been done is a huge operational responsibility for an organization of any size.

Techniques and tools that we look at throughout this book, including automating configuration management in code, and automating builds, testing, and delivery, can be used to help make this work safer and cheaper.

First, Understand What You Need to Scan

Your first step in understanding and managing vulnerabilities is to identify all the systems and applications that you need to secure, both on premises and in the cloud. Getting an up-to-date and accurate inventory of what you need to scan is difficult for most organizations and can be effectively impossible at enterprise scale; whereas a small security team may be responsible for thousands of applications in multiple data centers.

One of the many advantages of using automated configuration management tools like Ansible, Chef, and Puppet is that they are based on a central repository that describes all of your servers, how they are configured, and what software packages are installed on them.

UpGuard: Continuous Vulnerability Assessment

UpGuard (*https://www.upguard.com*) automatically discovers configuration information about Linux and Windows servers, network devices, and cloud services; identifies vulnerabilities and inconsistencies; and tracks changes to this information over time.

It continuously assesses vulnerability risks, automatically scanning systems or using information from other scanners, and assigns a compliance score for all of your systems.

UpGuard also creates tests to enforce configuration policies, and can generate runbook code that you can use with tools like Ansible, Chef, Puppet, Microsoft Windows PowerShell DSC, and Docker to apply updates and configuration changes.

You can use this information to understand the systems that you need to scan for vulnerabilities and to identify systems that need to be patched when you receive a vulnerability alert. Then you can use the same tools to automatically and quickly apply patches.

Then Decide How to Scan and How Often

Most vulnerability management programs run in a reactive, regularly scheduled scan-and-patch cycle, like Microsoft's "Patch Tuesday":

1. Set up a scan of your servers and network devices using tools like Core Impact, Nessus, Nexpose, or OpenVAS, or an online service like Qualys. These scanners

look for known vulnerabilities in common OS distributions, network devices, databases, and other runtime software, including outdated software packages, default credentials, and other dangerous configuration mistakes.

2. Review the vulnerabilities reported, filter out duplicates and false positives, and prioritize true positive findings based on risk.

3. Hand the results off to engineering to remediate by downloading and applying patches, or correcting the configuration, or adding a signature to your IDS/IPS or WAF/RASP to catch or block attempted exploits.

4. Re-scan to make sure that the problems were actually fixed.

5. Record what you did for auditors.

6. Rinse and repeat next month or next quarter, or however often compliance requires.

How Scanning Needs to Change in Agile and DevOps Environments

It's not enough to scan systems once a month or once a quarter when you are making changes every week or several times a day. You will never be able to keep up.

You'll need to automate and streamline scanning so that it can be run much more often, every day if possible, as part of your build pipelines.

To create an efficient feedback loop, you'll need to find a way to automatically remove duplicates and filter false positives from scanning results, and return the results directly into the tools that teams use to manage their work, whether it's a ticketing system like Jira, or an Agile backlog management system like Rally or VersionOne, or a Kanban system like Trello.

Tracking Vulnerabilities

As we will see in this book, there are other important ways to get vulnerability information besides scanning your network infrastructure:

- Scanning applications for common coding mistakes and runtime vulnerabilities using *automated security testing* (AST) tools that we'll explore in Chapter 11, *Agile Security Testing*

- Penetration testing and other manual and automated security testing

- Bug bounty programs (discussed in Chapter 12)

- Threat intelligence and vendor alerts

- Software component analysis (SCA) scanning tools that check for known vulnerabilities in open source components, something we'll look at in more detail later in this chapter

- Scanning runtime containers and container images for known vulnerabilities

- Scanning cloud instances for common vulnerabilities and unsafe configs using services like AWS Inspector (*https://aws.amazon.com/inspector/*)

- Manual code reviews or code audits of application code and infrastructure recipes and templates

- Bug reports from partners, users, and other customers (which is not how you want to hear about a vulnerability in your system)

To get an overall picture of security risk, all of this information needs to be consolidated, tracked, and reported for all of your systems. And it needs to be evaluated, prioritized, and fed back to operations and developers in ways that make sense to them and fit how they work so that problems can get fixed quickly.

Managing Vulnerabilities

Vulnerabilities in software or infrastructure are defects in requirements or design or coding or implementation. They should be handled like any other defect in the system: fixed immediately, or added to the team's backlog and prioritized along with other work, or dismissed because the team (including management) decides that the problem is not worth fixing.

But vulnerabilities introduce risks that engineering teams, product managers, and other people in the organization have a hard time understanding. It's usually obvious to users and to the team when there is a functional bug or operational problem that needs to be fixed, or if the system's performance is unacceptable. These are problems that engineering teams know how to deal with. Security vulnerabilities aren't as cut and dried.

As we'll see in Chapter 7, *Risk for Agile Teams*, to decide which security bugs need to be fixed and how quickly this has to be done, you need to know the answers to several questions:

- What is the overall threat profile for your organization? What kind of threats does your organization face, and what are the threat actors after?

- What is the risk profile of the system(s) where the vulnerability was found?

- How widespread is the vulnerability?

- How easy is it for an attacker to discover and to exploit?

- How effective are your existing security defenses in defending against attacks?

- What are the potential technical and business impacts to your organization of a successful attack?
- Can you detect if an attack is in progress?
- How quickly can you contain and recover from an attack, and block further attacks, once you have detected it?
- What are the costs of fixing the vulnerability, and what is your confidence that this will be done correctly and safely?
- What are your compliance obligations?

In order to understand and evaluate these risk factors, you need to look at vulnerabilities separately from the rest of the work that the engineering teams are doing. Tracking and reporting vulnerabilities is a required part of many organization's GRC (governance, risk, and compliance) programs and is mandated by regulations such as PCI DSS to demonstrate to management and auditors that due care and attention has been followed in identifying and managing security risks.

Vulnerability management involves a lot of mundane, but important bookkeeping work:

- Recording each vulnerability, when and where and how it was found or reported
- Scanning or checking to see where else the vulnerability might exist
- Determining the priority in which it should be fixed, based on a recognized risk rating
- Assigning an owner, to ensure that the problem gets fixed
- Scheduling the fix
- Verifying that it was fixed properly and tracking how long it took to get fixed
- Reporting all of this, and highlighting exceptions, to auditors

This is a full-time job in large enterprises. It's a job that is not done at all in many smaller organizations, especially in startups.

Application vulnerability management tools like bugBlast (*https://buguroo.com/prod ucts/bugblast-next-gen-appsec-platform*), Code Dx (*https://codedx.com*), and Denim Group's ThreadFix (*http://www.threadfix.it*) consolidate vulnerabilities found by different scanners as well as problems found in pen testing or manual reviews, and consolidate this information across multiple systems. This will help you to identify risks inside and across systems by identifying which systems or components have the most vulnerabilities, which types of vulnerabilities are the most common, and how long vulnerabilities have been left open.

You can assess which teams are doing the best job of remediation and whether teams are meeting their compliance requirements, and you can also evaluate the effectiveness of tools by looking at which tools find the most important vulnerabilities.

These tools simplify your job of managing findings by filtering out duplicate findings from multiple tools or different test runs and by giving you a chance to review, qualify, and prioritize vulnerability findings before asking developers to resolve them. Most vulnerability management tools have interfaces into popular development tools, so that you can automatically update the team's backlog.

CVEs, CWEs, and CVSS… Oh, My!

You can see how bad a job we've been doing as an industry of dealing with security bugs by looking at the extensive infrastructure and bureaucracy that has grown up around reporting, classifying, and prioritizing security problems. Instead of: "Hey, here's a bug; fix it!", we have an alphabet soup of CVEs, CWEs, CVSS, and CWSS to help keep track of all of these problems, why they happened, how they were found, how important they are, how to look for them, and how to know whether you fixed them or not.

CVE (*Common Vulnerabilities and Exposures*)
: The CVE (*https://cve.mitre.org/index.html*) is a long list of thousands of specific vulnerabilities found in software, maintained by MITRE for the US-CERT and US Department of Homeland Defense, and available to everybody else for free.

CWE (*Common Weakness Enumeration*)
: The CWE (*https://cwe.mitre.org/*) is a shorter, but still long, list that tries to describe and organize the mistakes that developers made which led to reported vulnerabilities in the CVE database. It has been built up by analyzing the CVEs to understand what the underlying cause or causes of each CVE was.

A CWE is a particularly dangerous mistake in programming or design that has been proven to lead to an exploitable vulnerability in software. The National Vulnerability Database lists the different types of CWEs (*https://nvd.nist.gov/cwe.cfm#cwes*).

For each CWE, there is information that explains the type of bug, examples, how to find it in testing or in code reviews and using static analysis tools, and how to fix it.

MITRE and SANS have come up with a list of the 25 most dangerous mistakes called, unsurprisingly, the "CWE/SANS Top 25 Most Dangerous Software Errors" (*http://cwe.mitre.org/top25/*).

NVD (*National Vulnerability Database*)
: The NVD (*https://nvd.nist.gov/home.cfm*) is a database sponsored by the same US government agencies, to track CVEs and what versions of software are affected,

---

who reported them and when, and then link to the other resources to help people deal with them.

The vulnerability feeds from this database are used by tools (such as OWASP Dependency Check) to track vulnerabilities in software packages.

CVSS and CWSS Scoring Systems

CVSS (*https://www.first.org/cvss*) and CWSS (*https://cwe.mitre.org/cwss/*) are alternative scoring models for determining how serious a CVE or CWE is. The score is based on balancing exploitability (how easy is it for an attacker to find the weakness and use it) against the potential damage that the attacker could cause.

Heartbleed example

Let's look at an example: the Heartbleed OpenSSL vulnerability.

In the National Vulnerability Database, you will find Heartbleed reported under CVE-2014-0160. Although it was a widespread and serious vulnerability that caused a lot of damage and received a lot of attention from the general press, Heartbleed was initially only given a CVSS v2 score of 5.0 on a scale of 1 to 10 (*https://web.nvd.nist.gov/view/vuln/detail?vulnId=CVE-2014-0160*). While the impact of Heartbleed was subsequently reassessed at 7.4 using the newer CVSS v3 scoring model, it pales against the equally infamous ShellShock vulnerability, which scored a perfect 10 (*https://www.first.org/cvss/examples*).

To understand how the vulnerability occurred, we need to look at the CWE information for this bug. Heartbleed's CWE is CWE-119 (*http://cwe.mitre.org/data/definitions/119.html*) Buffer Errors: Improper restriction of Operations within the Bounds of a Memory Buffer, or more specifically, CWE-126 (*http://cwe.mitre.org/data/definitions/126.html*) Buffer Over-read. This is a bounds-check violation in C/C++ caused by forgetting to validate an input value.

All of this trouble over a small and common coding mistake. We'll be looking more at the Heartbleed bug in other chapters of this book, because it is so well known and has been extensively analyzed to understand how and why it happened, and how we can stop problems like this from happening again—which is what this book is about.

What does this mean to developers?

You will see reports of vulnerabilities by CVE. This is how infrastructure security scanners like Nessus or OpenVAS work, and this is how IDS/IPS solutions like Snort, and application firewalls like ModSecurity, detect and block specific attack signatures. And this is how security researchers report and classify what they find.

You will also see bug reports with CWEs from static analysis tools and other scanning tools. This information is used to compare findings from different tools and to evaluate their effectiveness, although unfortunately, this isn't as easy as it sounds, given that different tools may report different, but related, CWEs for the same type of bug.

The CVE/CWE/CVSS/NVD ecosystem is interesting to know about. But unless you are writing a security tool or want to do some security research on the side, you can get through your day and still do a responsible job of building secure systems without worrying too much about CVEs, CWEs, and the rest, unless and until somebody reports a CVE in software that you've written or software that you use.

Dealing with Critical Vulnerabilities

When a critical vulnerability like Heartbleed or ShellShock is found that must be fixed quickly, you need to be able to rely on your vulnerability management program to ensure that:

- You are informed about the vulnerability through threat intelligence and vulnerability feeds, such as a CERT alert (*https://www.us-cert.gov/ncas/alerts*), or sometimes even from the press. In the case of Heartbleed, this wasn't that difficult, since, like the Anna Kournikova virus or ShellShock, it received wide coverage in the popular press, mostly because of its catchy name.

- You understand what the bug is and how serious it is, based on the risk score assigned to the CVE.

- You are confident that you can identify all the systems that need to be checked for this vulnerability.

- You can verify whether and where you have the vulnerability through scanning or configuration checks.

- You can quickly and safely patch or upgrade the vulnerable software package, or disable affected functions or add a signature to your IDS/IPS or firewall to block attacks as a workaround.

- You can verify that the patch was done successfully, or that whatever other step that you took to mitigate the risk of an attack was successful.

Vulnerability management ties security, compliance, development, and operations together in a continuous loop to protect your systems and your organization.

Securing Your Software Supply Chain

An important part of managing vulnerabilities is understanding and securing your software supply chain: the software parts that modern systems are built with. Today's Agile and DevOps teams take extensive advantage of open source libraries and frameworks to reduce development time and costs. But this comes with a downside: they also inherit bugs and vulnerabilities from other people's code.

According to Sonatype, which runs the Central Repository, the world's largest repository for open source software for Java developers: 80 to 90 percent of the code in today's applications comes from open source libraries and frameworks.

A lot of this code has serious problems in it. The Central Repository holds more than 1.36 million components (as of September 2015), and almost 1,500 components are being added every day. More than 70,000 of the software components in the Central Repository contain known security vulnerabilities. On average, 50 new critical vulnerabilities in open source software are reported every day.

Sonatype looked at 31 billion download requests from 106,000 different organizations in 2015. It found that large financial services organizations and other enterprises are downloading an average of more than 230,000 "software parts" each year. But keep in mind this is only counting Java components. The total number of parts, including RubyGems, NuGets, Docker images, and other goodies, is actually much higher.

Of these 230,000 downloads, 1 in every 16 download requests was for software that had at least 1 known security vulnerability.

In just one example, Sonatype reviewed downloads for The Legion of the Bouncy Castle, a popular crypto library. It was downloaded 17.4 million times in 2015. But one-third of the time, people downloaded known vulnerable versions of the library. This means that almost 14,000 organizations across the world unnecessarily and probably unknowingly exposed themselves to potentially serious security risks (*https://www.sonatype.com/2016-state-of-the-software-supply-chain-report*) while trying to make their applications more secure.

Scared yet? You should be.

It's clear that teams must ensure that they know what open source components are included in all their applications, make sure that known good versions were downloaded from known good sources, and that these components are kept up to date when vulnerabilities are found and fixed.

Luckily, you can do this automatically by using SCA tools like OWASP's Dependency Check project, or commercial tools like Black Duck (*https://www.blackducksoft ware.com/solutions/application-security*), JFrog Xray (*https://www.jfrog.com/xray/*), Snyk (*https://snyk.io/*), Sonatype's Nexus Lifecycle (*http://www.sonatype.com/nexus-lifecycle*), or SourceClear (*https://srcclr.com/*).

OWASP Dependency Check

OWASP's Dependency Check (*https://www.owasp.org/index.php/ OWASP_Dependency_Check*) is a free scanner that catalogs all the open source components used in an application and highlights vulnerabilities in these dependencies. It works for Java, .NET, Ruby (gemspec), PHP (composer), Node.js, and Python, as well as some C/C++ projects. Dependency Check integrates with common build tools, including Ant, Maven, and Gradle, and CI servers like Jenkins.

Dependency Check reports on any components with known vulnerabilities reported in NIST's National Vulnerability Database and gets updates from the NVD data feeds.

Here are some other popular open source dependency checking tools:

- Bundler Audit for Ruby (*https://github.com/rubysec/bundler-audit*)
- Retire.js for Javascript (*http://retirejs.github.io/retire.js/*)
- SafeNuGet for NuGet libraries (*https://www.owasp.org/index.php/OWASP_SafeNuGet*)

You can wire these tools into your build pipelines to automatically inventory open source dependencies, identify out-of-date libraries and libraries with known security vulnerabilities, and fail the build automatically if serious problems are found. By maintaining an up-to-date bill of materials for every system, you will be prepared for vulnerabilities like Heartbleed or DROWN, because you can quickly determine if you are exposed and what you need to fix.

These tools can also alert you when new dependencies are detected so that you can create a workflow to make sure that they get reviewed.

Vulnerabilities in Containers

If you are using containers like Docker in production (or even in development and test), you will need to enforce similar controls over dependencies in container images. Even though Docker scans images in official repos to catch packages with known vulnerabilities, there is still a good chance that someone will download a "poisoned image" containing out-of-date software or malware, or an image that is not safely configured.

You should scan images on your own, using an open source tool like OpenSCAP or Clair, or commercial scanning services from Twistlock, Tenable, or Black Duck Hub;

and then check these images into your own secure repository or private registry, where they can be safely used by developers and operations staff.

Fewer, Better Suppliers

There are obvious maintenance costs and security risks to overextending your software supply chain. Following Toyota's Lean Manufacturing model, your strategic goal should be to move to "fewer, better suppliers" over time, standardizing on libraries and frameworks and templates and images that are proven to work, that solve important problems for developers, and that have been vetted by security. At Netflix, they describe this as building a paved road, because developers—and security and compliance staff—know that if they take advantage of this code, the path ahead will be easier and safer.

Calculating Supply Chain Costs and Risks

Sonatype has developed a free calculator (*http://www.sonatype.com/ calculator/*) which will help developers and managers understand the cost and risks that you inherit over time from using too many third-party components.

But you need to recognize that although it makes good sense in the long term, getting different engineering teams to standardize on a set of common components won't be easy. It's difficult to ask developers supporting legacy apps to invest in making this kind of change. It's equally difficult in microservices environments where developers expect to be free to use the right tools for the job, selecting technologies based on their specific requirements, or even on their personal interests.

One place to start is by standardizing on the lowest layers of software: the kernel, OS, and VMs, and on general-purpose utility functions like logging and metrics collection, which need to be used consistently across apps and services.

How to Fix Vulnerabilities in an Agile Way

A major problem that almost all organizations face is that even when they know that they have a serious security vulnerability in a system, they can't get the fix out fast enough to stop attackers from exploiting the vulnerability. The longer vulnerabilities are exposed, the more likely the system will be, or has already been, attacked.

WhiteHat Security, which provides a service for scanning websites for security vulnerabilities, regularly analyzes and reports on vulnerability data that it collects. Using data from 2013 and 2014, WhiteHat found that 35 percent of finance and insurance websites are "always vulnerable," meaning that these sites had at least one serious vulnerability exposed every single day of the year. The stats for other industries and government organizations were even worse. Only 25 percent of finance and insurance sites were vulnerable for fewer than 30 days of the year.

On average, serious vulnerabilities stayed open for 739 days, and only 27 percent of serious vulnerabilities were fixed at all, because of the costs and risks and overhead involved in getting patches out.[1]

There are many reasons that vulnerabilities take too long to fix, besides teams being too busy with feature delivery:

- Time is wasted in bureaucracy and paperwork in handing off work between the security team and engineering teams.
- Engineering teams don't understand the vulnerability reports, how serious they are, and how to fix them.
- Teams are scared of making a mistake and breaking the system when putting in a patch because they don't have confidence in their ability to build and test and deploy updated software.
- Change management is expensive and slow, including all the steps to build, review, test, and deploy changes and the necessary handoffs and approvals.

As we've seen throughout this book, the speed of Agile development creates new security risks and problems. But this speed and efficiency can also offer an important edge against attackers, a way to close vulnerability windows much faster.

Agile teams are built to respond and react to new priorities and feedback, whether this is a new feature or a problem in production that must be fixed. Just-in-time prioritization, incremental design and rapid delivery, automating builds and testing, measuring and optimizing cycle time—all of these practices are about making changes cheaper, faster, and easier.

---

1 See the report by WhiteHat Security, "2017 Application Security Statistics Report: The Case for DevSecOps" (*https://www.whitehatsec.com/press-releases/featured/2015/05/21/pressrelease.html*).

Prioritizing Vulnerabilities

There are some factors that need to be considered in prioritizing the work to fix vulnerabilities:

Risk severity
> Based on a score like CVSS.

Exploitability
> The team's assessment of how likely this vulnerability can be exploited in your environment, how widespread the vulnerability is, and what compensating controls you have in place.

Cost and risk of making the fix
> The amount of work required to fix and test a vulnerability can vary widely, from rolling out a targeted minor patch from a supplier or making a small technical fix to correct an ACL or a default config setting, to major platform upgrades or overhauling application logic.

Compliance mandates
> The cost/risk of being out of compliance.

DevOps practices and tools like automated configuration management, continuous delivery, and repeatable automated deployment make it even cheaper and safer and faster to get changes and fixes to production. DevOps shops rely on this capability to minimize their MTTR in responding to operations incidents, knowing that they can get patches out quickly to resolve operational problems.

Let's look at how to take advantage of Agile practices and tools and feedback loops that are optimized for speed and efficiency, to reduce security risks.

Test-Driven Security

One way to ensure that vulnerabilities in your applications get fixed is to write an automated test (e.g., unit test or an acceptance test) which proves that the vulnerability exists, and check the test in with the rest of the code so that it gets run when the code is built. The test will fail until the vulnerability gets fixed. This is similar to the way that test-driven developers handle a bug fix, as we explain in Chapter 11, *Agile Security Testing*.

Testing for Heartbleed with GauntIt

In Chapter 11, we show how to write security tests using the GauntIt test framework. GauntIt comes packaged with a set of sample attacks, including an example of a test (*https://theagilead min.com/2014/04/08/gauntlt-test-for-heartbleed/*) specifically written to check for the Heartbleed vulnerability, which you can use as a template for writing your own security checks for other vulnerabilities.

Of course for this approach to be accepted by the team, the person writing the test needs to be accepted as a member of the team. This person needs the support of the Product Owner, who is responsible for prioritizing work and won't be happy to have the team sidetracked with fixing something if she doesn't understand why it is important or necessary.

This person also needs to understand and respect the team's conventions and how the code and test suite are structured, and he needs the technical chops to write a good test. The test must clearly show that a real problem exists, and it has to conform with the approach that the rest of the team is following so that the team is willing to own the test going forward. All of this will likely require help from someone on the team, and it will be much easier if the team is already heavily invested in test automation.

Writing tests like this gives you evidence that the vulnerability has been fixed properly. And it provides insurance that the vulnerability won't come back. As we've seen, it's a big step in the right direction from dropping a vulnerability report on a developer's desk.

Zero Bug Tolerance

Some Agile teams try to follow the ideal of "zero bug tolerance." They insist on fixing every bug that is found before they can move forward and call a feature done, or before they can start on a new feature or story. If a problem is serious enough, the team might all stop doing other work and swarm on it until it is fixed.

If you can explain to these teams that vulnerabilities are bugs, real bugs that need to be fixed, then they would be obliged to fix them.

For the team to take this seriously, you need to do a few things:

1. Be ruthless in eliminating false positives, and focus on vulnerabilities which are important to the organization, problems that are serious and exploitable.
2. Get these onto the Agile team's backlog in a form that the team understands.
3. Spend some time educating the team, including the Product Owner, about what these bugs are and why they are important.

4. Spend some more time helping the team understand how to test and fix each bug.

This approach is viable if you can start with the team early in development, to deal with vulnerabilities immediately as they come up. It's not fair to the team or the organization to come back months or years into development with a long list of vulnerabilities that were found from a recent scan and expect the team to stop everything else and fix them right away. But you can start a conversation with the team and come up with a plan that balances security risks with the rest of its work, and agree on a bar that the team can realistically commit to meeting.

Collective Code Ownership

Another common idea in Agile teams is that the code is open to everyone on the team. Anyone can review code that somebody else wrote, refactor it, add tests to it, fix it, or change it.

This means that if a security engineer finds a vulnerability, she should be able to fix it, as long as she is seen as part of the team. At Google, for example, most of the code base is open to everyone in the organization, which means that security engineers can fix vulnerabilities in any part of the code base, provided that they follow the team's conventions, and take ownership of any problems that they might accidentally introduce.

This takes serious technical skills (not a problem for security engineers at Google of course, but it might be more of a challenge in your organization) and confidence in those skills. But if you know that a bug is serious, and you know where the bug is in the code, and how to fix it properly, and how to check the fix in, then doesn't it make sense to go and do it, instead of trying to convince somebody else to stop what he is doing and fix it for you?

Even if you lack confidence in your coding skills, a pull request or just marking code for review can be a good way to move an issue closer to being fixed.

Security Sprints, Hardening Sprints, and Hack Days

Another way to get security problems corrected, especially if you have a lot of them to deal with, for example, when you are going through a pen test or an audit, or responding to a breach, is to run a dedicated "security sprint" or "hardening sprint."

For Agile teams, "hardening" is whatever you need to do to make the system ready for production. It's when you stop thinking about delivering new features, and focus most or all of your time on packaging, deploying, installing, and configuring the system and making sure that it is ready to run. For teams following continuous delivery or continuous deployment, all of this is something that they prepare for every time that they check in a change.

But for many other teams, this can come as an ugly and expensive surprise, once they understand that what they actually need to do is to take a working functional prototype that runs fine in development and make it into an industrial grade system that is ready for the real world, including making sure that the system is reliable and secure.

In a hardening sprint, the development team stops working on new features and stops building out the architecture and instead spends a dedicated block of time together on getting the system ready to be released.

There is a deep divide between people who recognize that spending some time on hardening is sometimes needed, especially in large programs where teams need to work through integration issues; and other people who are adamant that allocating separate time for hardening is a sign that you are doing things—or everything— wrong, and that the team is failing, or has already failed. This is especially the case if what the team means by "hardening" is actually a separate sprint (or sprints) for testing and bug fixing work that should have been done as the code was written, in what is called an "Agilefall" approach.

Hardening sprints are built into the SAFe (Scaled Agile Framework), an enterprise framework for managing large Agile programs. SAFe makes allowances for work that can only really be done in a final hardening and packaging phase before a big system is rolled out, including security and compliance checks. Disciplined Agile Delivery (DAD), another enterprise Agile method originally created by Scott Ambler at IBM to scale Agile practices to large projects, also includes a hardening phase before each release.

Planning a security sprint as part of hardening may be something that you have to do at some point, or several points, in a project, especially if you are working on a legacy system that has a lot of technical and security debt built up. But hardening sprints are expensive and hard to sell to the customer and management, who naturally will want to know why the team's velocity dropped to zero, and how it got into such a bad situation in the first place.

Try a Security Hack Day Instead of a Hardening Sprint

Some organizations hold regular *hack days*, where teams get to spend time off from their scheduled project work to learn new things, build or improve tools, prototype new ideas, and solve problems together.

Instead of hardening sprints, some teams have had success with security-focused hack days. In a hack day, which often ends late in the hack night, the team brings in some expert help and focuses on finding and fixing a specific kind of vulnerability. For example, you could get the team together, teach everyone all about SQL injection, how to find it and how to fix it properly. Then everyone works together, often in pairs, to fix as many of these vulnerabilities in the code as can safely get done in one day.

Hack days like this are obviously much cheaper and easier to make a case for than a dedicated sprint. They are also safer: developers are less likely to make mistakes or introduce regressions if they are all trained on what to do and focused on working on the same problem together for a short period of time. Hack days shine a light on security risks, help educate the team (after a few hours of fixing a specific vulnerability, everyone should be able to spot it and fix it quickly in the future), and they get important bugs fixed without slowing the team down too much.

Relying on a separate hardening sprint to find and fix vulnerabilities and other bugs before releasing code is risky, and over the long term, it's fighting a losing battle. Forcing teams to stop working on new development and instead focus on security issues for weeks or months at a time was an early, and desperate, part of Microsoft's Trustworthy Computing Initiative. But it didn't take Microsoft long to realize that this was costing too much and wasn't making a sustainable improvement in the security or reliability of its software. This is when the company switched its emphasis to building security practices directly into its development life cycle instead.

Taking On and Paying Down Security Debt

Agile teams have learned to recognize and find ways to deal with technical debt. Technical debt is the sum of all the things that the team, or the people who came before them, should have done when building the system, but didn't have the time to do, or didn't know that they should have done. These include shortcuts and quick-and-dirty hacks, tests that should have been written or that broke and were left broken, bugs that should have been fixed, code that wasn't refactored but should have been, and patches that should have been applied.

All of these things add up over time, making the system more brittle and harder to change, less reliable, and less secure. Eventually, some of this debt will need to be paid back with interest, and usually by people who weren't around when the debt was taken on: like children having to pay off their parents' mortgage.

When teams or their managers prioritize delivering features quickly over making sure that they are writing secure code, don't invest in training, cut back on reviews and testing, don't look for security problems, and don't take time to fix them early, they take on security debt. This debt increases the risk that the system will be compromised, as well as the cost of fixing the problem, as it could involve redesigning and rewriting parts of the system.

Sometimes this may be the right thing to do for the organization. For example, Lean startups and other teams building out a Minimum Viable Product (MVP) need to cut requirements back to the bone and deliver a working system as soon as possible in order to get feedback and see if it works. It's a waste of limited time and money to write solid, secure code and go through all the reviews and testing to make sure that the code is right if there is a good chance that they are going to throw the code out in a few days or weeks and start again—or pack up and move to another project or find another job because the system was a failure or they ran out of money.

There are other cases where the people paying for the work, or the people doing the work, need to cut corners in order to hit an urgent deadline—where doing things now is more important than doing things right.

What is key is that everybody involved (i.e., people doing the work of building the system, the people paying for this work, and the people using the systems to do their work) must recognize and accept that they are taking on real risks when they make these decisions.

This is how Microsoft and Facebook and Twitter achieved market leadership. It's a high-risk/high-reward strategy that can pay off and did pay off in these examples, but eventually all of these organizations were forced to confront the consequences of their choices and invest huge amounts of time and talent and money in trying to pay off their debts. It's possible that they may never succeed in this: Microsoft has been fighting with serious security problems since Bill Gates made "Trustworthy Computing" the company's highest priority back in 2002.

This is because just like credit card debt, security debt incurs interest. A little debt that you take on for a short period of time is easy to pay off. But lots of debt left over a long time can leave the system, and the organization, bankrupt.

Keep track of the security debt that you are taking on, and try to be deliberate and transparent about the choices you are making. Make security debt and other technical debt, such as the following, visible to the owners of the system when you are taking on risk:

- Open vulnerabilities and outstanding patches (i.e., how big your window of vulnerability is and how long it has been open)
- Outstanding pen test or audit findings
- High-risk code areas that have low automated test coverage
- Gaps in scanning or reviews
- Gaps in training
- Time-to-detect and time-to-repair metrics (i.e., how quickly the team can identify and respond to emergencies)

Write stories that explain what should be done to clean up the debt, and add these stories to the backlog so that they can be prioritized with other work. And make sure that everyone understands the risks and costs of not doing things right, right now and that it will cost more to make it right later.

Key Takeaways

Here are some of the keys to effectively dealing with vulnerabilities:

- New vulnerabilities are found in software every day. Vulnerability assessment and management needs to be done on a continuous basis.
- Leverage tooling and APIs to get vulnerabilities out of reports and into the team's backlog so that they can be scheduled and fixed as part of other work.
- Help the team, especially the Product Owner and Scrum Master, understand vulnerabilities and why and how they need to be fixed.
- Watch out for vulnerabilities in third-party dependencies, including open source frameworks, libraries, runtime stacks, and container images. Scan dependencies at build time, and stop the build if any serious vulnerabilities are found. Cache safe dependencies in artifact repositories or private image registries, and encourage developers to use them.
- Automated configuration management and continuous delivery pipelines enable you to respond quickly and confidently to serious vulnerabilities. Knowing that you can patch the software and push out a patch quickly is a major step forward in dealing with vulnerabilities.
- Security Hack Days can be an effective way to get the team focused on understanding and fixing security vulnerabilities.

CHAPTER 7

Risk for Agile Teams

Security professionals live and breathe risk management. But developers, especially developers on an Agile team, can get happily through their day without thinking about risk much, if at all.

Let's look at what's involved in bringing these two different worlds—or ways of looking at the world—together

Security Says, No

Before we get into how risk management is done, let's take a quick detour to the purpose of risk management and security in general.

Security teams have a reputation for being the people who say "No" in many organizations. A project team may be ready to deliver a new feature, but are using an approach or a technology that the security team doesn't understand, so it isn't allowed to go out. The operations team needs a firewall change to support a new system, but the security team owns the firewalls and can't coordinate the change in time, so the implementation of the system is blocked.

All of this is done in the name of risk management. Risk management is about enumerating and quantifying the unknown and attempting to control the risk. The easiest way to control the unknown and the risk is to prevent changes so that nothing can go wrong. However this fundamentally misses the point, and when tried in a fast-moving environment, results in a number of negative side effects to security overall.

Security should be about enabling the organization to carry out its goals in the most safe and secure manner possible. This means that an effective risk management process should be about enabling people in the organization to take appropriate risks in an informed manner. The key here being *informed*: risk management is not all about avoidance, but the mindful understanding, reduction, sharing, and acceptance of risk as appropriate.

Instead of saying "No," security should be saying "Yes, but," or even better "Yes, and," and providing guidance and help to carry out the actions in the safest and most secure way possible.

But that aside, let's look at how risk management is commonly understood.

Understanding Risks and Risk Management

Risk management is central to security and compliance, helping ensure that systems are safe from attack.

The security industry has over the last few decades gone to a lot of effort to define and standardize methods for understanding and controlling risks. Regulations like PCI DSS and SOX, and governance and control frameworks like NIST SP 800-53 and COBIT, expect you to follow a recognized and proven risk management approach, such as:

- ISO 27005
- NIST SP 800-30/39
- OCTAVE
- FAIR
- AS/NZS 4360

These risk management methodologies are about dealing with uncertainties. All risk management approaches start with identifying, rating, and ranking risks to help you to get some control over uncertainty.

Risk ratings take into account the likelihood of something bad happening, and the potential costs that your organization could incur if it does happen. This is done by assigning a numeric rating (quantitative) or a relative high-medium-low priority (qualitative) to each risk.

According to ISO 31010, the international standard for risk assessment, there are 31 different risk assessment techniques that you could choose from. Formal risk assessment techniques can help you to make difficult trade-offs and answer questions like, how much should you spend trying to protect your system your data, your organization, and your customers from something that may or may not go wrong?

But even using formal methods, security risks in software can be difficult to evaluate. What is the negative cost of a fully exploited XSS vulnerability in one of your web applications? And what is the chance of it occurring? How should your product owner or program manager decide which risks need to be addressed, and in what priority?

Compliance requirements often dictate how these decisions will be made. For example, PCI DSS requires that all vulnerabilities with a certain risk rating must be remediated within specific time guidelines. Tools such as OWASP's Top 10 Risk List can also help you to evaluate and decide how to deal with different security risks.

OWASP Top 10 Risk Management Tool

OWASP's Top 10 Risk List (*https://www.owasp.org/index.php/Category:OWASP_Top_Ten_Project*) identifies the most common and most serious software risks for web applications. This includes risks like injection, broken authentication and session management, and cross-site scripting. For each of these risks, it covers the following elements:

Threat agents
Which type of users to look out for.

Attack vectors and attack scenarios
What kind of attacks to expect.

Exploitability
How easy it is for attackers to exploit, and how widespread is the vulnerability.

Detectability
How easy it is for attackers to find.

Impacts
Technical and application-specific or business-specific impacts.

This information is a great first stop on your road to greater risk understanding and will help you to understand where to focus your training, design and coding, reviews, and testing effort.

Risk management is not static: it will change in response to threat intelligence, regulatory changes, and changes that you make to your system or your operations procedures. This is why regulations like PCI DSS also mandate regular risk reviews.

Risks and Threats

We introduced the concepts of risk and threats earlier in this book, and we'll talk more about threats and how to deal with them in another chapter. Here we want to make clear the difference between threats and risks, and how they interplay:

Threats
> What and who you have to protect your system/data/customers from, what could go wrong, and what harm could this cause to your system or the data. Threats are specific.

Risks
> Your system's exposure to threats (probability and costs), what you can/should do to reduce this exposure, and the cost trade-offs. Risks are abstract.

Security threats and risks are everywhere if you know where to look for them.

If your industry is under active attack, if your organization is holding a lot of valuable personal data or financial data, and if your application is popping with SQL injection and XSS vulnerabilities when you scan it, then you're in a lot trouble, and you need to do something about it.

But if your organization might be under attack, and you don't know what your threats are, and you aren't testing your systems, and you don't know what vulnerabilities you have or how serious they are, then you are probably in a lot more trouble. Sticking your head in the sand does not cause those risks or threats to disappear.

Everyone is under a range of threats today, across every industry, in every geography. You can't pretend that you don't have to worry about data security or software security because your organization is small or just a startup or you're working in a legacy environment. That doesn't cut it anymore.

As a starting point, you need to understand the threats that your organization and system face, and how serious they are. This is the goal of threat intelligence and threat assessment, which we explain in Chapter 8, *Threat Assessments and Understanding Attacks*.

Then you need to look at how well prepared your system and your organization are to meet these threats, or what you need to do to reduce the risks. That's the point of this chapter.

What is important to regulators, your management, your customers, and other stakeholders is that you take a serious and consistent approach to identifying, assessing, communicating, and addressing risks that could impact the security of your systems.

Dealing with Risk

There are different strategies for handling risks:

Reducing
> Implementing countermeasures or controls, compensating controls (such as activity auditing, or runtime IPS or application firewalls), plans to manage risks, tools, training, testing, and scanning

Avoiding
> Deciding not to do something, disabling or simplifying a feature or an interface, and not using unsafe or unproven technology

Accepting
> Recognizing that bad things will probably happen, and then preparing to deal with them: monitoring, incident response, and continuous delivery (proven ability to deploy patches quickly)

Sharing or transferring
> Outsourcing to third parties like data center operators or cloud services providers or managed security service providers (MSSPs) to share risk; or taking on an insurance policy

The key thing to be aware of is that any given risk mitigation technique or control has a cost associated with it. That might be a financial cost, performance impact, delay in time to market, or loss of changeability or usability. We need to be sure that the approach we select aligns with the organization's needs and priorities, and doesn't hamper the organization beyond the value of what we are trying to protect.

Outsourcing Doesn't Make Risks Go Away

Outsourcing responsibilities for coding, testing, or operations doesn't make your risks go away.

Outsourcing to a third party can make good business sense, as well as help to reduce operational and security risks: a good example could be using an enterprise cloud services provider like AWS to host your application, rather than trying to set up your own secure data center. However, you are still responsible for understanding and managing these risks, as well as new ones that may arise from the act of outsourcing. Regulators and insurers will insist on this.

You need to be confident that whoever is doing work on your behalf is taking responsible steps to protect your data and your customer's data, and has appropriate operational risk management and security capabilities in place.

If you have enough leverage (your organization is large enough, or the size of the deal is big enough), you can insist on specific requirements during contracting. Big and small firms should also do regular reviews on key service providers as part of their operational risk management programs.

One tool that can help you with this is a Structured Information Gathering (SIG) questionnaire, available from *https://sharedassessments.org* for a small fee, which will walk you through how to do a risk assessment of a service supplier. It asks organizations to describe their IT, privacy, security, and risk management controls. You can use it in RFP situations, as part of regular check-ups, or even as a self-assessment of your own controls.

The SIG guide is a standardized and comprehensive set of questions that is designed to help meet regulatory requirements and guidelines such as PCI DSS, FFIEC, NIST, and ISO. You can customize it to meet specific compliance or governance requirements. The SIG Lite is a smaller, simpler questionnaire that you can use for less critical suppliers or for initial risk assessments.

You can gain some confidence that you have mitigated specific risks by testing the system against vulnerabilities and other events that you anticipate. Traditionally, software development teams do this at point of release with penetration testing or some other kind of security review.

Leaving these checks until the end means that risk owners are often forced to choose between inadequate security solutions and not releasing on time. It's this that results in security having a bad name in many circles, and results in unusable and insecure systems in the wild.

Modern Agile teams have to follow a different approach, where they integrate risk management directly into their design, development, testing, and deployment activities, and leverage automation and iteration and feedback loops to maintain a high level of confidence in the face of high-velocity delivery. They need to do all of this in ways that don't slow them down or add unnecessary cost.

Making Risks Visible

Of course it isn't possible to mitigate every risk. You need to have have a good understanding of what risks (the risks that you know about) you haven't addressed yet or were only able to partially address.

On traditional software projects, this is done with a risk register maintained by the project manager, and by reporting the "residual risks," those risks that reside in the system after deployment.

Modern teams can track security risks in several ways:

- Continuously scanning infrastructure and code, including open source libraries and frameworks, for out-of-date packages and known vulnerabilities
- Tracking vulnerabilities and metrics on how they are managed, as we described in Chapter 6, *Agile Vulnerability Management*
- Measuring automated test coverage and code complexity in high-risk code areas
- Watching for security stories and attacker stories in the backlog that have not been implemented
- Measuring lead time for changes and MTTR (mean time to recovery) for problems in production, which tell you how fast the team can respond to a severe vulnerability or security breach
- Tracking technical debt on the backlog as stories, or using automated code analysis platforms like SonarQube (*https://www.sonarqube.org/*) or Code Climate (*https://codeclimate.com/*)

Some Agile teams also maintain a risk register in the form of a risk backlog or a risk wall that lists risks that they've identified, their rating, and notes on how the team plans to deal with them. This risk backlog is managed the same way as the team's story backlog: items are prioritized and scheduled depending on priority and cost.

The team's progress working through the risk backlog can be measured in the same way that they measure their velocity delivering stories, and reported using tools like Risk Burndown Charts.[1]

Accepting and Transferring Risks

There are some risks that you can't manage effectively, at least not now, or that you may decide are not worth trying to minimize because you believe that they are unlikely to occur, or because they are so low impact that they won't cause a significant cost to the organization if they do occur.

In these cases, you have a couple of choices:

1. Someone in the organization with the appropriate authority can accept the consequences of the risk, should it trigger. In Agile teams this could be a decision made by the Product Owner or the entire team together, with or without the security team or management involved.

   It's important to make sure that the whoever makes this decision has enough information to do it responsibly. And it is important to understand that accepting a risk doesn't make the risk go away. Each time that you accept a risk, you are taking on a kind of debt, just like you do with financial debt, or technical debt; and never forget that debt accrues interest.

   You and your management should be prepared to pay off this debt some day.

   One way to prepare is by making sure that you have a good incident response capability in place and exercising it so that you know that you can deal with problems if they come up, something that we cover in Chapter 13, *Operations and OpSec*.

2. You can also transfer the risk or part of the risk on to another party, by outsourcing responsibilities to another organization that is better prepared to deal with risk (for example, outsourcing your data center facilities management to a high-quality cloud services provider), or you can take out insurance to cover some of your risk.

   An insurance policy is not a get out of jail free card. Insurers will check to ensure that you've done a responsible job of reducing your and their risks to an acceptable minimum; and they will use these to determine premiums and deductibles, as well as to draw clear lines around what will and will not be covered.

---

1 See Mike Cohn's article, "Managing Risk on Agile Projects with the Risk Burndown Chart" (*https://www.moun taingoatsoftware.com/blog/managing-risk-on-agile-projects-with-the-risk-burndown-chart*), April 8, 2010.

Changing Contexts for Risks

If you decide to accept a risk with a system, then it is critical that you record that fact somewhere and review it regularly, especially in an Agile team.

Risks are not just static concepts. Risks are the manifestation of threats and vulnerabilities in the system. This means that the status, significance, and importance of risks will change over time; and in particular, they tend to change as the system changes.

In traditional risk management, this isn't necessarily a hard problem to manage. If the system is only changed when significant projects are completed (e.g., say an annual basis), then the risk management process may only need to be redone once a year or so.

But with an Agile team continuously changing the system in response to new information, the context in which a risk is accepted can change dramatically in a fairly short time.

It is very difficult and therefore rare for traditional risk management processes to be managed at the same speed as an Agile team, which means that risk decisions are often made within the context of individual changes. However, risk accretes or compounds, and it can be difficult to model or catch this appropriately.

For example, one of us worked on a single sign-on system. The system had a bug in the password reset flow that at the end of the process logged you into the system without needing to type your password again.

This created a vulnerability, because someone following a link in an email and not having to enter the old password could potentially hijack an account. However the risk of somebody intercepting the email and exploiting it was deemed low, and the risk was accepted by the team and added to a backlog of risks.

Fast forward 12 months, and the same issue was rediscovered in a security test. However, now it was a much bigger deal, because in the preceding 12 months, the single sign-on system had been reused to provide login to a number of other sensitive systems.

When those new systems were added, one of the agreed security practices was that the sign-on would require a second factor, in this case a code from an OTP (one-time password) application, entered at login time in addition to the password. This requirement was implemented, and the system was considered acceptable.

However, the password-reset-bypass bug now also bypassed the two-factor authentication, which was a much more significant vulnerability.

The team was able to fix this issue and roll out the fix within hours of being identified. What they learned from this incident was that while the decision to accept the risk was appropriate for the initial context, it was not easy to recognize that this decision needed to be re-evaluated when they made other context-changing decisions such as enrolling new sensitive systems or adding the two-factor requirement.

Risk Management in Agile and DevOps

Agile development and DevOps practices cause problems for traditional risk management practices. We are in some fairly new territory without a clear set of rules. The community of risk management practitioners has not yet agreed on a methodology of risk management that is compatible with Agile, and as such we can find a number of culture clashes when trying to manage risk in a way that is acceptable to everyone within your organization, as well as to your auditors.

In particular, Agile practices are commonly perceived to introduce whole new kinds of risk.

Speed of Delivery

The biggest new risk is that the Agile focus on speed of delivery leads to a rate of change that traditional approaches to managing risks aren't designed for.

Common change control practices, such as specified by ITIL or COBIT, are designed to deal with Waterfall projects that push large change sets a handful of times per year and cannot possibly keep up with continuous delivery or continuous deployment approaches.

Manual testing practices and quality gates, including penetration testing and compliance audits, are slow, intensive processes that can take weeks to assess a single build. These processes need a fundamental shift in thinking to cope with the speed of Agile delivery.

As such, risk practices tend to get left out, ignored, or bypassed for many Agile teams. This creates a new risk: that the baby is thrown out with the bathwater, that risk controls are put aside completely instead of replacing them with something that provides a similar, but simpler set of checks and balances at lower cost.

However, speed of delivery can also be an advantage in dealing with security risks.

Few organizations working in a traditional project delivery environment acknowledge that slow, closely managed deployments are themselves a source of risk, because changes involve so many people and so many moving parts, and because this forces emergency changes to bypass many of the control processes involved in order to get things done in time.

Agile teams make changes on a regular and repeated basis, meaning that the risk of any individual change affecting or damaging the system's security properties is much reduced, while the team's ability to revert or roll back a change is much increased.

Fast-moving Agile teams can also quickly respond to risks, vulnerabilities, and issues when they recognize them.

Incremental Design and Refactoring

Traditional practices are highly reliant on development artifacts, such as written design specifications and models, detailed requirements, and so forth.

The traditional practices tend to assume that when changes are made to the system, these artifacts will be updated inline with the changes, enabling the risk management process to review changes to the system design for security vulnerabilities and risks, and propose mitigations or changes.

Agile methodologies focus on incremental and iterative design, meaning that the design of the system is not available to review before work starts, nor is there necessarily a set of artifacts that are updated with changes.

This approach increases the risk that teams will miss important compliance constraints or fail to anticipate security requirements in design and planning in favor of focusing on feature delivery, and it eliminates Waterfall control gates and review checkpoints that managers and regulators have come to rely on.

It can also mean a lack of auditable decision points and artifacts that can be traced later by auditors and compliance officers. Instead they need to go to the code to find the history of design decisions.

Equally, security is very hard to add later to a system design, and Agile techniques do not naturally encourage security thinking by default (if they did, this book would be unnecessary!).

Agile methods are optimized for the capability to change as the environmental context changes; so as the security landscape emerges and threats change, the team is able to respond quickly, fixing design issues and adjusting the behavior of the system.

Furthermore, Agile practitioners maintain that while they don't produce as much documentation, their experience of projects is that the documentation rarely matches the reality of the system, meaning that the *configuration drift* between what is understood in the documentation, and the way the system actually behaves, can be enormous.

By pushing security, auditors, and compliance teams to look at the actual code, they encourage an understanding of the reality of the system rather than the imagined reality of a design document.

Self-Organized, Autonomous Teams

Agile teams tend to work in a highly self-organized and autonomous manner. They have control over their workload, the product backlog, and the manner of delivery.

This means that unlike in some more traditional software engineering shops, Agile teams may resist or avoid review boards, design authorities, and other control mechanisms imposed from outside if they believe that these outside forces will get in the way of delivery. This is a problem for security professionals who are used to working with architecture review boards and other central authorities to set guiding principles and rules to ensure the security of all systems.

Furthermore, this tends to mean that management has less insight into, and control over, each team's detailed development processes and the bill of materials for the software: the libraries and frameworks used in development. This can raise concerns for audit and compliance teams that want to know exactly how work was done and which software products are using which versions of libraries.

Agile teams ask management to rely on the team to do the right thing, and on the individual capability and competence of the Product Owner to ensure that quality is built in.

Agile advocates argue that top-down control and decision making in traditional engineering methodologies often result in decisions that are inefficient for the individual team or product, and that changing those decisions becomes harder and slower due to the larger *blast radius* of a decision.

For example, an individual product team deciding to upgrade a library to the latest version affects only that team, but getting an architecture review board to approve the change might require understanding the impact on every team in the organization.

Self-organized and autonomous teams reduce the risk of slow decision making and create firewalls between distinct teams, meaning that vulnerabilities affecting a single team may not necessarily affect all the teams in the organization. It also gives the organization the ability to respond in a more targeted and appropriate way within each team.

Automation

Agile teams rely on automation heavily in order to get the speed, repeatability, and consistency that they need to keep moving forward.

However automation itself comes with its own risks. The tools themselves can be the target of attack and an attack vector in themselves, something we will look at in Chapter 13, *Operations and OpSec*.

Automated systems can allow mistakes, errors, and attacks to be propagated and multiplied in far more damaging ways than manual systems. As the DevOps comedy account @DevOpsBorat says, "To make error is human. To propagate error to all server in automatic way is #devops." [2]

Furthermore, automated tooling is fallible; and as we know so well in the security world, it can be easy for humans to begin to trust in the computer and stop applying sense or judgment to the results. This can lead to teams trusting that if the tests pass, the system is working as expected, even if other evidence might indicate otherwise.

Automated configuration management and build and deployment pipelines can help enforce separation of duties by providing authenticated and audited systematic access for making system changes, minimizing or eliminating the need for developers to log on directly to production systems. But automation can also interfere with separation of duties, making it hard to define who actually has access to a system and who has the ability to change the system. We'll explore this issue in detail in Chapter 14, *Compliance*.

Agile Risk Mitigation

Agile methods also provide some risk mitigations to existing practices.

Waterfall, V-model, and other traditional software engineering systems are known to be subject to cost, scope, and schedule overruns. Agile projects are just as subject to overruns, but managers of Agile projects tend to have greater awareness of overruns earlier, and the principles of YAGNI (you aren't gonna need it), just-in-time prioritization, and continuous delivery of working software with iterative improvement means that it's easier to cancel a project and still deliver value to the organization.

Furthermore, frequent demos, shorter feedback loops, designing around a Minimum Viable Product, and the ability to respond to change means that the business risks of delivering software that doesn't actually meet the user needs are significantly reduced.

Evidence has shown repeatedly over the decades that changes to the system later in the development cycle are more expensive than changes early on. However, the traditional response to this has been to lengthen and ossify the earlier stages in development, attempting to build more complete and comprehensive requirements and designs, rather than focusing on minimizing the cost of change.

Even if a project is delivered well in a Waterfall or V-model system (as many are), systems are only being built for a very short period of their active life and spend most of their life being in service and requiring maintenance and change. Agile methods can

---

2 *https://twitter.com/DEVOPS_BORAT/status/41587168870797312*

help to reduce the costs and the risk to the business of implementing these whole life cycle changes.

Finally, a symptom of this problem is that many systems build in large amounts of configurability and design complexity to anticipate or minimize the cost of future changes. Some common examples are the use of "Business Rules Engines" and "Enterprise Service Bus" platforms to externalize the more frequently changed components of the system and make them easier to change.

However, these approaches add further complexity and operational management overhead to the systems that the organization needs to run. They also add huge complexity to testing and replication of the environments, as changes need to be tested in the presence of many possible configurations.

Software developed following incremental Agile and Lean approaches should be simpler by design; and if the organization is capable of writing and releasing code to change the system at speed, then it can be significantly simpler. Simple systems contain far fewer moving parts and significantly less risk. They are easier to understand and reason about, and this gives us better security properties.

Finally, the more often that you make changes, the more chances that you have to break things. Agile, and especially DevOps teams, make changes much more frequently. Counterintuitively, research shows that organizations that change the most often actually have lower failure rates and higher reliability.[3]

How do they do this?

- Releasing changes in smaller batches, and using dark launching and progressive canary releases to manage the risk of deploying changes.
- Optimizing for MTTR (mean time to recovery) by anticipating failure and preparing to deal with it.
- Automating configuration management and deployment to ensure consistency and repeatability.
- Building feedback loops into production operations and from production into development to catch problems quickly so that they can be fixed quickly, and building an effective incident response capability.

Agile and DevOps teams don't have to think too much about how to deal with these kinds of risks, as long as they follow the patterns and use their tools properly. Their success depends a lot on the Product Owner understanding the importance of minimizing technical and operational risks and agreeing to prioritize the work necessary,

---

3 See Puppet Labs' "2016 State of DevOps Report" (*https://puppet.com/resources/white-paper/2016-state-of-devops-report*).

and on the Scrum Master and the rest of the team to work responsibly, and on trust and open collaboration at all levels to eliminate misunderstandings and to bring problems to the surface so that they can be solved.

For larger projects, enterprise Agile program management frameworks like SAFe (*http://www.scaledagileframework.com/*) (the Scaled Agile Framework) and DAD (*http://www.disciplinedagiledelivery.com/*) (Disciplined Agile Development) take risk management beyond the team level. They add explicit up front planning and design, reporting and integration checkpoints between teams, and additional roles for architecture and program management to manage risks and dependencies between teams and programs.

Many experienced Agile practitioners and experts are skeptical of these promises, since it has proven to be incredibly difficult to reconcile traditional Waterfall and project management approaches with the principles of Agile. These enterprise management frameworks may help your organization transition to Agile without throwing away all the management best practice that it has built up over time, but we recommend that you tread carefully and ensure you don't miss out on the full benefits of Agile in following them.

Handling Security Risks in Agile and DevOps

Security professionals often separate themselves from risk management professionals. They like to argue that business risks are significantly different from security risks, that security is a special approach in software development.

This is true to a certain extent. Security risks tend to be far less well understood than traditional business risks, far more easily described as "unknown unknowns," and far harder to measure in terms of loss or impact.

However, security is another quality of software, in the same way that performance, quality, efficiency, and usability are qualities of the software.

Agile development techniques have sometimes struggled with these qualities, usually referred to as *nonfunctional requirements*, because it is very difficult to write these into user stories in the same way that user features can be described.

These qualities, including and especially security, have to become something that the team is aware of, owns, and manages internally throughout every story that is delivered.

Security risks can be managed the same way as other risks, by building risk management into how you design, develop, test, and deploy software, and how you run the system.

In a traditional software development life cycle, risk assessment is done based on the system requirements and design specifications and models created up front. A risk analyst uses those documents to identify the risks that will reside in the system and puts together a plan to monitor and mitigate these risks. Then audits are done to ensure that the system built matches the documented design specifications and that the risk management plan is still valid.

In iterative, incremental, Agile development environments, risk needs to be continuously reassessed and continuously managed.

There are several opportunities in Agile methods, such as Scrum, where security and compliance risk management activities can be wired in:

Sprint planning
Review and record risks.

Story writing
Watch out for stories that add security and privacy risks, and counter security and compliance risks by writing security stories, attacker stories, and compliance stories.

Test writing
Add automated security tests and compliance checks.

Coding
Use vetted libraries and patterns.

Code reviews
Ensure that code (especially high-risk code) is reviewed for security risks and ensuring that all code is scanned using automated static analysis tools.

Refactoring
Reduce technical complexity in code and design through disciplined refactoring.

Design
Conduct threat modeling when high-risk changes are made to the system's attack surface.

Retrospectives
When the team meets to look at improvement opportunities, consider security risks, compliance risks, and other technical and operational risks, and how to manage them.

Postmortem reviews
Use feedback from a failure or incident to examine underlying risks and to come up with solutions.

Risk management also builds on and drives automation and standardization in testing and deployment through continuous integration and continuous delivery. And risk management informs configuration management, monitoring, and other operations practices.

Essentially, all the practices, tools, and methods described in this book are part of your risk management program.

Key Takeaways

Most developers, especially in Agile environments, don't explicitly deal with risk management, because they don't have to. Agile techniques and practices help developers take care of many basic project risks, technical risks, and business risks.

Managing security risks, privacy risks, and compliance risks has to be integrated into how developers think and work in the same way as other risks:

- Help the team to understand common security risks, such as the OWASP Top 10, and how they are commonly managed.
- Make security risks and other risks visible to the team (and to management) in a risk register, or as security stories or compliance stories in the backlog.
- Risks and risk management should be explicitly considered in the team's retrospectives and continuous improvement feedback loops.
- By continuously making small, frequent changes, Agile teams reduce operational and security risks. Small changes are easier to understand and test, safer to roll out, and easier to fix if something goes wrong.
- Risk management in Agile needs to be done on an interactive basis. Decisions to accept or otherwise mitigate risks need to be re-evaluated over time as the design of the system changes.
- Take advantage of Agile and DevOps practices and built-in control points to add risk management controls and provide evidence for auditors. We look at this in more detail in Chapter 14, *Compliance*.

CHAPTER 8

Threat Assessments and Understanding Attacks

You can't defend yourself effectively against adversaries that you can't see and that you don't understand. You need to understand the threats to your organization, your systems, and your customer's data, and be prepared to deal with these threats (see "Threat Assessment" on page 127).

You need up-to-date, accurate threat information to aid in this understanding:

- Inform your security monitoring systems so that you know what to look for, and to arm your runtime defenses so that you can protect organization and systems from attacks.

- Prioritize patching and other remediation work.

- Drive operational risk assessments so that you can understand how well prepared (or unprepared) your organization is to face attacks.

- Help write security stories by modeling threat actors as anti-personas.

- Define test scenarios so that you can attack your own systems using tools like Gauntlt and find security weaknesses before adversaries find them.

- Guide education and awareness.

- Assess your design for security risks through threat modeling.

Understanding Threats: Paranoia and Reality

If you read the news or follow security commentators, the world can seem like a fairly terrible place. A steady stream of large-scale systems compromises and breaches are featured in the news each week: high-profile organizations falling to a range of attacks and losing control of sensitive information.

It can be easy when reading these accounts to assume that these organizations and systems were exceptional in some way. That they were unusual in the way that they were attacked or targeted, or perhaps they were especially poorly configured or built. The reality is that all systems and networks connected to the internet are under attack, all the time.

The internet is inhabited by an entire ecosystem of potentially harmful individuals, groups, and automated entities that are continuously working to identify new vulnerable systems and weak points that can be exploited. Attacks emanating from this diverse group can be targeted with a clear objective in mind, or can be indiscriminate and opportunistic, taking advantage of whatever is stumbled across.

With so much hostile activity going on around us, we can easily become overwhelmed. While it's dangerous to ignore threats, you can't be afraid of everything: you will only end up paralyzing your organization.

So how do we look at these threats in a way that allows us to take action and make good decisions? Let's begin by asking some basic questions: Who could attack your system? Why would they want to? How would they go about succeeding? Which threats are most important to you right now? How can you understand and defend against them most effectively?

Understanding Threat Actors

In the security world, the phrase "threat actor" is often used to describe people, organizations, or entities that might pose risk (or threat) to your systems, organization, and people. One way we can begin to understand these threat actors, their capabilities, and intentions is to start to profile and understand how they might behave toward us, and subsequently how to identify and defend against them.

Before we dive into some of the common threat actor archetypes that exist, we should look at what each threat actor has in common. We can break down each of these threat actors into the following five elements. These elements line up with the questions we would want to ask about this person, group, or entity during our analysis:

Narrative

Who is this person, group, or entity, and what is their background?

Motivation

Why would they wish to attack our organization, technology, or people?

Objective

What would they want to achieve by attacking us?

Resources

How skilled, funded, and capable are they? Do they have access to the tools, people, or funds to go through with the attack?

Characteristics

Where in the world are they location? What is their typical attack behavior (if known)? Are they well known?

Using Attack Stories and Threat Modeling as Requirements

Remember that threat modeling and defining attack stories are linked. Revisit Chapter 5, *Security and Requirements* to refresh how to build this thought pattern into your requirements capture.

Now that we have a structured way to think about these threat actors, let's use that structure to look at some common profiles and attacker types.

Threat Actor Archetypes

There are many ways to split and sort the common threat actors faced by organizations. For simplicity we will group them based on their relative position to our organization.

Insiders

Insiders have access and are operating from a trusted position. Here are insiders to look out for:

- Malicious or disenfranchised employees
- Former employees who might still have privileged access (e.g., to internal systems, cloud applications, or hardware)
- Activists inside the organization: someone with insider access who has a grudge or a cause against the organization or who wants to damage it for his own purposes

- Spies: corporate espionage or foreign intelligence moles (yes, this doesn't just happen in the movies)
- Puppets: employees who are being coerced or social engineered into using their privileged access on behalf of someone else
- Staff who make honest but expensive mistakes (especially admins with privileged system access)

Outsiders

Outsiders may choose to attack, but do so from an external, untrusted position. They can be:

- Users who are sloppy or careless, or simply curious and might cause trouble by accident.
- Fraudsters.
- Bots that are automatically scanning everything everywhere all the time for common vulnerabilities.
- Hackers and script kiddies: random jerks with limited skills out to show off.
- Security researchers and "security researchers": skilled professionals who are out to show off.
- Hacktivists: groups with a moral or political agenda that target your organization or industry for ideological reasons. Such attacks can take a variety of forms ranging from denial of service and website defacement to the leaking of sensitive (and potentially embarrassing) documents and data.
- Organized criminals looking to steal data or IP, or to conduct ransomware attacks or DDOS attacks and other blackmail.
- Nation-state attack teams looking to steal data or IP, or conducting reconnaissance or sabotage for cyber warfare (for a vast majority of situations, these will be well outside of your threat model and would not be something you would likely be able to discover or prevent).

Threat Actors and Motivations

Taking our groupings a little further, we can also categorize these examples by motivation and objective. If we disregard those threat actors who cause harm accidentally or through negligence, we can broadly group these actors into the following five motivations:

Financial
> Attackers aiming to increase their own wealth through theft of information, money, or assets (or the manipulation of data or markets).

Political
> Attackers looking to further a political or belief-based agenda.

Egotistical
> Attackers who want to prove themselves or acting for self promotion.

Personal
> Attackers motivated by personal grievances and emotional response.

Chaotic
> Attackers who just want to cause as much damage and turmoil as possible because they can, *for the lulz* can be all the motivation that such threat actors need.

While it is possible for threat actors to have multiple motivations from this list, normally one from the list will be their primary focus and determine the resource, enthusiasm, and time given to an attack.

A few years ago, most organizations outside financial services could pretend that their systems were generally safe from professional criminals and focus most of their attention on how to protect against insiders, script kiddies, and other opportunistic hackers. But today, criminals, as well as hacktivist groups and other highly motivated adversaries, have much easier access to the tools and information needed to conduct sophisticated and damaging attacks, making it possible to scale their activities across more and more systems.

Given the current attack landscape of the internet, it would be prudent to assume that every system will be seen as a valid target of attack. While it is important to be aware of the presence of indiscriminate opportunistic attempts at compromise, it is also important to accept that more sophisticated and targeted threat actors will also be looking at your systems. Even if you don't think you're important enough to hit their radar, the range of motivations driving them will inevitably make you a more worthwhile target than you may think.

For those of us working in the government, critical infrastructure, or financial sectors, as well as those in startups working on advanced technologies, we must also consider the more sophisticated threat actors. While nation-state attackers are not the primary threat for the majority of businesses, in some industries, the threat posed by these groups is very present.

Identifying the threat actors that are relevant to your organization is often not trivial, but is worth taking the time to do if you want to be able to invest your limited resources in defenses that will actually make a difference to your security when those actors come knocking. Considering the motivations of threat actors and what they could gain by attacking your organization can give you a solid foundation to identify how you might be attacked.

Threats and Attack Targets

Different organizations and systems face different threats, depending on their industry, size, type of data, connectivity, and other factors. To begin to understand the threats you face, you need to answer questions like, what could be the target of an attack?

Your organization
Because of your industry, brand, reputation, or your people.

Your data
Because of the value it holds and/or information it pertains to.

Your service
Because of the functionality that it provides.

Your resources
Because of the compute, storage, or bandwidth you have available.

Your ecosystem
Because of its connectivity with other's systems (can it be used as a launchpad to attack other systems and organizations, like Target's HVAC supplier?).

Data is the most common target of attack: people trying to steal it, compromise it, or destroy it. Here are some data-related questions to ask:

1. What data does your system store, process, or have access to that is confidential or sensitive?

2. Who might want to steal it?

3. What would happen if they stole it? What could they do with it? Who would be hurt? How badly would they be hurt?

4. How much data do they need to steal before it matters to customers, to competitors, to regulators, or law enforcement?

5. Could you tell if they stole it?

6. What if they destroy it? What is the cost/loss? Ransomware attacks are rapidly changing how organizations think about this threat.

7. What if they tamper with it? What is the cost/loss? Could you tell if it happened?

Threat Intelligence

There are different sources of information about threats to help you understand threat actors and the risks that they pose to your organization. While this is an area of the security industry that is widely considered to be hyped and to have not returned on the promises of value that have been made (see the "Threaty Threats" warning ahead), it can still have a place in your security program. The following are a few categories of threat intelligence that you can take advantage of:

Information sharing centers
    Closed, managed communities that allow government agencies and industry participants to share pertinent threat intelligence and risk information, including indicators of compromise, as well as a forum for sharing best practices and for voluntarily reporting incidents. Examples include FS ISAC for the US financial industry, Auto ISAC for automakers, the US Defense Security Information Exchange (DSIE), the UK Cybersecurity Information Sharing Partnership (CISP), and the Canadian Cyber Incident Response Centre (CCIRC).

Government advisories
    Threat and risk advisories from government services and law enforcement agencies such as US-CERT and FBI Infragard.

Vendor-specific threat feeds
    Updates on vulnerabilities reported by software and network vendors.

Internet whitelists and blacklists
> Updated lists of valid or dangerous IP addresses which can be used to build network whitelists and blacklists for firewalls, IDS/IPS, and monitoring systems.

Consolidated threat feeds
> Open source and commercial threat feed services that consolidate information from multiple sources and may offer value-add risk analysis.

Analyst studies and reports
> In-depth analysis such as Mandiant's M-Trends or Verizon's Data Breach Investigation Report.

 For more information, see "A curated list of Awesome Threat Intelligence resources" (*https://github.com/hslatman/awesome-threat-intelligence*).

These sources provide information about threats against your industry or industry sector, against customers or suppliers including new malware or malware variants seen in the wild, new vulnerabilities that are actively being exploited, known sources of malicious traffic, fraud techniques, new attack patterns, zero days and compromise indicators, news about breaches, government alerts, and alerts from law enforcement.

The following are platforms for reporting, detecting, collecting, and aggregating threat intelligence:

- Open Threat Exchange (*https://www.alienvault.com/open-threat-exchange*)
- OpenTPX (*https://www.opentpx.org*)
- PassiveTotal (*https://www.passivetotal.org*)
- Critical Stack (*https://intel.criticalstack.com*)
- Facebook's ThreatExchange (*https://www.facebook.com/threatexchange*)

Threat information comes in many different forms, including reports, email notifications, and live structured data feeds. Two open community projects help make it easier to share threat information between different organizations and between tools by defining standards for describing and reporting threats.

STIX (*https://stixproject.github.io*) is a community project to standardize threat information using a common format that can be easily understood and aggregated by automated tooling, in the same way that SCAP or CWE is used. It defines a structured language to describe threats, including information about threat indicators (what other organizations are seeing in the wild).

TAXII (*http://taxiiproject.github.io*) is another standards initiative to define common ways of sharing threat data and how to identify and respond to threat information. HailaTaxii.com (*http://hailataxii.com*) provides a repository of open source threat feeds available in STIX format.

Threaty Threats

For many in the security industry, threat intelligence has unfortunately evolved into something of a running joke, with outlandish claims of value not being realized, and competition between suppliers seeming to focus on information quantity, not quality or relevance. Visually fascinating but operationally questionable *pew pew* maps, where threats are animated in ways taken straight from Hollywood, have done little to help the situation in terms of demonstrable value. Such is the derision that this part of the industry attracts parody services like Threatbutt (*http://threatbutt.com*) have been created just to mock.

As with many parts of information security, you need to clearly understand and investigate the actual value the various parts of threat intelligence can bring to your organization rather than jumping on the bandwagon just because it looks cool.

Threat Assessment

Your next step is to determine which threats matter most to your organization and to your system: what threats you need to immediately understand and prepare for.

Threat Intel for Developers

Most threat intelligence consists of updates on file signatures (to identify malware), alerts on phishing and DDOS and ransomware attacks and fraud attempts, and network reputation information identifying potential sources of attacks. This is information that is of interest to the security team, operations, and IT, but not necessarily to developers.

Developers need to understand what types of threats they need to protect against in design, development, and implementation. What kind of attacks are being seen in the wild, and where are they coming from? What third-party software vulnerabilities are being exploited? What kind of events should they be looking for and alerting on as exceptions, or trying to block?

The best source of this information is often right in front of developers: their systems running in production. Depending on the solutions being developed, it may also be worth understanding whether there is any value that can be realized from integrating threat intelligence data into the solution itself.

Threats that other organizations in your industry sector are actively dealing with should be a high priority. Of course, the most urgent issues are the threats that have already triggered: attacks that are underway against your organization and your systems.

Coming up, we talk about *attack-driven defense*, using information that you see about attacks that are underway in production to drive security priorities. Information from production monitoring provides real, actionable information about active threats that you need to understand and do something about: they aren't theoretical; they are in progress. This isn't to say that you can or should ignore other, less imminent threats. But if bad guys are pounding on the door, you should make sure that it is locked shut.

Attack-driven defense creates self-reinforcing feedback loops to and from development and production:

1. Use live attack information to update your threat understanding and build up a better understanding of what threats are your highest priority.

2. Use threat intelligence to help define what you need to look for, by adding checks in production monitoring to determine if/when these attacks are active.

3. Use all of this information to prioritize your testing, scanning, and reviews so that you can identify weaknesses in the system and find and remediate, or monitor for, vulnerabilities before attackers find them and exploit them.

In order to make use of this, you will need the following:

1. Effective monitoring capabilities that will catch indicators of attack and feed this information back to operations and developers to act on.

2. Investigative and forensics skills to understand the impact of the attack: is it an isolated occurrence that you caught in time, or something that happened before that you just noticed.

3. A proven ability to push patches or other fixes out quickly and safely in response to attacks, relying on your automated build and deployment pipeline.

Your System's Attack Surface

To assess the security of your system and its exposure to threats, you first need to understand the *attack surface*, the parts of the system that attackers care about.

There are actually three different attack surfaces that you need to be concerned about for any system:

Network
All the network endpoints that are exposed, including all the devices and services listening on the network, the OSes, VMs, and containers. You can use a scanning tool like *nmap* to understand the network attack surface.

Application
Every way that an attacker can enter data or commands, and every way that an attacker could get data out of the system, especially anonymous endpoints; and the code behind all of this, specifically any vulnerabilities in this code that could be exploited by an attacker.

Human
The people involved in designing, building, operating, and supporting the system, as well as the people using the system, who can all be targets of social engineering attacks. They could be manipulated or compromised to gain unauthorized access to the system or important information about the system, or turned into malicious actors.

Mapping Your Application Attack Surface

The application attack surface includes, among other things:

- Web forms, fields, HTTP headers and parameters, and cookies
- APIs, especially public network-facing APIs, which are easy to attack; and admin APIs, which are worth the extra effort to attack

- Clients: client code such as mobile clients present a separate attack surface
- Configuration parameters
- Operations tooling for the system
- File uploads
- Data stores: because data can be stolen or damaged once it is stored, and because you will read data back from data stores, so data can be used against the system in Persistent XSS and other attacks
- Audit logs: because they contain valuable information or because they can be used to track attacker activity
- Calls out to services like email and other systems, services, and third parties
- User and system credentials that could be stolen, or compromised to gain unauthorized access to the system (this also includes API tokens)
- Sensitive data in the system that could be damaged or stolen: PII, PHI, financial data, confidential or classified information
- Security controls: your shields to protect the system and data: identity management and authentication and session management logic, access control lists, audit logging, encryption, input data validation and output data encoding; more specifically, any weaknesses or vulnerabilities in these controls that attackers can find and exploit
- And, as we look at in Chapter 11, your automated build and delivery pipeline for the system.

Remember that this includes not only the code that you write, but all of the third-party and open source code libraries and frameworks that you use in the application. Even a reasonably small application built on a rich application framework like Angular or Ruby on Rails can have a large attack surface.

Managing Your Application Attack Surface

The bigger or more complex the system, the larger the attack surface will be. Your goal should be to keep the attack surface as small as possible. This has always been hard to do and keeps getting harder in modern architectures.

Using Microservices Explodes the Attack Surface

Microservices are one of the hot new ideas in application architecture, because they provide development teams with so much more flexibility and independence. It's hard to argue with the success of microservices at organizations like Amazon and Netflix, but it's also worth recognizing that microservices introduce serious operational challenges and security risks.

The attack surface of an individual microservice should be small and easy to review. But the total attack surface of a system essentially explodes once you start using microservices at any scale. The number of endpoints and the potential connections between different microservices can become unmanageable.

It is not always easy to understand call-chain dependencies: you can't necessarily control who calls you and what callers expect from your service, and you can't control what downstream services do, or when or how they will be changed.

In engineering-led shops that follow the lead of Amazon and Netflix, developers are free to choose to the best tools for the job at hand, which means that different microservices could be written in different languages and using different frameworks. This introduces new technology-specific risks and makes the job of reviewing, scanning, and securing the environment much more difficult.

Containers like Docker, which are often part of a microservices story, also impact the attack surface of the system in fundamental ways. Although containers can be configured to reduce the system attack surface and improve isolation between services, they expose an attack surface of their own that needs to be carefully managed.

This seems like too much to track and take care of. But you can break down the problem—and the risk.

Each time that you make a change to the system, consider how the change impacts the attack surface. The more changes that you make, the more risk you may be taking on. The bigger the change, the more risk that you may be taking on.

Most changes made by Agile and DevOps teams are small and incremental. Adding a new field to a web form technically increases the size of the attack surface, but the incremental risk that you are taking on should be easy to understand and deal with.

However, other changes can be much more serious.

Are you adding a new admin role or rolling out a new network-facing API? Are you changing a security control or introducing some new type of sensitive data that needs to be protected? Are you making a fundamental change to the architecture, or moving a trust boundary? These types of changes should trigger a risk review (in design or code or both) and possibly some kind of compliance checks. Fortunately, changes like this are much less common.

Agile Threat Modeling

Threat modeling is about exploring security risks in design by looking at the design from an attacker's perspective and making sure that you have the necessary protection in place. In the same way that attacker stories or misuse cases ask the team to re-examine requirements from an attacker's point of view, threat modeling changes the team's perspective in design to think about what can go wrong and what you can do about it at the design level.

This doesn't have to be done in a heavyweight, expensive Waterfall-style review. All that you need to do is to build a simple model of the system, and look at trust, and at threats and how to defend against them.

Understanding Trust and Trust Boundaries

Trust boundaries are points in the system where you (as a developer) change expectations about what data is safe to use and which users can be trusted. Boundaries are where controls need to be applied and assumptions about data and identity and authorization need to be checked. Anything inside a boundary should be safe. Anything outside of the boundary is out of your control and should be considered unsafe. Anything that crosses a boundary is suspect: guilty until proven innocent.

Trust Is Simple. Or Is It?

Trust is a simple concept. But this is also where serious mistakes are often made in design. It's easy to make incorrect or naive assumptions about the trustworthiness of user identity or data between systems, between clients (any kind of client, including browsers, workstation clients, mobile clients, and IoT devices) and servers, between other layers inside a system, and between services.

Trust can be hard to model and enforce in enterprise systems connected to many other systems and services. And, as we'll see in Chapter 9, *Building Secure and Usable Systems*, trust is pervasive and entangled in modern architectures based on microservices, containers, and cloud platforms.

Trust boundaries become especially fuzzy in a microservices world, where a single call can chain across many different services. Each service owner needs to understand and enforce trust assumptions around data and identity. Unless everyone follows common patterns, it is easy to break trust relationships and other contracts between microservices.

In the cloud, you need to clearly understand the cloud provider's *shared responsibility model*: what services they provide for you, and how you need to use these services safely. If you are trusting your cloud provider to do identity management and access management, or auditing services, or encryption, check these services out carefully and make sure that you configure and use them correctly. Then write tests to make sure that you always configure and use them correctly. Make sure that you understand what risks or threats you could face from co-tenants, and how to safely isolate your systems and data. And if you are implementing a hybrid public/private cloud architecture, carefully review all data and identity passed between public and private cloud domains.

Making mistakes around trust is #1 on the IEEE's Top 10 Software Security Design Flaws.[1] Their advice is: "Earn or Give, But Never Assume Trust."

How do you know that you can trust a user's identity? Where is authentication done? How and where are authorization and access control rules applied? And how do you know you can trust the data? Where is data validated or encoded? Could the data have been tampered with along the way?

---

1 IEEE Center for Secure Design, "Avoiding the Top 10 Software Security Design Flaws" (*https://www.computer.org/cms/CYBSI/docs/Top-10-Flaws.pdf*), 2014.

These are questions that apply to every environment. You need to have high confidence in the answers to these questions, especially when you are doing something that is security sensitive.

You need to ask questions about trust at the application level, as well as questions about the operational and runtime environment. What protection are you relying on in the network: firewalls and proxies, filtering, and segmentation? What levels of isolation and other protection is the OS or VM or container providing you? How can you be sure?

Trusted Versus Trustworthy

The terms *trusted* and *trustworthy* are often used interchangeably, but when it comes to security their difference is actually very important, and the widespread incorrect usage of them illustrates some deeper misunderstandings that manifest across the space. It could well be that the seeds of confusion were planted by the famous Orange Book (Trusted Computer System Evaluation Criteria) (*https://en.wikipedia.org/wiki/Trusted_Computer_System_Evaluation_Criteria*) developed by the US Department of Defense in the early 1980s.

If something is *trusted*, then what is being said is that someone has taken the action of placing *trust* in it and nothing more. However, if something is *trustworthy*, then a claim is being made that the subject is *worthy* of the trust being placed in it. These are distinctly different and carry with them different properties in terms of security.

You will often see advice stating not to open *untrusted* attachments or click on *untrusted* links, when what is really meant is not to open or click *untrustworthy* links or attachments.

When discussing users and systems in terms of threat models, it's important to understand the difference between entities that are *trusted* (they have had trust placed in them regardless of worthiness) and entities that are *trustworthy* (they have had their worthiness of trust evaluated, or better yet proven).

While this may all seem grammatical pedantry, the actual impact of understanding the differences that manifest from *trusted* versus *trustworthy* actors can make a very real-world difference in your security approaches.

A great short video by Brian Sletten discussing this as it relates to browser security can be found at *https://www.oreilly.com/learning/trusted-vs-trustworthy* and is well worth the 10-minute investment to watch.

Threats are difficult for developers to understand and hard to for anyone to quantify. Trust is a more straightforward concept, which makes thinking about trust a good place to start in reviewing your design for security weaknesses. Unlike threats, trust can also be verified: you can walk through the design or read the code and write tests to check your assumptions.

Building Your Threat Model

To build a threat model, you start by drawing a picture of the system or the part of the system that you are working on, and the connections in and out to show data flows, highlighting any places where sensitive data including credentials or PII are created or updated, transmitted, or stored. The most common and natural way to show this is a data flow diagram with some extra annotations.

Once you have the main pieces and the flows described, you'll want to identify trust boundaries. A common convention is to draw these as dotted lines demarcating the different trust zones, as we show in Figure 8-1.

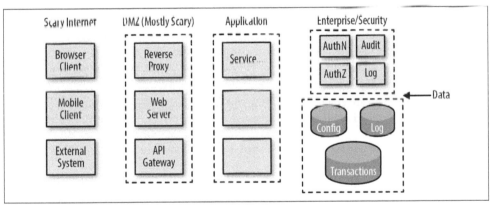

Figure 8-1. Simple trust/threat boundary model

Trust zones can be established between organizations, between data centers or networks, between systems, between layers of an application, or between services or components inside a service, depending on the level that you are working at.

Then mark out the controls and checks at these boundaries:

- Where is authentication done?
- Where are access control checks applied?
- Data validation
- Crypto—what information is being encrypted and when/where
- Rate limiting

- Sensors and detectors

"Good Enough" Is Good Enough

Don't spend a lot of time making pretty pictures. Your model can be rough, especially to start. Like any Agile modeling, the point is to have just enough that everyone can understand the pieces and how they fit together; anything more is waste. Version 0.1 could be nothing more than a whiteboard diagram that is captured via a photo on a mobile phone.

Free Threat Modeling Tool from Microsoft

Microsoft provides a free tool called Microsoft Threat Modeling Tool 2016 (*http://bit.ly/ms-threat-modeling-tool*) which will help you create threat models and save them so that you can review and update the model as you make changes to the system.

As with all free tools, there are advantages and disadvantages to using this to help with your threat models. Using a modeling tool like this will allow you to easily drag and drop components onto your diagram without having to remember what the specific symbol should be at any stage. They also have a wide range of symbols and example components available to choose from.

There are challenges to using this tool though. The very Microsoft-specific language and suggested components can make it difficult to decide which items to use on your diagram. Often there are dozens of components which share a symbol but have a different name in the menu.

Furthermore, this tool has a built-in *report generation* feature that will export a threat assessment based on your model (and the attributes you completed for each component). While this can seem very impressive, it can turn into hundreds of generic threats in HTML format that need to be triaged and assessed before they can be used. These reports often take a lot longer to triage than a manual threat assessment would have taken; and without this triage process, the assessment can be an impressive-looking distraction.

We recommend using tools for the modeling of systems, and conducting the threat assessment itself manually or outside of the tool, preferably in a way that tightly integrates with your issue tracking and pipeline.

Once you have a good enough diagram drawn up, get the team together to walk through the diagram and do some brainstorming about threats and attacks. Look carefully at information that crosses trust boundaries, especially sensitive information. Be realistic when it comes to threats and attack scenarios. Use the threat intelligence that you've captured and attack patterns that you've observed in production to focus your attention. At this stage it would also be recommended to call out the things that are not in your threat model and you are consciously placing out of scope, a clear articulation of what you won't be focusing on helps you center on what you will be.

Threat modeling is more effective if you can get people with different viewpoints involved. Developers who know the system or part of the system that you are reviewing, architects and developers who know other parts of the system, testers who know how the system actually works, operations engineers and network engineers who understand the runtime environment, and security specialists will all look for different problems and risks.

Try not to get bogged down in arguing about low-level details, unless you are already reviewing at a low level and need to verify all of these assumptions.

Spend time identifying risks and design weaknesses before switching into solution mode. Then look at what you could change to protect your system from these threats. Can you move responsibilities from outside of a trust boundary to inside? Can you reduce the number of connections between modules, or simplify the design or workflow to reduce the size of the attack surface? Do you need to pass information across a trust boundary, or can you pass a secure key or token instead?

What changes can you, or must you, make now, and what changes can be added to the backlog and scheduled?

Learning More About Threat Modeling

SAFECode has a 45-minute free online course on Threat modeling that provides a good overview (*https://training.safecode.org/course/threat_modelling_101*).

Microsoft popularized the practice of application threat modeling. For a quick introduction to how they do (or at least used to do) threat modeling at Microsoft, read Peter Torr's Blog, "Guerrilla Threat Modelling (or 'Threat Modeling' if you're American)" (*http://bit.ly/guerilla-threat-modelling*).

If you really want to dig deep into everything about threat modeling, you should read Adam Shostack's book *Threat Modeling: Designing for Security* (Wiley) (*https://threatmodelingbook.com*).

Shostack was one of the leaders of Microsoft's software security practice and helped to pioneer the threat modeling approach followed in Microsoft's SDL. His book covers threat modeling in detail, including different techniques and games and tools for building threat models, as well as an analysis of the different types of threats that you need to consider.

Thinking Like an Attacker

In Chapter 5, we asked developers to put on a black hat and think like an attacker when writing attacker stories or negative scenarios. But how do you do that? How do you think like an attacker? What is it like to see a system through an attacker's eyes?

Adam Shostack, a leading expert on threat modeling, says that you can't ask someone to "think like an attacker" and expect them to be really effective at it if they haven't actually worked as a pen tester or done some serious hacking. It's like being told to "think like a professional chef." You might know how to cook at home for family and friends, and you might even be good at it. But this doesn't mean that you know what it's like to work in a Michelin star restaurant or work as a short-order cook in a diner during the morning rush.[2]

You need real experience and context to understand how attackers think and work. You can learn something over time from working with good pen testers (and from Red Teaming exercises and bug bounties) and through training. Using pen testing tools like OWASP ZAP in your testing programs will open a small window into the world of an attacker. Capture the Flag exercises and hands-on exploitation training systems can help people become more familiar with the ways in which attackers think

---

2 Read Bill Buford's *Heat: An Amateur's Adventures as Kitchen Slave, Line Cook, Pasta-Maker, and Apprentice to a Dante-Quoting Butcher in Tuscany* (Vintage) to get an appreciation of just how hard this is.

about the world. But at least in the short term you'll need to rely on a security expert (if you have one available) to play the role of the attacker.

STRIDE: A Structured Model to Understand Attackers

Even if you know how attackers work, it's a good idea to follow a structured model to help make sure that you remember to review the design for different security threats and risks. One of the best known approaches for this is Microsoft's *STRIDE*.

STRIDE is an acronym that stands for the following:

	Threat	Solution
Spoofing	Can you trust the user's identity?	Authentication and session management, digital certificates.
Tampering	Can you trust the integrity of the data? Can someone change it on purpose, or accidentally?	Digital signatures, checksums, sequence accounting, access control, auditing.
Repudiation	Can you prove who did something and when they did it?	End-to-end auditing and logging, sequence accounting, digital certificates and digital signatures, fraud prevention.
Information disclosure	What is the risk of data theft or leaks?	Access control, encryption, data tokenization, error handling.
Denial of service	Can someone stop authorized users from getting valid access to the system—on purpose, or accidentally?	Rate limiting, boundary protection, elastic resourcing, availability services.
Elevation of privilege	Can an unprivileged user gain privileged system access?	Authorization, least privilege, type safety and parameterization to prevent injection attacks.

STRIDE is a simple way of thinking about the most common paths that attackers can take to get at systems and data. There are other approaches that are just as effective, such as *attack trees*, which we looked at in Chapter 5. What's important is to agree on a simple but effective way to think about threats and how to defend against them in design.

Don't Overlook Accidents

When you are thinking about what can go wrong, don't overlook accidents. Honest mistakes can cause very bad things to happen to a system, especially mistakes by operations or a privileged application admin user. (See the discussion of blameless postmortems in Chapter 13.)

Incremental Threat Modeling and Risk Assessments

Where does threat modeling fit into Agile sprints or Lean one-piece continuous flow? When should you stop and do threat modeling where you are filling in the design as you go in response to feedback, where there are no clear handoffs or sign offs because the design is "never finished," and where there may be no design document to hand off because "the code is the design"?

Assess Risks Up Front

You can begin up front by understanding that even if the architecture is only roughed out and subject to change, the team still needs to commit to a set of tools and a run-time stack to get started. Even with a loose or incomplete idea of what you are going to build, you can start to understand risks and weaknesses in design and what you will need to do about them.

At PayPal, for example, every team must go through an initial risk assessment, by filling out an automated risk questionnaire, whenever it begins work on a new app or microservice. One of the key decision points is whether the team is using languages and frameworks that have already been vetted by the security team in another project. Or, is it introducing something new to the organization, technologies that the security team hasn't seen or checked before? There is a big difference in risk between "just another web or mobile app" built on an approved platform, and a technical experiment using new languages and tools.

Here are some of the issues to understand and assess in an up-front risk review:

1. Do you understand how to use the language(s) and frameworks safely? What security protections are offered in the framework? What needs to be added to make it simple for developers to "do the right thing" by default?

2. Is there good continuous integration and continuous delivery toolchain support for the language(s) and framework, including static code analysis tooling, and dependency management analysis capabilities to catch vulnerabilities in third-party and open source libraries?

3. Is sensitive and confidential data being used or managed in the system? What data is needed, how is it to be handled, and what needs to be audited? Does it need to be stored, and, if so, how? Do you need to make considerations for encryption, tokenization and masking, access control, and auditing?

4. Understanding trust boundaries between this app/service and others: where do controls need to be enforced around authentication, access control, and data quality? What assumptions are being made at a high level in the design?

Review Threats as the Design Changes

After this, threat modeling should be done whenever you make a material change to the system's attack surface, which we explained earlier. Threat modeling could be added to the acceptance criteria for a story when the story is originally written or when it is elaborated in sprint planning, or as team members work on the story or test the code and recognize the risks.

In Agile and DevOps environments, this means that you will need to do threat modeling much more often than in Waterfall development. But it should also be easier.

In the beginning of a project, when you are first putting in the architectural skeleton of the system and fleshing out the design and interfaces, you will obviously be making lots of changes to the attack surface. It will probably be difficult to understand which risks to focus on, because there is so much to consider, and because the design is continuously changing as you learn more about the problem space and your technology.

You could decide to defer threat modeling until the design details become clearer and more set, recognizing that you are taking on technical debt and security debt that will need to be paid off later. Or keep iterating through the model so that you can keep control over the risks, recognizing that you will be throwing away at least some of this work when you change the design.

Later, as you make smaller, targeted, incremental changes, threat modeling will be easier and faster because you can focus in on the context and the impact of each change. It will be easier to identify risks and problems. And it should also get easier and faster the more often the team goes through the process and steps through the model. At some point, threat modeling will become routine, just another part of how the team thinks and works.

The key to threat modeling in Agile and DevOps is recognizing that because design and coding and deployment are done in a tight, iterative loop, you will be caught up in the same loops when you are assessing technical risks. This means that you can make—and you need to make—threat modeling efficient, simple, pragmatic, and fast.

Getting Value Out of Threat Modeling

The team will need to decide how much threat modeling is needed, and how long to spend on it, trading off risk and time. Like other Agile reviews, the team may decide to time box threat modeling sessions, holding them to a fixed time duration, making the work more predictable and focused, even if this means that the review will not be comprehensive or complete.

Quick-and-dirty threat modeling done often is much better than no threat modeling at all.

Like code reviews, threat modeling doesn't have to be an intimidating, expensive, and heavyweight process; and it can't be, if you expect teams to fit it into high-velocity Agile delivery. It doesn't matter whether you use STRIDE, CAPEC (*https:// capec.mitre.org/*), DESIST (a variant of STRIDE; dispute, elevation of privilege, spoofing, information disclosure, service denial, tampering), attack trees (which we looked at in Chapter 5), Lockheed Martin's Kill Chain (*http://www.lockheedmartin.com/us/ what-we-do/aerospace-defense/cyber/cyber-kill-chain.html*), or simply a careful validation of trust assumptions in your design. The important thing is to find an approach that the team understands and agrees to follow, and that helps it to find real security problems—and solutions to those problems—during design.

In iterative design and development, you will have opportunities to come back and revisit and fill in your design and your threat model, probably many times, so you don't have to try to exhaustively review the design each time. Do threat modeling the same way that you design and write code. Design a little, then take a bite out of the attack surface in a threat modeling session, write some code and some tests. Fill in or open up the design a bit more, and take another bite. You're never done threat modeling.

Each time that you come back again to look at the design and how it has been changed, you'll have a new focus, new information, and more experience, which means that you may ask new questions and find problems that you didn't see before.

Focus on high-risk threats, especially active threats. And make sure that you cover common attacks.

Minimum Viable Process (and Paperwork)

A common mistake we see when working with teams that are threat modeling for the first time is the focus on documentation, paperwork, and process over outcomes.

It can be very tempting to enforce that every change be documented in a template and that every new feature have the same "lightweight" threat assessment form completed. In fact, sometimes even our lightweight processes distract us from the real value of the activity. If you find your team is more focused on how to complete the diagram or document than the findings of the assessment, revisit your approach.

Even in heavy compliance environments, the process and documentation requirements for threat assessment should be the minimum needed for audit and not the primary focus of the activity.

Remember, for the most part, we are engineers and builders. Use your skills to automate the process and documentation so that you can spend your time on the assessment, where the real value lies.

Common Attack Vectors

Walking through common attack vectors, the basic kinds of attacks that you need to defend against and the technical details of how they actually work, helps to make abstract threats and risks concrete and understandable to developers and operations engineers. It also helps them to be more realistic in thinking about threats so that you focus on defending against the scenarios and types of vulnerabilities that adversaries will try first.

There are a few different ways to learn about common attacks and how they work:

Scanning
> Tools like OWASP ZAP, or scanning services like Qualys or WhiteHat Sentinel, which automatically execute common attacks against your application.

Penetration testing results
> Take the time to understand what pen testers tried, why, what they found, and why.

Bug bounties
> As we'll see in "Bug Bounties" on page 233, bug bounty programs can be an effective, if not always efficient, way to get broad security testing coverage.

Red Team/Blue Team games
> Covered in Chapter 13, force defensive Blue Teams to actively watch for, and learn how to respond to, real attacks.

Attack simulation platforms
> AttackIQ (*https://www.attackiq.com*), SafeBreach (*https://safebreach.com*), and Verodin (*https://verodin.com*) automatically execute common network and application attacks, and allow you to script your own attack/response scenarios. These are black boxes that test the effectiveness of your defenses, and allow you to visualize if and how your network is compromised under different conditions.

Industry analyst reports
> Reports like Verizon's annual "Data Breach Investigations Report" (*http://www.verizonenterprise.com/verizon-insights-lab/dbir/*) provide an overview of the most common and serious attacks seen in the wild.

OWASP's Top 10 (https://www.owasp.org)
> Lists the most serious risks and the most common attacks against web applications and mobile applications. For each of the Top 10 risks, OWASP looks at threat agents (what kind of users to look out for) and common attack vectors and examples of attack scenarios. We'll look at the OWASP Top 10 again in Chapter 14 because this list of risks has become a reference requirement for many regulations.

Event logs from your own systems
> This will show indicators of real-world attacks and whether they are successful.

Common attacks need to be taken into account in design, in testing, in reviews, and in monitoring. You can use your understanding of common attacks to write security stories, to script automated security tests, to guide threat modeling sessions, and to define attack signatures for your security monitoring and defense systems.

Key Takeaways

To effectively defend against adversaries and their threats against your organization and system, you need to take the following measures:

- Threat intelligence needs to be incorporated into Agile and DevOps feedback loops.

- One of the best sources of threat intelligence is what is happening to your production systems right now. Use this information in attack-driven defense to find and plug holes before attackers find and exploit them.

- Although Agile teams often don't spend a lot of time in up-front design, before the team commits to a technology platform and runtime stack, work with them to understand security risks in their approach and how to minimize them.

- In Agile and especially DevOps environments, the system's attack surface is continuously changing. By understanding the attack surface and the impact of changes that you are making, you can identify risks and potential weaknesses that need to be addressed.

- Because the attack surface is continuously changing, you need to do threat modeling on a continuous basis. Threat modeling has to be done a lightweight, incremental, and iterative way.

- Make sure that team understands common attacks like the OWASP Top 10, and how to deal with them in design, testing, and monitoring.

CHAPTER 9

Building Secure and Usable Systems

What does it mean to build a secure system?

Building a secure system means designing and implementing a system that deals with the risks that you are taking, and leaves only acceptable risks behind.

The level of *security* that you apply will depend on your organization, on your industry, on your customers, and on the type of system. If you are building an online consumer marketplace, or a mobile game, you'll have a very different set of security concerns than someone building an encryption device designed to be used in the field by Marines in the advance guard.

However some patterns are common in most security-based situations.

Design to Resist Compromise

A secure system must be built to resist compromise, whether that's resisting remote SQL injection attacks, being resistant to power differential attacks, or not leaking electromagnetic spectrum information. The point is that you understand the operating environment and can build in protection against compromise.

You do this by changing your design assumptions.

We know from years of crypto research that you should assume that all user input is compromised, and that attackers can repeatedly and reliably introduce whatever input they want. We should also assume that attackers can reliably read all output from your system.

You can even go so far as to assume that the attackers know everything about your system and how it works.[1] So where does that leave you?

Resisting compromise is about carefully checking all input data, and providing as little information on output as you can get away with. It's about anticipating failures and making sure that you handle them safely, and detecting and recording errors and attacks. And making life as difficult as you can for an attacker, while still making sure that the system is usable and understandable.

For almost all of us, we can assume that our attackers have bounded resources and motivation. That is, if we can resist long enough, they will either run out of time and money, or get bored and move elsewhere. (If you aren't in that camp, then you need specialist help and probably shouldn't be reading this book!) If a nation state decides to attack you, they are probably going to succeed anyway—but you still want to make it as difficult for them as possible, and try to catch them in the act.

Security Versus Usability

People often talk about security and usability being the opposite faces of the same coin. That security forces us to build unusable systems and that usability experts want to remove the security features that we build in.

This is increasingly understood to be wrong. It shows a tunnel-vision view of security as a technical mission rather than a holistic mission.

Systems that are not usable due to over-engineered security controls tend to push users to find unauthorized workarounds that compromise the security of the system: passwords written on Post-it notes, to teams sharing accounts because it's easier, to systems with default passwords so the administrators can sort things out when they break.

We, as security, need to think holistically about the systems that we build, and ensure that the user is encouraged and able to use the service in the most secure manner possible. Take whatever steps you need to protect the system, but do this in ways that don't get in the way of what the system is designed to do or how it is supposed to be used.

---

1 This idea goes back over 100 years, and is commonly known as Shannon's Maxim: "the enemy knows the system."

Technical Controls

When we think about securing a system, most people think of technical controls. These are solutions that prevent an attacker (or user) from accessing unauthorized or unintended functionality or system control functions.

Technical controls are often bolted on to the design of a system to solve security problems. They suffer from the dual problem of being an attractive vendor space and being highly limited in scope.

It's common for vendors to get excited about how amazing their technical black box is and how much it will do to make your system safe. But ask yourself this: do you really think that all the organizations that suffered intrusions last year were not running next-generation firewalls, intrusion detection systems, advanced endpoint protection, or other magic black boxes?

Some natural skepticism is healthy when choosing technical controls and products. Although they are an important part of most security architectures, in most cases they only address low-hanging fruit (common vulnerabilities) or specific edge cases. Much as locking the door to your home won't protect it from all thieves, technical controls and products won't protect your system from all threats. They must be considered as part of a wider, more holistic approach.

We divide security controls in systems into a few different categories. Like all categorical systems, they overlap and aren't perfect, but it helps us start to talk about such things.

Deterrent Controls

Deterrent controls deter or make clear to people what will happen if they attack your system. These are the technical equivalent of a signpost on your gate warning visitors to "Beware of the dog" or that "This building is under surveillance."

In a physical sense, this can include other highly visible controls, so CCTV or electrified or barbed wire fences are just as much a deterrent as they are a highly effective resistive control (see below).

In a digital system, this can include things like modifying service headers to include warnings, and warning messages or customized error handling. The visible presence of such things makes it clear that you know what you are doing, and makes it clear to attackers when they are crossing a legal line.

Resistive Controls

Resistive controls are designed to slow down an attacker, not stop them. Limiting the number of sign-in attempts from a single address, or rate-limiting uses of the system are resistive. A clever attacker can get around these controls, but they slow down attackers, increasing the chance that they will get caught or making them want to look elsewhere.

As these controls aim to slow down and frustrate an attacker, we can also include simple steps like code obfuscation, generic error messages, and responsive session management.

Code obfuscation has been an area of much debate as a resistive control and allows us to consider the cost of such choices. Running your code through an obfuscation system renders it difficult to read and often makes it difficult to review and understand. While this will slow down less skilled attackers, remember there is a cost to this control. Obfuscated code is also difficult to debug and can cause frustration for support teams.

Resistive controls are useful but should be applied with care. Slowing down and frustrating attackers is rarely acceptable if it means frustrating and causing confusion or friction for genuine system users.

Protective Controls

Protective controls actually prevent an attack from occurring. Most technical security controls are this kind of control, so firewalls, access control lists (ACLs), IP restrictions, and so forth are all designed to prevent misuse of the system.

Some protective controls, such as making systems only available for set time periods or from a finite set of physical locations, may have a high impact on usability. While there may be strong business cases for these controls, we must always consider the edge cases in our environments.

For example, controls that prevent users from logging in from outside office hours or location can prevent staff from checking their emails when traveling to a conference.

People (including attackers) are like water when it comes to protective controls that get in their way. They will work around them and come up with pragmatic solutions to get themselves moving again.

Detective Controls

Some controls are designed not to prevent or even slow the attackers, but merely to detect an intrusion. These can vary from simple log auditing or security event tools to more advanced tools like honeypots, traffic flow graphs, and even monitoring of CPU load for abnormalities.

Detective controls are widely applied and familiar to operations and infrastructure teams alike. The core challenges with these controls are ensuring that they are tuned to detect the right things for your environment and that someone is watching the logs and ready to respond if something is detected.

Compensating Controls

Finally, there are times when the control you want might not be available. So if you want to prevent staff from accessing the login system from outside the country, but a significant proportion of your staff travels for work, you might be stuck.

What you often do is apply other controls that you might not otherwise require to compensate for the lack of the controls that you do have. For example, in that situation, you can instead use a physical, second-factor token on authentication, and monitor any changes of location compared to staff travel records to detect misuse.

We take a look at several other examples of compensating controls in Chapter 13, *Operations and OpSec* where we cover controls such as WAFs, RASP, and runtime defense.

Security Architecture

So what does all this mean? How can we build a secure system?

We can use the controls, combined with some principles to build a system that resists and actively defends against attack.

We need to be aware from the beginning what the system does and who is going to attack it. Hopefully, by following the guidance in Chapter 7 on threat assessments, you will understand who is likely to attack the system, what they are after, and the most likely ways that they will attack you.

Next, you need to think about your system itself. We often talk about systems as being a single, monolithic black box. That's an artifact of traditional systems engineering thinking. Back in the *old days*, building a system required buying sufficient computers to run the system, and the physical hardware might be a major proportion of the cost.

These days, with containerization, microservices, virtual machines, and cloud-based compute being cheap, and looking to get much cheaper, we can instead start to see more separation between the components of the system.

From a security perspective, this appears to be much better. Each component can be reasoned about much more easily and can be secured in its normal operation. Components are often smaller, more singular in their purpose, and able to be deployed, changed, and managed independently.

However, this creates a new set of security risks and challenges.

The traditional model of security is to think of a system as being similar to an M&M or a Smartie (depending on American or British upbringing, I guess), or in New Zealand, an *armadillo* (because apparently New Zealanders have more wildlife than candy, or think that wildlife is candy). All of these things have a hard outer shell, but a soft gooey interior.

Perimeterless Security

Historically, when we defined the architecture of an M&M (or armadillo) system, the system would only have a few perimeters or trust boundaries. Anything outside of a trust boundary (such as third-party systems or users) would be treated as untrusted, while all systems and entities within the trust boundary or hardened perimeter, behind the DMZ and firewalls, would be considered to be safe.

As we saw in the previous chapter on threats and attacks, understanding trust and trust boundaries is relatively simple in monolithic, on-premises systems. In this model, there are only a few entities or components inside the perimeter, and no reason to consider them to be a risk.

But too much depends on only a few perimeters. Once an attacker breaches a perimeter, everything is open to him.

As we separate and uncouple our architectures, we have to change this way of thinking. Because each entity is managed separately and uncoupled, we can no longer simply trust that other components in the system are not compromised. This also means that we cannot allow admin staff on internal networks to have unlimited access across the system (absolutely no "God mode" admins or support back doors).

Instead, systems should be built so that they do not assume that other points anywhere on the physical or virtual network are trustworthy. In other words, a low-trust network, or what is now being called a *zero trust network*.

To learn more about how to design and operate a zero trust network, you should read up on what Google is doing with its BeyondCorp initiative (*http://static.googleusercontent.com/media/ research.google.com/en//pubs/archive/43231.pdf*).

And read *Zero Trust Networks: Building Trusted Systems in Untrusted Networks* (O'Reilly) by Evan Gilman and Doug Barth.

In this environment, everything on the network needs to be protected against malicious insiders or attackers who have breached your perimeter or other defenses:

- Reassess and audit-identity at every point. You must always know who you are dealing with, whether through time-sensitive tokens issued by an authentication server, or cryptographically safe keys or similar techniques to prove identity.

- Consider using TLS for secure network communications between services, at the very least when talking to edge services, authentication services, and other critical services.

- Revalidate and check inputs, even from core services and platform services. This means validating all headers, and every field of every request.

- Enforce access control rules on data and on API functions at each point. Make these rules as simple as you can get away with, but ensure that they are consistently enforced, and that they follow the principle of least privilege.

- Treat all sensitive data (any data that somebody might want to steal) as toxic.[2] Always know where it is and who owns it, handle it safely, be careful with who you share it with and how you store it (if you must store it), and keep it encrypted whenever possible.

- Log traffic at each point—not just at the perimeter firewall—so that you can identify when and where a compromise actually occurred. Log records should be forwarded to a secure, central logging service to make it possible to trace requests across services and to protect the logs if a service or node is compromised.

- Harden all runtimes (OS, VMs, containers, databases) just as you would if these boxes were in your DMZ.

- Use *circuit breakers* and *bulkheads* to contain runtime failures and to minimize the "blast radius" of a security breach. These are stability patterns from Michael Nygards's book *Release It!* (Pragmatic Bookshelf) (*https://pragprog.com/book/mnee/release-it*), which explains how to design, build, and operate resilient online systems.

  Bulkheads can be built around connections, thread pools, processes, and data. Circuit breakers protect callers from downstream malfunctions, automatically detecting and recovering from timeouts and hangs when calling other services. Netflix's Hystrix (*https://github.com/Netflix/Hystrix*) is a good example of how to implement a circuit breaker.

- Take advantage of containers to help manage and protect services. Although containers don't provide the same level of runtime isolation as a VM, they are much lighter weight, and they can be—and should be—packaged and set up with only the minimal set of dependencies and capabilities required for a specific service, reducing the overall attack surface of the network.

- Be very careful with handling private keys and other secrets. Consider using a secure key management service like AWS KMS (*https://aws.amazon.com/kms*), or

---

2 See Bruce Schneier's blog entry, "Data Is a Toxic Asset" (*https://www.schneier.com/blog/archives/2016/03/data_is_a_toxic.html*), March 4, 2016.

a general purpose secrets manager like Hashicorp's Vault (*https://www.vaultpro ject.io/intro*), as we explain in Chapter 13, *Operations and OpSec*.

Assume Compromised

One of the key new mandates is to assume that all other external-facing services are compromised. That is to say that if you have a layered architecture, then you should assume that the layer above is compromised at all times.

You could treat services in the layer below as compromised; but in most cases, if the layer below you is compromised, then it's game over. It's incredibly difficult to defend from an attack from lower down the call stack. You can and should try to protect your service (and the services above you) from errors and runtime failures in layers below.

Any service or user that can call your service is at a higher level and is therefore dangerous. So it doesn't matter whether the requests are coming from the internet, from a staff terminal, another service, or from the administrator of the system; they should be treated as if the thing sending the requests has been compromised.

What do we do if we think the layer above is compromised? We question the identity of the caller. We check all input carefully for anything attempting to come down to our layer. We are careful about what information we return back up: only the information needed, and nothing more. And we audit what happened at each point: what we got, when we got it, and what we did with it.

Try to be paranoid, but practical. Good defensive design and coding, being careful about what data your services need to share, and thinking about how to contain runtime failures and breaches will make your system more secure and more resilient.

Complexity and Security

Complexity is the enemy of security. As systems become bigger and more complex, they become harder to understand and harder to secure.

> You can't secure what you don't understand.
>
> —Bruce Schneier, *A Plea for Simplicity*

Agile and Lean development help to reduce complexity by trying to keep the design of the system as simple as possible.

Incremental design starting with the simplest model that works, Lean's insistence on delivering a working Minimum Viable Product (MVP) to users as quickly as possible, and YAGNI (you aren't gonna need it) (*https://martinfowler.com/bliki/Yagni.html*), which reminds the team to focus on only what's needed now when implementing a feature instead of trying to anticipate what might be needed in the future, are all forces against complexity and "Big Design Up Front."

Keeping the feature set to a minimum and ensuring that each feature is as simple as possible help to reduce security risks by making the attack surface of the application small.

Complexity will still creep in over time. But iterative and continuous refactoring help ensure that the design is cleaned up and stays simple as you go forward.

However there's an important distinction between irreducibly simple and dangerously naïve.

A clean architecture with well-defined interfaces and a minimal feature set is not the same as a simplistic and incomplete design that focuses only on implementing features quickly, without dealing with data safety and confidentiality, or providing defense against runtime failures and attacks.

There's also an important distinction between essential complexity and accidental complexity.

Some design problems, especially in security, are hard to solve properly: cryptography and distributed identity management are good examples. This is essential complexity that you can manage by offloading the work and the risk, using proven, trusted libraries or services instead of trying to figure out how to do this on your own.

But as we'll see in Chapter 10, *Code Review for Security*, there are many cases of unnecessary complexity that introduce unnecessary risks. Code that is difficult to understand and code that cannot be thoroughly tested is code that you cannot trust to be secure or safe. Systems that you cannot build repeatably and cannot deploy with confidence are not secure or safe.

Again, many of the Agile practices that we've looked at in this book can help to drive down unnecessary complexity and reduce risk:

- Test-driven development and behavior-driven design
- Shared code ownership following common code guidelines
- Automated code scanning to catch bad coding practices and code smells
- Pair programming and peer reviews
- Disciplined refactoring
- Continuous integration

These are all forces for making code simpler and safer. Automating build chains, automated deployment, and continuous delivery reduces complexity and risk in delivering and implementing changes by standardizing steps and making them testable, and by making it safer and cheaper to roll out small, incremental improvements and fixes instead of big-bang upgrades.

Breaking large systems down into smaller parts with clear separation of concerns helps to reduce complexity, at least at first. Small, single-purpose services are trivially easy to understand and test in isolation and safe to deploy on their own. However, at some point as you continue to create more small services, the total complexity in the system increases significantly and so does the security risk.[3]

There are no simple answers on how to deal with this kind of complexity. You will need to enforce consistent patterns and design policies and controls across teams, provide deep visibility into the system and how it works, and regularly reassess your architecture for gaps and weaknesses. And, as we've explained, make sure that each component is designed to work in a hostile, untrusting, and unpredictable environment.

Key Takeaways

Building a secure system requires that you change your design assumptions in the following ways:

- Design the system to resist compromise. Assume that attackers know everything about your system and how it works. Build protection in against failures, mistakes, and attacks.

- Technical security controls can be bolted on to the architecture of the system to help deter, resist, detect, or protect against attacks, or to compensate for weaknesses in your system. Or security controls can be threaded through the architecture and design of the system as part of your code.

- Always assume that the system is compromised, and that you cannot rely on perimeter defenses or black boxes.

- While security adds necessary complexity to design, unnecessary complexity is the enemy of security. Take advantage of Agile principles and practices to reduce complexity in design and code. This will make the system easier to change and safer to run.

---

3 To understand more about these issues and how to deal with them, watch Laura's presentation on "Practical Microservice Security" (*https://www.youtube.com/watch?v=EJ86JSFQVOE*), presented at NDC Sydney 2016.

CHAPTER 10

Code Review for Security

We've looked at how to deal with security in planning, in requirements, and in design. Now it's time to deal with security at the code level.

At least half of security vulnerabilities are introduced in coding, by developers making simple programming mistakes, by not being careful, missing a requirement, or misunderstanding or misusing the language, libraries, and frameworks.

There are two different basic approaches for catching problems, including security issues, in code:

Testing
> Whether automated or manual, including black-box scanning for security vulnerabilities.

Code reviews
> Including pair programming and peer reviews, code audits, and automated code scanning.

We'll look at the strengths and weaknesses of both approaches in the next two chapters. Let's start by understanding how code reviews fit into Agile development, and how they can be used to find important problems in development.

Why Do We Need to Review Code?

Code reviews are done for many different reasons:

Governance
> Peer reviews can play an important step in change control by ensuring that at least one other person is aware of and, implicitly or explicitly, approved the code change.

Transparency

Code reviews provide team members with information about what is happening in the project, creating awareness of how the system works and how it is changing. By shining a light on every change, reviews also minimize the threat of a malicious insider planting a logic bomb or back door or trying to commit fraud.

Compliance

Code reviews are required by compliance regulations such as PCI DSS.

Consistency

Code reviews help reinforce coding conventions, style, and patterns across the team.

Learning

Code reviews provide an opportunity for less experienced developers to learn about good practices and tricks of the trade. Both authors and reviewers can learn from each other.

Sharing

Reviewing each other's code creates a shared sense of ownership. If reviews are done regularly, developers become less protective about their code, and more open to change and feedback.

Accountability

Knowing that somebody else is going to look closely and critically at your work encourages developers to be more careful and thoughtful and take fewer shortcuts, which means better code.

But what's most important for our purposes is that *code reviews are an effective way to find bugs, including security vulnerabilities*, as long as they are done properly.

Types of Code Reviews

There are many different ways to review code:

- Formal inspections
- Rubber ducking (self-review)
- Pair programming
- Peer code reviews
- External code audits
- Automated code reviews

Let's look at the strengths, weaknesses, and costs of each approach.

Formal Inspections

Formal code inspections are done in meetings by a review team (involving the author of the code, a code reader who walks through the code, one or more reviewers, and a moderator or a coach) sitting around a table carefully looking at code printouts or code projected onto the wall. They are still done by some teams, especially in high-risk, life-critical systems development. But they are an expensive and inefficient way to find problems in code.

There are several recent studies which prove that setting up and holding formal code inspection meetings significantly adds to development delays and costs without adding significant value. While it can take hours to do all the planning, paperwork, and follow up, and weeks to schedule a code inspection meeting, less than 5% of defects are actually found in the meeting itself. The rest are all found by reviewers looking through code on their own while preparing for the meeting.[1]

Rubber Ducking or Desk Checking

The term "rubber ducking" is based on the idea that if you don't have anyone else to review your code, walking through the code and explaining it to an imaginary other person (or a rubber duck) is better than not reviewing the code at all.

Self-reviews don't meet governance, compliance, transparency, and information sharing requirements. But if they are done in a disciplined way, self-reviews can still be an effective way to find defects, including security vulnerabilities.

In one study on code reviews at Cisco Systems, developers who double-checked their work found half of the defects that other reviewers found, without any help.

Take a Break Before Reviewing Your Own Code

If you can afford to wait a few days between coding and reviewing your own code, you will be more likely to see your mistakes.

Pair Programming (and Mob Programming)

Pair programming, where two developers write code together, one at the keyboard driving, and the other navigating and assisting (like a couple on a road trip), is a fundamental practice in Extreme Programming (XP). Pair programming provides immediate, continuous code reviews: developers work together closely, share ideas,

---

1 See the article by Lawrence G. Votta, Jr., "Does every inspection need a meeting?" (*http://dl.acm.org/cita tion.cfm?id=167070*), 1993.

look at problems, and help each other write better code. Organizations such as Pivotal Labs are famous for their success with pair programming.

Pair programming is about joint problem-solving, driving, and navigating toward a solution. It's a great way to bring a new team member up to speed or to debug a tricky problem. Pairing tends to result in cleaner, tighter code, with clearer abstractions, and fewer logical and functional errors. But unless you are pairing developers with a security expert or a technically strong experienced developer, pair programming won't necessarily result in more secure code.

Pair programming also comes with costs. While two heads are better than one, it's obviously more expensive to have two developers working on the same piece of code together. Pairing is also an intensive, highly disciplined practice, which many people find socially straining, mentally exhausting, and difficult to sustain. Few developers pair up more than a few hours a day or a few days in a week.

A more extreme version of pair programming is *mob programming* (*http://mobprog ramming.org*), where an entire team works together on the same piece of code, using a single computer. This approach emphasizes collaboration, team problem-solving, and learning. Only a small number of organizations have had success working this way, but the benefits should include complete transparency and even better quality code.

Peer Code Reviews

Lightweight, informal peer code reviews are common practice in many Agile and DevOps teams. Organizations like Google, Microsoft, Facebook, and Etsy all encourage, or insist on, peer reviews before code can be released to production. Code reviews are also a key part of the workflow for making changes in most large open source projects, such as the Linux kernel, Apache, Mozilla, and Chromium.

Peer reviews are either done by people sitting side by side (in over-the-shoulder reviews), or by requesting a code review through email, through a Git pull request, or using a collaborative code review tool like Phabricator, Gerrit, Review Board, Code Collaborator, or Crucible. Using these tools, reviewers—even in distributed teams— can share feedback with the author and with each other, comment or annotate code that should be changed, and open discussion threads. This automatically creates records that can be used for governance and compliance.

Where peer code reviews are already part of the engineering culture and practices of a team, you can take advantage of this in your security program by teaching the team to include checking for secure coding practices and security-related risks and issues.

Code Audits

While pair programming and peer reviews are generally done as part of the day-to-day job of writing code, code audits are separate and outside of development. In a code audit, an expert security reviewer (or a small team of reviewers) from outside of the team examines the code base for security vulnerabilities, or at least as much of the code base as they can within the time allowed. These reviews are often required for compliance reasons or to manage important risks.

Code audits usually take several days of reviewer time, as well as time from the team to help the reviewer(s) understand the design and context of the system and the structure of the code, and then more time from the team to understand what the reviewers found (or think that they found) and to put together a plan to address the findings.

Code auditors bring specialized security knowledge or other expertise that most developers won't have. But because this work can be so mentally fatiguing, and because reviewers usually have limited time and limited familiarity with the code, they may miss important issues. A successful audit depends on the reviewer's experience, understanding of the language and technology platform, ability to come up to speed with what the system does and how it does it, and mental stamina.

We'll look more at code audits in Chapter 12, *External Reviews, Testing, and Advice*.

Automated Code Reviews

Code scanning tools can be used to automatically review code for bad coding practices, and common coding mistakes and vulnerabilities. At a minimum, automated reviews using code scanning tools act as a backstop to manual reviewers, by catching careless and often subtle errors that are hard to see in the code.

We will look at the strengths and weaknesses of automated code reviews in more detail later in this chapter.

What Kind of Review Approach Works Best for Your Team?

To be effective and sustainable in a fast-moving environment, code reviews need to be Agile: lightweight, practical, inexpensive, and fast.

Formal inspections are rigorous, but they are expensive and too slow to be practical for most Agile teams.

As we've seen, getting developers to carefully review their own work can catch bugs early. But self-reviews do not meet compliance or governance requirements, they don't provide increased transparency into changes or help with sharing information and ideas across the team, so this approach will not "do," even if it is better than not doing a review at all. Unless of course there's only one of you.

Code audits sit outside of the development cycle: they are a point-in-time risk assessment or compliance activity. You can't rely on them as part of day-to-day development.

Pair programming isn't for everyone. People who like it, like it a lot. People who don't like it, don't like it one bit. While pair programming is a great way for developers to share ideas and solve hard problems together, mentor new team members, and refactor code on the fly, it is not necessarily an effective way to find and prevent security issues.

This leaves peer reviews. Practiced properly, asking team members to review each other's code is probably the most effective approach for Agile environments. This kind of review can be done often, in small bites, without adding significant delays or costs. We'll focus on how to incorporate peer reviews into development, and how to include security checking into peer reviews, in this chapter.

When Should You Review Code?

There are different points in development where you can and should review code: before the code is committed to the mainline, before code changes are released, and after problems are found.

Before Code Changes Are Committed

The most natural and the most valuable time for code reviews is before the change is committed to the code mainline. This is how many Agile teams and open source teams, especially teams using collaborative code review tools like Gerrit, work today.

Modern source code management systems such as Git make this easy to do. In Git, engineers create a pull request when they want to push code changes to a source repo. The pull request tells the rest of the team about the change and gives them an opportunity to review and discuss the change before it can be merged. Repo administrators can enforce rules to require approvals and set other contributing guidelines.

In many environments, enforcing code reviews up front is the only way to ensure that reviews get done at all: it can be difficult to convince developers to make code changes after they have already checked code in and moved on to another piece of work.

This is also a good place to add some automated checking. For example, Thought-Works has built a pre-commit tool for teams using Git, called Talisman (*https:// github.com/thoughtworks/talisman*), which looks for suspicious things in code, like secrets, and blocks the code from being checked in. You could extend this tool (or build your own) to implement other checks that are important in your environment.

Gated Checks Before Release

Security and compliance can insist that code reviews are completed at least for certain stories, or for high-risk fixes before the the code can be considered done. This means that the team cannot move forward and can't deploy changes until these reviews have been completed and any issues found during the reviews are resolved.

Your goal should be to work with the team and keep it moving in a safe way. Instead of leaving these checks to the end as a final check before release, build steps into the team's workflow so that the security team is immediately notified when these reviews are required and can do them as early as possible. Force the team to stop work only when necessary to keep risks under control.

Postmortem and Investigation

Another important time to do code reviews is in a postmortem situation, after a security breach or outage, or if nasty surprises are found in an external audit or a pen test. We will look more at postmortems and how to do them properly in Chapter 13, *Operations and OpSec*.

A postmortem code review is usually done by senior members of the team and may include outside experts, depending on how bad the problem was. The goals of these reviews are to ensure that you understand what went wrong, that you know how to fix it, and to help with root cause analysis—to dig deep into why the problem happened and find a way to prevent problems like this in the future.

There will also be some kind of paperwork required, to prove to somebody—senior management, auditors, regulators—that the code review was done properly, and to document follow-up actions. This can be expensive, serious work. Make sure that people learn as much as they can from the "opportunity" that a bad problem presents.

How to Review Code

The team, including security and compliance, the Product Owner, and management, needs to agree on how code reviews are done.

This includes rules of conduct that guide the team on how to give and accept feedback constructively without hurting people and pulling the team down.

Giving critical feedback isn't easy for developers. Accepting critical feedback can be even harder. Even if you are careful not to tell somebody they are stupid or did something stupid, they might take your feedback that way. Enforce a "no asshole rule": be critical, but polite. Encourage reviewers to ask questions rather than pass judgments whenever possible. Remember, you are reviewing the code, not the person. Instead of saying, "You should not do X," try, "The code should do Y instead of X."

Another important rule of conduct is that reviewers must commit to responding to review requests in a reasonable time frame. This is important in scheduling and to ensure that the team doesn't lose momentum.

Take Advantage of Coding Guidelines

Coding guidelines are important in Agile teams to support *collective code ownership*, the principle that anybody on the team should be able to take on any coding assignment or fix any bug (within his or her ability), and everyone can refactor each other's code. In order to do this effectively, the code has to be consistent and follow a common style and conventions.

The team's code guidelines should prescribe surface issues like element naming and code indentation and formatting, as well as more important underlying issues: proper use of frameworks and libraries, auditing and logging patterns that need to be followed, and banned practices and banned function calls.

There are some good freely available coding guidelines that you can use:

- Google's coding guidelines (*https://github.com/google/styleguide*) for various languages
- CERT coding standards (*http://bit.ly/cert-coding-standards*) for C, C++, Java, Android, Java, and Perl
- Microsoft's secure .NET coding guidelines (*http://bit.ly/msdn-coding-standards*)
- Oracle's Java SE coding guidelines (*http://bit.ly/oracle-coding-standards*)
- OWASP Secure Coding Practices (*http://bit.ly/owasp-coding-standards*)
- Mozilla's Web Application Secure Coding Guidelines (*http://bit.ly/mozilla-coding-standards*)

Even if your team and your code are wildly outside compliance with these guides, it's worth picking one as a target and defining a plan to iterate toward that target. This will be easier than trying to create your own guide from scratch.

By following one of these guides, you should end up with cleaner, more consistent code that is easier to understand and review, and code that is more secure by default.

Using Code Review Checklists

Code review checklists are an important tool in reviews. But these checklists can be, and should be, short and focused.

You don't need a checklist item to tell the reviewer to check whether the code is understandable, or that it actually does what it is supposed to do. Basic rules of programming or language-specific rules don't need to be on a checklist. Automated static analysis tooling, including checkers in the developer's IDE, should catch these issues.

Checklists are used by airline pilots and ICU nurses and surgeons to remind them about small, but important things that are easy to forget while they are trying to focus on the main task.

For more on checklists, read Dr. Atul Gawande's excellent book, *The Checklist Manifesto* (Metropolitan Books) (*http://atulga wande.com/book/the-checklist-manifesto*).

Use checklists to remind people to look for things that aren't obvious. Remind reviewers to look out for things beyond code clarity and correctness—for things that are important, but easy to overlook and forget, and things that tools won't find for you. As we'll see in this chapter, this should include things like correct error handling, looking out for secrets in code and configuration, tracing the use of private or sensitive data, and watching for debugging code or test code left in by accident. Build your checklists up from issues that you find in production or in pen testing so that you don't repeat the mistakes of the past.

Don't Make These Mistakes

There are some common mistakes and anti-patterns that you need to avoid when it comes to code reviews:

1. Believing that senior people don't need their code reviewed. Everyone on the team should follow the same rules, regardless of seniority. In many cases, senior team members are the ones who take on the most difficult coding tasks and problem-solving work, and this is the most important code to review.

2. Not reviewing legacy code. A study on the honeymoon effect in software development proves that there is a honeymoon period after new software features and changes are deployed before attackers have the chance to understand them and attack them. Most successful attacks are made against code that has been out long enough for bad guys to identify vulnerabilities and to find a way to exploit them. This is especially the case for popular third-party and open source libraries and

platform code. Once attackers have found a vulnerability in this code and learned to fingerprint it, the risk of compromise increases significantly.[2]

So while you need to review changes as they are being made, because it is much easier and cheaper to fix the mistakes that you find right away, it is still important to look at older code, especially if you have code written before the team got training on secure development.

3. Relying only on automated code reviews. Automated code scanning tools can help you to find problems in code and identify where code needs to be cleaned up, but as we'll show later, they are not a substitute for manual code reviews. This is a case of AND, not OR.

Avoiding these fundamental mistakes will help you improve the security and quality of your code.

Review Code a Little Bit at a Time

Another common mistake is forcing team members to review large change sets. Experience backed up by research proves that the effectiveness of code reviews negatively correlates with the amount of code reviewed. The more files and lines of code that a reviewer has to look at, the more tired he will get, and the less he will be able to find.

A reviewer who is forced to look at 1,000 lines of code changes might comment on how hard it is to understand or how something might be made simpler. But she won't be able to see all the mistakes that are made. A reviewer who only has to look at 50 or 100 lines of code will have a much easier job of finding bugs, especially subtle mistakes. And he will be able to do this much faster.

In fact, research shows that the effectiveness of code reviews starts to drop off after around 200 lines of code, and that the number of real defects that reviewers find falls off sharply when they are asked to review code for more than an hour (see the "Modern Code Review" chapter of *Making Software* [O'Reilly]).

This is an unavoidable problem in code audits, where auditors need to scan through thousands of lines of code each day, often for several days at a time. But it should be much less of a concern for Agile teams, especially teams following continuous integration, because they tend to make small, iterative changes, which can be reviewed immediately on each check-in.

---

2 See the report by Rebecca Gelles, "The Unpredictable Attacker: Does the 'Honeymoon Effect' Hold for Exploits?" (*http://dreuarchive.cra.org/2011/Gelles/rdreureport.pdf*), 2/6/2012.

What Code Needs to Be Reviewed?

The team needs to agree on what code has to be reviewed, and who needs to be involved in code reviews.

In a perfect world, all code changes should be reviewed for maintainability, for correctness, and for security. This demands a high level of engineering discipline and management commitment.

If you aren't ready for this yet, or can't convince your management or your customer to give you the time to review all code changes across the board, you can still get a lot of benefit by taking a pragmatic, risk-based approach. Most changes in continuous integration are small and incremental, and carry limited security risk, especially code that will be thrown away quickly when the team is experimenting and iterating through design alternatives.

For many of these changes, you can lean on automated code scanning tools in the developer's IDE and in continuous integration to catch common coding mistakes and bad coding practices. As we'll see later in this chapter, there are limitations to what these tools can find, but this might be good enough to contain your risks and help you to meet your compliance requirements (regulations like PCI DSS require all changes to be reviewed, but also allow for automating code reviews).

But some code, such as the following, needs to be looked at more closely and carefully, because the risk of making and missing a mistake is too high:

- Security features like authentication and access control, crypto functions, and code that uses crypto functions
- Code that deals with money, or with private or confidential data
- APIs with other systems that deal with money or with private or confidential data
- Web and mobile UIs (i.e., big changes or new workflows)
- Public network-facing APIs and file imports from external sources (i.e., code that is frequently exposed to attack)
- Framework code and other plumbing
- First-of code using a new framework or design approach, until the team gets comfortable with how to do this properly
- Code written by new team members (at least if they aren't pairing up with a more experienced team member) to make sure that they follow the team's coding patterns and guidelines

Changes to frameworks or security features or public APIs should also be reviewed in design, as part of threat modeling, which is discussed in Chapter 8, *Threat Assessments and Understanding Attacks*.

High-Risk Code and the 80:20 Rule

The 80:20 rule reminds us that most problems in a system tend to cluster in specific parts of the code:

80% of bugs are found in 20% of the code

Some studies have found that half of your code might not have any bugs at all, while most bugs will be found in only 10–20% of the code, likely the 10–20% of the code that is changing most often.[3]

Tracking bugs can help you to understand where to focus your reviews and testing. Code with a history of bugs should also be a strong candidate for careful refactoring or rewriting.

Although it will usually be obvious to the team what code changes carry risk, here are some steps to identify and track code that should be reviewed carefully:

- Tagging user stories for security features or business workflows which handle money or sensitive data.

- Grepping source code for calls to dangerous function calls like crypto functions.

- Scanning code review comments (if you are using a collaborative code review tool like Gerrit).

- Tracking code check-in to identify code that is changed often: code with a high rate of churn tends to have more defects.

- Reviewing bug reports and static analysis to identify problem areas in code: code with a history of bugs, or code that has high complexity and low automated test coverage.

- Looking out for code that has recently undergone large-scale "root canal" refactoring. While day-to-day, in-phase refactoring can do a lot to simplify code and make it easier to understand and safer to change, major refactoring or redesign work can accidentally change the trust model of an application and introduce regressions.

Netflix has an interesting way to identify high-risk code. It wrote a tool called Penguin Shortbread, which maps out call sequences for microservices. Services that are called by many other services or that fan out to many other services are automatically tagged as high-risk dependencies that need to be reviewed.

---

3 See the report by Forrest Shull, et al., "What We Have Learned About Fighting Defects" (*http://cite seerx.ist.psu.edu/viewdoc/download?doi=10.1.1.12.7165&rep=rep1&type=pdf*).

At Etsy, as soon as high-risk code is identified through code reviews or scanning, its developers hash the code and create a unit test that automatically alerts the security team when the code hash value has been changed through a check-in.

Finally, you can make the team responsible for watching out for risks in code, and encourage developers to ask for a code review whenever they think they need help.

Who Needs to Review Code?

Once you agree on what code needs to be reviewed and when reviews should be done, you need to decide who needs to be involved in code reviews, and how many reviewers need to be involved.

Can anyone on the team act as a reviewer, or do you need to include somebody who has worked on the code before, or a subject matter expert? When do you need to get more than one person to review the code?

How Many Reviewers?

Reviews (and pair programming) are based on the reasonable principle that two people will find more problems than one person can on her own. So if two heads are better than one, why not have more reviewers, and get even more eyes on the code?

At Google and Microsoft, where they've been doing code reviews successfully for a long time, experience shows that two reviewers seems to be the magic number. Most teams in these organizations require two reviews, although there are times when an author may ask for more input, especially when the reviewers don't agree with each other.

Some teams at Microsoft specifically ask for two different kinds of reviews to get maximum value from each of the reviewers:

1. A review before the code is checked in, focused more on readability and clarity and maintainability
2. A second review (done before or after check-in) to look for risks and bugs

Studies have found that a second reviewer will only find half as many new problems as the first reviewer. Beyond this point, you are wasting time and money. One study showed no difference in the number of problems found by teams of three, four, or five individuals, while another showed that two reviewers actually did a better job than four.[4]

This is partly because of overlap and redundancy. More reviewers means more people looking for, and finding, the same problems (and more people coming up with false positive findings that the author has to waste time sifting through). You also encounter a "social loafing" problem. Complacency and a false sense of security set in as you add more reviewers: because each reviewer knows that somebody else is looking at the same code, they are under less pressure to find problems on their own.

But what's even more important than getting the right number of reviewers is getting the right people to review your code.

What Experience Do Reviewers Need?

A new team member will learn a lot by having an experienced team member review his code, reinforcing his understanding of how the system and the team work. By reviewing code for other people on the team, a new developer will gain exposure to more of the code base and learn something about the system. But this is an inefficient way to learn. And it misses the main point of asking for a code review, which is to find and correct as many problems with the code as early as possible.

Research backs up what should be obvious: effective code reviews depend heavily on the reviewer's skill and familiarity with the problem domain and platform, and her ability to understand the code. A study on code reviews at Microsoft found that reviewers from outside of the team, or who were new to the team and didn't know the code or the problem area, could only do a superficial job of finding formatting issues or simple logic bugs. Like other areas in software development, the range of individual performance can be huge: top performers are 10 times more effective in finding problems and providing valuable feedback.

This means that your best, most experienced developers will spend a lot of time reviewing code, and they should. You need reviewers who are good at reading code and good at debugging, and who know the language, frameworks, and problem area. They will do a much better job of finding problems and can provide much more valuable feedback, including suggestions on how to solve the problem in a simpler or more efficient way, or how to make better use of the language and frameworks. And they can do all of this much faster.

---

4 Chris Sauer, D. Ross Jeffery, Lesley Land, and Philip Yetton, "The Effectiveness of Software Development Technical Reviews: A Behaviorally Motivated Program of Research" (*http://dl.acm.org/citation.cfm?id=331521*), *IEEE Transactions on Software Engineering*, Vol 26, Issue 1, January 2000: 1-14.

Regulations may also dictate how much experience reviewers require. For example, PCI DSS 6.3.2 requires that reviewers must be "knowledgeable in code review techniques and secure coding practices."

If you want new developers to learn about the code and coding conventions and architecture, it will be much more effective to partner them up with an experienced team member in pair programming or pair debugging exercises than asking them to review somebody else's code. If you have to get inexperienced developers to review code, lower your expectations. Recognize that you will need to depend a lot more on automated static analysis tools and testing to find real problems in the code.

Automated Code Reviews

Automated static analysis scanning tools should be part of your code review program for the following reasons:

- Automated code scanning is the only practical way to ensure coverage on a large legacy code base and to provide a level of insight into the security and quality of this code.

- Static scanning can be done on a continuous basis against all of your code. The tools never get sick or tired of looking for the same kinds of problems and are much more consistent than manual reviewers.

- Unlike human reviewers, good static analysis tools won't get held up by bad element naming or indentation or other cosmetic issues.

- While as we'll see, automated code scanners may miss finding many important vulnerabilities, they are good at finding certain bugs that are important for reliability and security. This is especially valuable if you don't have strong security skills in-house to do effective manual reviews.

- Automated code review tools are an accepted alternative to manual code reviews in regulations such as PCI DSS. For many teams this is a practical and cost-effective way to meet compliance requirements.

Some static analysis tools scan byte code or binaries. These are the easiest to set up and get started with, because you can point the scanner at a deployed package and run it, or upload binaries to a scanning service like Veracode and let them scan the code for you. This approach is especially useful for checking code that you don't have source for.

Other tools scan source code directly, which means that you don't need to wait to compile the code before you scan it, and you can scan individual pieces of code or change sets. But in order to get a complete scan of the system, you need to understand the application's library structures and all the code dependencies.

Automated tools will usually point you to the specific line of code where problems are found (and often showing you how this statement was reached). Some tools do simple pattern matching or linting, while other tools build up an abstract model of the application, map out data flows, and walk code execution paths to find vulnerabilities like SQL injection and cross-site scripting. Because this can take a long time for large code bases, some analysis engines will save the abstract model, scan only the code that has been changed, and update the model incrementally.

Code analysis tools can catch common but important coding mistakes and can help enforce good coding practices, so that reviewers can focus on other important problems. They are generally good at finding the following issues:

- Sloppy code, including code that is poorly structured, dead or unreachable code, copy-and-pasted code sections, and code that violates recognized good coding practices.

- Subtle coding mistakes that compilers should catch but don't: the kind of mistakes that are hard to find in testing and in manual code reviews, like errors in conditional logic, buffer overflows and memory corruption problems in C/C++, null pointers in Java.

- Missed data validation and injection vulnerabilities, where programmers fail to check the length of input strings or pass unsanitized "tainted data" on to an interpreter such as a SQL database engine or a browser.

- Common mistakes in security functions like applied crypto (weak ciphers/hash functions, weak keys, weak random number generators).

- Common configuration problems such as insecure HTTP headers or cookie flags.

These tools should be a part of your code review program, but they shouldn't be the only part of your code review program. To understand why, let's start by looking at the different types of tools and what they are good for.

Different Tools Find Different Problems

For most environments you have a choice of static analysis tools, designed to look for different problems.

Compiler warnings

Static code analysis should start with checking for compiler warnings. The compiler writers put these warnings in for a reason. You don't need to buy a tool to tell you something that your compiler will already find for you up front. Turn the warning levels up, carefully review the findings, and clean them up.

Code style and code smells

Tools that check for code consistency, maintainability, and clarity (PMD and Checkstyle for Java, Ruby-lint for Ruby) help developers to write code that is easier to understand, easier to change, easier to review, and safer to change. They can help to make sure that all of your code is consistent. They will also point out areas where you could have bad code, including code that doesn't follow safe conventions, and common mistakes in copy-and-paste, or merge mistakes that could be serious.

But unless you are following a recognized style guide from the beginning, you will need to customize some of the coding style rules to match your team's coding conventions.

Bug patterns

Tools that look for common coding bugs and bug patterns (tools like FindBugs and RuboCop) will catch subtle logic mistakes and errors that could lead to runtime failures or security vulnerabilities.

Security vulnerabilities (SAST)

Tools that identify security vulnerabilities through control flow and data flow analysis, heuristics, pattern analysis, and other techniques (Find Security Bugs, Brakeman, Fortify) can find common security issues such as mistakes in using crypto functions, configuration errors, and potential injection vulnerabilities.

These tools are sometimes referred to as "SAST" for "Static Analysis Security Testing," a classification popularized by Gartner, to differentiate them from black-box "DAST" tools like ZAP or Burp, which are used to dynamically scan a running application. We will look at DAST scanning tools in the next chapter.

Custom greps and detectors

Simple, homemade tools that grep through code looking for hardcoded credentials, unsafe or banned function or library calls (such as gets and strcpy and memcpy in C/C++, or eval in PHP and Javascript), calls to crypto libraries, and other things that the security team or the development team want to watch out for.

You can also write your own custom checks using extensions provided by other tools, for example, writing your own bug detector in FindBugs, or your own PMD coding rule, although only a few teams actually do this.

Catching mistakes as you are coding

You can catch some issues automatically in a developer's IDE, using plug-ins for Eclipse or Visual Studio or IntelliJ, or the built-in code checkers and code completion features that come with most modern development toolsets.

These tools can't do deep data flow and control flow checking, but they can highlight common mistakes and questionable code as you are working on it, acting like a security spell-checker.

The following are free IDE plug-ins:

- Eclipse plug-ins for FindBugs (*https://marketplace.eclipse.org/content/findbugs-eclipse-plugin*) and Find Security Bugs (*http://find-sec-bugs.github.io/*) for Java
- Puma Scan (*https://www.pumascan.com/*), a Visual Studio plug-in for C#

Other IDE plug-ins for tools like HPE Fortify take results from batch scans done previously and present them to the developer in the IDE as they are working on those areas of code. This makes it easier for developers to see existing problems, but they won't immediately catch any new mistakes.

Vulnerable dependencies

Tools like OWASP's Dependency-Check, Bundler-Audit for Ruby projects, or Retire.JS for JavaScript will inventory your build dependencies and check to make sure that they do not contain any known vulnerabilities.

You can decide to automatically fail the build if the checks find a serious security vulnerability or other issue. We reviewed these tools in more detail in Chapter 6, *Agile Vulnerability Management*.

Code complexity analysis and technical debt metrics

Other tools can be used to report on metrics such as code complexity or other measurements of technical debt, identifying problem areas in the code (hot spots and clusters) or trends. Mapping code complexity against automated test coverage, for example, is a way to identify potential risks in the code base.

SonarQube (*http://www.sonarqube.org*), a popular code quality and security analysis platform, includes a technical debt cost calculator as well as other code quality and security measurements in its dashboard. It calculates technical debt by assigning weightings to different static analysis findings (coding best practices, dead code, code complexity, bugs, and security vulnerabilities) and gaps in test coverage, and calculates the cost of remediating all of these issues in dollars. Even if you don't agree with SonarQube's costing model, the dashboard is useful for tracking technical debt over time.

What Tools Are Good For, and What They're Not Good For

Make sure that you and the team members understand what they are getting out of a static analysis tool and how much they can rely on them.

Some tools are much better at finding some problems than others, and this can depend a lot on your use of language, frameworks, and design patterns.

There are several good open source and commercial static analysis tools available today for mainstream languages like Java, C/C++, and C#, using common frameworks like Struts and Spring and .NET, and for other popular development environments like Ruby on Rails.

But it's difficult to find good tool support for hot new languages such as Golang or Swift or F# or Jolie, and it's especially difficult to find tools that can catch real problems in dynamically typed scripting languages like Javascript, PHP, and Python, which is where you need the best checking. Most code analyzers (at least the open source ones) for these languages are still limited to linting and basic checking for good practices, which helps to make for better code, but won't ensure that your code is secure or even that it will run without crashing.

IAST or RASP: Alternatives to Static Code Analysis

IAST (Interactive or Instrumented Application Security Testing) and RASP (Runtime Application Self-Protection) are new technologies that offer an alternative to static code analysis. These tools instrument the runtime environment (for example, the Java JVM) and build a model of the application as it is executing, inspecting the call stack and variables to identify vulnerabilities in running code.

However, like static code analysis tools, language and platform support varies widely, and so does the effectiveness of the rules. The quality of coverage from these tools also depends on how thoroughly you exercise the code in your tests.

A static analysis tool can tell you when code makes unsafe library calls, but it can't tell you if somebody forgot to make a call that he should have. Tools can tell you if you made a basic mistake in applied crypto, but can't tell you if you forgot to encrypt or tokenize sensitive data, or forgot an ACL check, or if the code accidentally exposes sensitive data in exception handling. Only an experienced human reviewer can do this.

There is important research that can help us to understand the effectiveness, and limits, of automated static analysis tools.

In one study, researchers ran 2 different commercial static analysis tools against a large application that contained 15 known security vulnerabilities (found earlier in a structured manual audit done by security experts). The tools together found less than half of the known security bugs: only the simplest problems, the bugs that didn't require a deep understanding of the code or the design.[5]

The tools also reported thousands of other issues that needed to be reviewed and qualified, or thrown away as false positives. Some of these findings included runtime correctness problems, null pointers, and resource leaks that probably needed to be fixed, and code quality issues (dead code, unused variables), but they did not uncover any other security vulnerabilities.

NIST has run a series of benchmarks to assess the effectiveness of static analysis tools called SAMATE (*https://samate.nist.gov/Main_Page.html*). In its most recent analysis (2014) NIST tested 14 different static analysis tools on C/C++ and Java code with known vulnerabilities. This is what was found:

1. Over half of the vulnerabilities were not detected by any of the tools.

2. As the complexity of code increased, the ability of tools to find problems decreased significantly. Many tools simply gave up. This was also shown in the case of the Heartbleed bug in OpenSSL, which could not be found by any of the automated code analysis tools available, partly because the code was too complex.

3. NIST also found a significant and disappointing lack of overlap between tools: *less than 1%* of the vulnerabilities were found by all the tools.[6]

More recently, OWASP's Benchmark Project (*https://www.owasp.org/index.php/Benchmark*) was started to create a test suite with known security vulnerabilities, designed to evaluate the effectiveness of different static analysis and application scanners. This project scores tools by subtracting false positive findings from true positives. The average score for the commercial SAST tools that they evaluated was only 26%.

While tools continue to get better—more accurate, faster, easier to understand, and with better support for more languages and frameworks—they can't replace reviews done by smart people. But they can act as an effective backstop to manual reviews by catching common mistakes; and, by enforcing good coding practices and consistency, they can make manual reviews easier and more effective.

---

5 James A. Kupsch and Barton P. Miller, "Manual vs. Automated Vulnerability Assessment: A Case Study" (*http://pages.cs.wisc.edu/~kupsch/va/ManVsAutoVulnAssessment.pdf*) (2009).

6 Aurelien Delaitre, Delaitre, Aurélien, Bertrand Stivalet, Elizabeth Fong and Vadim Okun. "Evaluating Bug Finders — Test and Measurement of Static Code Analyzers." (*http://bit.ly/eval-bug-finders*), *2015 IEEE/ACM 1st International Workshop on Complex Faults and Failures in Large Software Systems (COUFLESS)* (2015): 14-20.

Getting Developers to Use Automated Code Reviews

You want to reach a point where engineering teams treat static analysis findings like they do unit tests: when they check in a change, and a tool reports something wrong, they will fix it immediately, because they have learned to trust the tool and know that they can rely on it to find important problems for them.

It should be easier to introduce static analysis checking for security vulnerabilities into teams that have already had good experience with static analysis tools for code quality and have learned to depend on them. Start with getting the team to use a good bug-finding tool, and the team has accepted it and successfully made it part of its day-to-day work, introduce security checking.

Dropping off a report on a developer's desk with thousands of static analysis warnings isn't going to get buy in from the team. Try taking an incremental, low-friction approach.

Take some time to understand how the tool works and how to configure the rules and checkers properly. Many teams rely on the default setup, which is almost never the right thing to do. Some tools come with conservative defaults, which means that they don't apply rules and checkers that could be important for your application. Many other tools want to be as thorough as possible, enforcing checks that aren't relevant and flooding developers with false positives.

Install the tool and run a set of scans with different rules and settings. Measure how long the scans take, and how much CPU and memory the tool uses. Review the results, and look for the sweet spot between maximizing true positive findings and minimizing false positives. Find the rules and checkers that have the highest confidence. Turn the other rules off, at least to start.

Check the Rules In

Make sure to check in the rules and settings that you are using to a repo so that you can review the rules that were in effect at any point in time. You may need to show this to an auditor to prove that you aren't just performing security theater, by trying to get away with checks that are too easy on developers and that miss too many real problems in the code.

Establish a baseline. Run a complete scan, go over the results with the team, or maybe just a couple of the strongest developers to start, to explain what the tool can do and show that it works. Then mark everything that the tool found so that these findings won't show up in future scans by default. This is security debt that you will pay off later.

Get the team agree to take a zero bug tolerance approach to any findings moving forward: from this point on, if the tool finds any serious problems, the team will agree to review them and fix all true positives.

Instead of having to sift through pages of review results, team members will see only a handful of findings each day, or each time that they check in code—however often you decide to run the scanner. This shouldn't add much to their work, and eventually will become just another part of their day-to-day workflow.

After the team has gained confidence in the tool and learned how to work effectively with the results, it can schedule time to go back and review and fix the problems found in the baseline scan.

Rinse and Repeat

Because of the limited overlap between what each tool finds, to get effective coverage, you'll have to use more than one static analysis tool. This means you you'll need to go through all of these steps more than once. While it should get easier each time, be prepared for the costs.

Of course if you take this approach, you will be leaving some bugs in the system and vulnerabilities open for attack, at least for a while. But now at least you know what the problems are and where they are, and you can work with the Product Owner and the team and management on a plan to reduce the risks.

Self-Service Scanning

In many large enterprises, code scanning is done by the security team, in what Dr. Gary McGraw at Cigital calls a "scanning factory" model. The security team schedules and runs scans across different projects, reviews and triages the results, and reports the results back to development.

Working this way introduces unnecessary delays in feedback to the team. It can take days to complete the scans, review the results, and prepare reports. By the time that developers learn about problems, they may have already moved on to other features, which means that they have to stop what they are working on, switch back to their earlier work, restore the context, find the problem, fix it, test it, build it, and then switch back again. This is the kind of waste that Agile and Lean methods are intended to avoid.

Another disadvantage of this model is that it makes scanning "somebody else's problem," taking away any sense of ownership from the developers.

A more effective, more scalable, and more Agile way of working is to make code scanning available to developers on a self-service basis while they are working, in ways that make natural sense to them.

Instead of choosing standardized tools that are convenient for the security team to use across multiple projects, let the team choose tools that work best for its specific needs and that fit into its workflows.

The first place to include self-service scanning is in each developer's IDE, using plug-ins or the IDE's built-in rules to check for problems as they are coding, or when they save changes or compile code in their IDE. It's especially important to have high-confidence, high-impact rules in place here, rules that highlight real problems; otherwise developers will quickly learn to ignore all alerts and highlighting.

But keep in mind that there's no visibility to the rest of the team at this point into what problems were found, and no way to prove that developers are fixing these problems up front. So you will still need to add incremental code analysis and fast code scanning each time that the code is built, to catch any problems that might get past.

Most scanning tools have APIs that you can use to push results directly back into each developer's IDE or automatically create bug reports in backlog tracking tools like Jira or VersionOne. Or you can use one of the application vulnerability management tools that we looked at in Chapter 6 to help with this.

Provide High-Fidelity Feedback

If you want developers to take the results of scanning seriously, you have to provide them with actionable feedback, highlighting real problems that they need to fix. Any time that a developer spends chasing down false positives or findings that aren't relevant to her project is time wasted. If too much time gets used up this way, you will lose her cooperation, and her manager's support.

Try to be ruthless when making trade-offs between completeness against speed and accuracy of results. Keeping the feedback loop tight and high fidelity is generally more important than completeness in continuous integration or continuous delivery.

As part of the feedback loop, make it simple for developers to report back when they see false positives or noise. Twitter provides a "bullshit" button which allows developers to report and suppress false positive findings.

Self-service, fast-feedback scanning requires tools that run quickly, and that provide clear context for each finding so that developers don't need a security expert's help to understand what the problem is, how serious it is, where it was found, how it was found, or how to fix it.

If you have the resources, you can still run deep, full code scans out of band in your security scanning factory, review and qualify the results, and feed them into the development backlog to get fixed. While this could take hours or days to run on large code bases, these scans should only pick up a small number of important exceptions that make it through the earlier, faster, high-certainty checking in development. So the cost of reviewing these issues and the impact on the team's velocity to come back and deal with them should be minimal, and the risk of missing an important problem should be low.

Reviewing Infrastructure Code

Today's systems are built using automated programmable configuration management tools like Ansible, Chef, Docker, and Puppet. Chef recipes, Puppet manifests, Ansible playbooks, Dockerfiles, and AWS CloudFormation templates should follow the same life cycle as your other code, from check-in, manual review, automated build checks, lint checks and other static analysis checks, and automated unit and integration and acceptance testing.

Code reviews for recipes and playbooks are done for many of the same reasons as application code:

- Ensure that all changes to system configuration have been checked by at least one person (governance).
- Check for maintainability and compliance with code conventions.
- Check for correctness.
- Make sure that test configurations are not accidentally pushed to production.
- Enforce operational and security policies.

Reviewers can use the same code review methods, workflows, and code review tools that application developers use, such as Gerrit or Review Board. They should pay attention to style and structure problems, proper separation of code and data, reuse, and readability. Reviewers should also check to make sure that there are good tests written for each module. But most important, they should be on the lookout for configuration mistakes and oversights that could leave the system vulnerable to attack.

Engineers can't lean too heavily on static analysis tools for this type of code. Tools like Foodcritic for Chef or Puppet-lint for Puppet do basic syntax checks and look for common coding mistakes, which is important in these scripting languages, where you want to find problems before runtime. Out of the box they won't find serious security issues for you. You will need to write your own custom rules to do this.[7]

We'll look more at how and where security comes in when working with these tools in Chapter 13, *Operations and OpSec.*

Code Review Challenges and Limitations

There are a lot of coding problems that a good reviewer will catch, if she has the skills and time. A good reviewer will find logical mistakes and oversights that automated code scanning tools and testing will often miss, such as the following:

- Inconsistencies (the author changed *a*, *b*, and *d*, but forgot to change *c*).
- Common coding mixups, like using < instead of < = or sometimes even > in comparisons.
- Off-by-one errors.
- Using the wrong variables in calculations or comparisons (buyer when they should have used seller).

Code reviewers can also find mistakes or weaknesses in design as they read through the code—if they know the system design well. But as we discussed in Chapter 8, *Threat Assessments and Understanding Attacks*, separate reviews should be done at the design level to examine trust assumptions, threats, and protection against threats.

It's easy for code reviewers to find test or debugging code left in by accident, and they are likely to trip on redundant code and checks that don't seem to be necessary, and other signs of copy-and-paste or merge mistakes.

Code reviews are probably the best way to find concurrency and timing problems (threading, locking, time of check/time of use), and mistakes in cryptography. As we'll see later, they're probably the only way to find back doors and time bombs.

But experience and research show that instead of finding bugs, reviewers end up spending most of their time finding and reporting problems that make the code harder to understand and harder to maintain. They get held up on things like poor element naming, misleading or missing comments, poorly structured code, and dead and unused code.[8]

---

7 For an example of security checks that you could add, see this plug-in for puppet-lint: *https://github.com/floek/puppet-lint-security-plugins.*

8 Mika V. Mantyla and Casper Lassenius, "What Types of Defects Are Really Discovered in Code Reviews?" (*http://dl.acm.org/citation.cfm?id=1592371*), *IEEE Transactions on Software Engineering*, Volume 35, Issue 3, May 2009: 430-448.

There are some good reasons that code reviews don't find as many bugs as they should:

- Reviews take time to do properly.
- Understanding somebody else's code is hard (especially in complex or diverse technical environments, or large code bases).
- Finding security vulnerabilities in somebody else's code is even harder.

Let's look at each of these issues in some more detail.

Reviews Take Time

First, it takes time to review code properly. The team, including and especially the Product Owner, as well as management, all need to understand that code reviews will take up a significant part of each developer's day, and that waiting for code reviews will slow down delivery.

At an organization like Microsoft, developers spend on average between two and six hours a week reviewing code changes. Developers wait a day on average for code review feedback. But in some cases, reviewers may take days, or even weeks, to get back with their findings. These code changes can't be checked in to the mainline, can't be tested, and can't be factored into delivery timelines.

So it is critical that teams build up the discipline and a collaborative and supportive culture, ensuring that everyone is prepared to step up and help other team members by getting their reviews done. And it is even more important that they have the discipline to take reviews seriously, and are willing to put the necessary work in to do a good job. Because, as we'll see, doing code reviews properly isn't easy.

Understanding Somebody Else's Code Is Hard

One of the main reasons that reviewers don't find as many bugs as they should or could is because in order to find problems, they need to understand what the code does and how and why it was changed.

Understanding all of this takes most of a reviewer's time, which is why most review comments are about readability (naming, commenting, formatting) and how to make code simpler or clearer, instead of about more fundamental problems.

 This is where code analysis tools that focus on enforcing coding style and conventions can help, by making code cleaner and more consistent.

If reviewers aren't familiar with the code, they will also need to read more code to establish context, which means that they may run out of time before they can find anything materially wrong.

This is another reason why it's important to have code reviews done by experienced team members. People who have worked with the code before—changed it themselves or reviewed it previously—have a clear edge over someone who has never seen the code before. They can work much faster, and provide more effective feedback.[9]

Finding Security Vulnerabilities Is Even Harder

Finding functional or logical defects in somebody else's code is hard, as we've seen. A reviewer has to understand the purpose of the change, the context, and understand the code well enough to find mistakes in implementation or logic errors.

Finding security vulnerabilities is even harder. You start off with the same challenges —the need to understand the purpose and context, the structure and the coding style, and so on—and the reviewer also needs to understand secure coding and what to look out for.

Let's look at some more research to see how hard reviewing for security vulnerabilities really is.

In a 2013 study, 30 PHP developers (including some security experts) were hired to do independent manual security code reviews of a small web app with 6 known vulnerabilities. The reviewers were given 12 hours to complete the reviews, and were not allowed to use static analysis tools.

None of the reviewers found all the known bugs (although several found a new XSS vulnerability that the researchers hadn't known about), and 20% of the reviewers didn't find any vulnerabilities at all. Reviewers with more coding experience didn't necessarily find more security bugs—because even experienced developers don't always understand what to look for in a security code review.[10]

We can see how difficult, and how important, code reviews are in security by looking closely at one of the most high-profile security vulnerabilities of the past few years: the OpenSSL Heartbleed vulnerability. This critical weakness in SSL handshaking was caused by not checking for a buffer over-read in C, a simple, low-level coding mistake.

---

9 Amiangshu Bosu, Michaela Greiler, and Christian Bird, "Characteristics of Useful Code Reviews: An Empirical Study at Microsoft" (*https://www.microsoft.com/en-us/research/publication/characteristics-of-useful-code-reviews-an-empirical-study-at-microsoft*), Proceedings of the International Conference on Mining Software Repositories, May 1, 2015.

10 Anne Edmundson, et al., "An Empirical Study on the Effectiveness of Security Code Review" (*https://www.cs.princeton.edu/~annee/pdf/coderev-essos13.pdf*), ESSoS (2013).

What was surprising was that even though the original change was reviewed by someone who had worked on the OpenSSL code before, and the code was open source and available to anyone to read, it took more than two years before a security team at Google found the bug in a code audit.[11]

The author of the change, the original reviewer, several static analysis tools, and almost everyone in the open source community who downloaded and used the code all missed the bug because the code was simply too complicated to understand, which also meant that it was too complicated to change safely. This should never be the case for security-critical code.

Understanding code, making it simpler and cleaner and clearer, emphasizing coding guidelines and continuous refactoring, isn't just about making code easier to change for the next person. It's also about making the code more secure.

Adopting Secure Code Reviews

What should you expect from secure code reviews? How can you make them effective?

Introduce secure code reviews into a team in a low-overhead, incremental way. Work inside of Agile practices, and work in an Agile way. Start with small steps and keep reinforcing good ways of working. Continuously learn and improve. It takes time to change the way that people think and work—but this is what Agile and Lean development is all about.

Build on What the Team Is Doing, or Should Be Doing

If the team is already doing pair programming or peer reviews, help it understand how to include security in reviews, using the guidance in this book. Work with managers and the team's Product Owner and Scrum Master to make sure that the team members are given enough time to learn, and time to learn about security as they are working.

Make sure developers are trained in the fundamentals of secure coding, so that they will write safer code, and so that they know what kinds of problems to look for when they are reviewing code. Take advantage of SAFECode's free training courses and public information from OWASP. Be practical when it comes to training. You don't need to train everyone on the team on the low-level details of how to do encryption properly. But everyone needs to understand when and how to correctly call crypto functions.

---

11 David A. Wheeler, "How to prevent the next Heartbleed" (*http://www.dwheeler.com/essays/heartbleed.html*), 2017-01-29.

Don't rely on reviews by inexperienced team members. Insist on experienced, qualified reviewers, especially for high-risk code.

If the team isn't doing pair programming or peer reviews:

- Find people that the team trusts and respects, senior developers who care about writing good code and who like to take on challenges.
- Do everything you can to convince these people (and their managers) that it is an important and valuable use of their time to review code, starting with high-risk framework code and security features.
- Make sure that they have the information and training to know what problems to look for.
- If you work in a regulated industry, use compliance as a stick, if you have to.

Make code reviews as easy as possible

Introduce static analysis into the team, using some of your security budget, to help developers write better code. If you don't have a budget for tools, take advantage of the open source alternatives mentioned earlier. Follow the guidelines that we've already laid out on how to get engineers to use these tools effectively.

If the team is using a collaborative code review platform like Gerrit or Review Board, take advantage of the team's workflows and the data that collected, to:

- Ensure that high-risk code is being reviewed.
- Spot-check reviews to ensure that they are being done responsibly.
- Use the comment information as an audit trail for compliance.
- Feed static analysis results back into code reviews as comments, to help reviewers find more problems.

Build on collective code ownership in Agile

If the code is open to anyone on the team to review or work on, make your security people part of the team. This means that they shouldn't need a reason to look at code to find problems. And, if they know what they are doing and are trusted by the rest of the team, they shouldn't need permission to fix vulnerabilities either, as long as they follow the team's conventions and workflows.

Make sure that reviewers also look at tests, especially for high-risk code. Code without tests is dangerous code that could be broken. If you care about the reliability and security of code, you need to check on the quality and coverage of automated tests, and ensure that negative tests are being written. We'll look at this more in Chapter 11, *Agile Security Testing*.

And if you care about the long-term sustainability of the system, you should also review tests to make sure that they are reasonably well-written, understandable, and maintainable.

Refactoring: Keeping Code Simple and Secure

Code that is clean and clear and consistent is less likely to have bugs (including security bugs) and easier and safer to change and fix. And much easier to review: if reviewers can't understand the code, they will waste time trying to figure out what is going on. And they will miss the opportunity to find bugs.

This is why, for example, post-Heartbleed, the OpenSSL team spent months reformatting the code and deleting unused code and doing other simple cleanup work. The team needed to do this before it could take on more important, and more fundamental improvements.[12]

Fortunately, many Agile teams, especially teams following Extreme Programming, understand the importance of writing clean code and enforcing consistent coding guidelines. If you are working on one of these teams, your job as a reviewer will be much easier—and more valuable.

If not, you should encourage the team to take advantage of refactoring, another common Agile practice. *Refactoring*—a well-defined, consistent set of patterns and practices for cleaning up and restructuring code in small, incremental steps—is built in to most modern IDEs. Developers can rename fields and methods and classes, extract methods and classes, change method signatures, and make other, more fundamental structural changes safely and predictably—especially if they have a good regression test safety net in place, something we will look at more in the next chapter.

---

12 Matt Caswell, "Code Reformat Finished" (*https://www.openssl.org/blog/blog/2015/02/11/code-reformat-finished/*), OpenSSL Blog, Feb 11th, 2015.

Using refactoring tools in their IDEs, reviewers can do their own quick-and-dirty, throwaway "scratch refactoring" until they understand the code better, suggest refactorings in review comments, or submit refactoring changes in a separate patch back to the author. But if reviewers need to reformat code in their IDE or refactor the code before they can review it, the team is doing something wrong.

Fundamentals Will Take You a Long Way to Secure, Safe Code

If you can get past the point of understanding, either because the code is clean, or because you cleaned it up yourself, or because you have worked with it enough that you can make sense of it, then you can start to review what the code actually does—or doesn't do.

As part of code reviews, even without a strong understanding of secure coding, reviewers can also look out for:

1. Hardcoded passwords or other credentials, hardcoded paths, hardcoded magic numbers, and other hardcoded things which could be dangerous.

2. Test code or debugging code left in by accident.

3. Ensuring that sensitive data is encrypted or tokenized or otherwise handled safely—whether encryption is done properly is a security specialist problem, but whether it is done at all is a business problem that can be handled by anyone on the team who is familiar with the requirements.

4. Mistakes in error handling—good error handling is another part of defensive programming, and because error handling is hard to test and rarely tested, it is important to check that errors will be handled properly during code reviews.

5. Access control checks, making sure that they are applied and maintained correctly and consistently. Who can do what or see what in the system are business rules, not a security problem for expensive pointy-hat security wizards.

6. Consistent auditing for add/change/delete actions.

7. Consistent use of approved frameworks and standard libraries—especially when dealing with security functions like crypto or output encoding.

8. Thread safety, including time-of-check/time-of-use and deadlocks: these problems are hard to find in testing, so it is particularly important to look out for concurrency and timing and locking problems in code reviews.

None of the things in the list requires specialized security knowledge. You don't need to bring in a security auditor to make sure that your team is writing clean, solid, and safe defensive code.

All Input Is Evil

When it comes to security, the most important thing that reviewers need to look out for is making sure that data is safe to be used. Michael Howard at Microsoft, coauthor of *Writing Secure Code* (Microsoft Press), said that if there was one rule that developers should follow, it is to understand that "all input is evil."

Checking that data is validated for type, length, and range of values is part of defensive programming. It's tedious, but every developer should have learned how important it is, either in school or through painful experience when he had to troubleshoot a crash or a breach. Luckily, this is one of the areas where static analysis tools can help: tools that do taint analysis and data-flow checking can catch missing validation checks.

But data validation isn't enough to make modern web or mobile applications secure, because the fundamental technology that we rely on to get things done, web browsers and database engines and XML interpreters, have problems clearly differentiating between instructions and data. This is something that attackers have learned to take advantage of in cross-site scripting attacks and SQL injection and other dangerous attacks.

In addition to data validation, you also need to encode or escape data, or otherwise template it, to make it safe for a browser or before writing it to a database. Using Prepared Statements in SQL will prevent SQL injection by clearly laying out the commands from the data variables. Modern web frameworks like Angular.js, Ember, React, Rails, and Play provide some built-in protection for XSS and other injection attacks, as long as you use them properly— and as long as you make sure to keep the frameworks up to date if vulnerabilities are reported.

For defense-in-depth protection, you can also take advantage of secure HTTP headers such as Content Security Policy (CSP). Check out the Secure Headers that Twitter's engineering team has contributed at: *https://github.com/twitter/secureheaders*.

Reviewing Security Features and Controls

Reviewing security features and controls is much harder than reviewing the rest of the application code. To find problems, reviewers need to understand the nuts and bolts and screws of security, as well as how to read the code. Luckily, this is code that isn't changed much, and if you are doing things properly, most of this should be done using the built-in security capabilities of your web framework or mobile framework, or special-purpose security libraries like Apache Shiro (*http://shiro.apache.org*) or Google's KeyCzar crypto toolkit (*https://github.com/google/keyczar*).

Probably the best reference for a security code review checklist is OWASP's ASVS project (*http://bit.ly/owasp-asvs*). Although ASVS is designed as an auditing tool, you can pull checks from it to ensure that reviewers—and coders—have covered all of the important bases, especially for security controls. Skip the boring parts up front about auditing yadda yadda and go straight to the checklists.

Let's look at how to use the ASVS to guide code reviews for important security functions and considerations. In the authentication section, ASVS lists a number of things to look out for, including the following:

- All pages and other resources require authentication by default, except for those made public to anonymous users.
- Password fields do not echo the user's password when entered.
- All authentication controls are enforced on the server, not just on the client.
- Authentication code fails securely to ensure that attackers cannot log in if there is an error (i.e., that access is denied by default, and only granted if all the steps pass).
- All suspicious authentication decisions are logged.

ASVS covers session management, access control, handling of malicious input, cryptography at rest, error handling and logging, data protection, communications security, and more.

Reviewing Code for Insider Threats

The threat of a malicious insider planting a time bomb or a Trojan or some other malcode into your system, or tampering with application logic to commit fraud, is relatively low, but it is still real.

Fortunately, reviewing code to prevent honest mistakes can also help you to catch and contain many insider threats. Whether it is accidental and foolish, or deliberate and evil, you look for many of the same things, what Brenton Kohler at Cigital calls "red flags":[13]

1. Small, accidental or (accidental-seeming) mistakes in security functions, including authentication and session management, access control, or in crypto or secrets handling.

   As Bruce Schneier points out, trivial, but highly damaging mistakes, like Apple's "goto fail" bug in SSL, could be a cause for concern:

   "Was this done on purpose? I have no idea. But if I wanted to do something like this on purpose, this is exactly how I would do it."[14]

2. Support back doors (or things that could be used as back doors), such as hardcoded URLs or IPs or other addresses, hardcoded user IDs and passwords or password hashes or keys in the code or in configuration. Hidden admin commands, hidden parameters, and hidden runtime options.

   While code like this is often intended for production support and troubleshooting purposes (or left in accidentally after debugging and testing), it could also be used for malicious purposes. In any case, back doors are potentially dangerous holes that could be exploited by attackers;

3. Test code or debugging code or diagnostics.

4. Embedded shell commands.

5. Logic errors in handling money (for example, penny shaving (*https://en.wikipe dia.org/wiki/Salami_slicing*)), or mistakes in risk limits or managing credit card details, or in command and control functions, or critical network-facing code.

6. Mistakes in error handling or exception handling that could leave the system open.

7. Missing logging or missing audit functions, and gaps in sequence handling.

8. Code that is overly tricky, or that just doesn't seem to make sense, especially if it involves time-based logic, crypto, or any high-risk functions. A malicious insider is likely to take steps to obfuscate what they are trying to do. It should be obvious by now that even if code like this isn't intentionally malicious, you don't want it in your system.

9. Self-modifying code—for the same reasons as above.

---

13 Brenton Kohler, "How to eliminate malicious code within your software supply chain" (*https://www.synop sys.com/blogs/software-security/eliminate-malicious-code-from-software-supply-chain*), Synopsys, March 9, 2015.

14 Bruce Schneier, "Was the iOS SSL Flaw Deliberate?" (*https://www.schneier.com/blog/archives/2014/02/ was_the_ios_ssl.html*), Schneier on Security, February 27, 2014.

If you are concerned about potential collusion between developers, you can regularly rotate reviewers, or assign them randomly, and spot-check reviews to make sure that the team is taking this seriously. If the stakes are high enough, you could hire eyes from outside to audit your code, like the Linux Foundation Core Infrastructure Initiative is doing, paying experts to do a detailed audit of OpenSSL, NTP, and OpenSSH.

You also need to manage all the steps from check-in through build and test to deployment, to ensure that you are deploying exactly what developers checked in and built and tested, and that nothing has been tampered with along the way. Take the steps that we outlined in Chapter 13, *Operations and OpSec* to lock down your repos and build pipelines. Carefully manage secrets and keys. Use checksums or digital signatures and change detection tools like OSSEC to watch out for unexpected or unauthorized changes to important configs and code.

But you should be doing all of this anyway. These controls will minimize the risk of insider attacks, and will also help you to catch attackers who somehow compromised your network and your development or build environment.

Key Takeaways

Code reviews can be a powerful tool for catching security vulnerabilities early, as long as they are done properly:

- Code reviews need to be done in ways that don't hold the team up. Forcing reviews through the security team will create a bottleneck that developers will try to work around.

- Peer reviews before code is checked in to the mainline, using Git pull requests or a similar workflow, are probably the most effective way to ensure that code reviews actually get done.

  The security team only needs to get involved in reviewing high-risk security functions and framework code—code that should rarely change.

- Code review tools like Gerrit or Review Board or Phabricator can automatically enforce consistent workflows, and make reviews easier and more transparent, especially in distributed teams. Team members can see and build on each other's feedback, and the electronic record that these tools create will make auditors happy.

- Reviewing code takes time and is mentally exhausting. Reviews are more effective if they are done in small, frequent bites—luckily, this is the way that most changes are made by Agile teams.

- Train developers in secure coding and provide brief checklists so that they understand what to avoid in coding, and what to look for in code reviews.

- Developers need to feel safe in reviews: safe to ask for feedback, safe to provide feedback, safe to ask questions when they don't understand. Make sure reviewers focus on the code, not the coder.

  Code reviews are a powerful opportunity for continuous learning and improvement. Use feedback from code reviews to improve the team's coding guidelines and templates, and share what they learn in code reviews during team retrospectives.

- Everyone's code should be reviewed—including, and especially, senior team members, because they most often take on the harder, and riskier, coding problems.

  Help the team to identify high-risk code (tag high-risk stories in Jira or Pivotal Tracker or other story tracking tools), and make sure that this code is carefully reviewed by one or more experienced developers.

  Code needs to be reviewed even if it was developed through pair programming, because reviews tend to find different problems than pairing.

- Automated static code analysis tools are not a substitute for manual reviews. This is a case of *AND*, not *OR*. Take advantage of static analysis tools to enforce good coding guidelines, and to catch insecure dependencies and dangerous functions and common coding mistakes. Running these checks before reviewers see the code will make code reviews easier, faster, and much more effective.

- While automated static analysis tools look like a cheap and easy way to ensure that code gets reviewed (at least if you are using open source tools), they are not plug and play. You need to implement them carefully and correctly, and work with developers so that they understand what the tool does and buy in to using it consistently.

  Because these tools all look for different problems or work in different ways, to get good coverage you will need to run more than one tool against the code.

- Developers hate false positives. Take time to understand and tune static analysis tools so that they provide efficient and reliable feedback.

- Make static analysis checking available to developers on a self-service basis. Provide static analysis on the desktop so that developers can catch problems in the IDE as they are coding, and wire static analysis checking into CI/CD build pipelines.

- Don't forget to review configuration directives and tests: this is an important part of your code base, and needs to be treated like other code.

Code reviews and static analysis checking need to be part of the team's Definition of Done: the contract between team members that determines when features or fixes are complete before they can move on to the next piece of work. The team needs to agree on what code will be reviewed (all code changes, or only high-risk code), how many reviewers need to be involved, when code reviews are done (before the code is checked in or after), what automated code review tools will be run in continuous integration, and how to deal with the findings.

CHAPTER 11

Agile Security Testing

One of the most fundamental changes in Agile development is in how testing is done. Because Agile teams move so fast, testing relies heavily, and often exclusively, on automation. If you are delivering working software every week, or if you're pushing each change to production immediately in continuous deployment, manual testing isn't a viable option.

Throwing code over to an independent test team at the end of a sprint is an anti-pattern in Agile. Testing has to be done in phase as changes are made. Hardening sprints, where the team blocks off time to focus on testing, debugging, and patching the code before it can be deployed to production, is another practice that most modern teams avoid.

Organizations that depend on independent test teams for quality assurance, and on manual penetration testing gates or scheduled scans or audits for security, need to change the way that they think and work.

How Is Testing Done in Agile?

In many Agile and DevOps teams, there are no testers. Developers take on the responsibility for testing their own code, because they have to. The Product Owner or someone else on the team playing the role of the "customer" may write acceptance test scenarios using tools supplied by the team. But developers are responsible for writing all the other tests and making sure that they pass. Testing becomes an integral part of coding, instead of a separate Waterfall phase.

Because developers are constantly making iterative changes to code as they run experiments, refactor, and respond to feedback, they need to protect themselves from accidentally breaking existing system behavior. They do this by building up a safety net of automated regression tests which they will run several times each day. These tests must be:

- Cheap and easy for the team to run often
- Fast and efficient so that the team will run them often
- Repeatable and predictable so that the team can rely on the results

The same requirements apply to security testing. Security tests need to be fast, repeatable, efficient, and automated as much as possible. As much as possible, security testing should fit into engineering workflows like the other testing that the team is doing, without causing unnecessary delays or adding unnecessary costs.

If You Got Bugs, You'll Get Pwned

We know that there is a strong connection between code quality and security. The more bugs you have, the more security problems you will have.

Research has found that up to half of software security vulnerabilities are caused by simple coding mistakes. Not design oversights or misunderstanding security black magic. Just silly, sloppy things like copy-and-paste or merge errors, not checking input parameters, bad—or no—error handling, brackets in the wrong spot.

Carnegie Mellon's Software Engineering Institute has found that between 1% and 5% of all software defects are security vulnerabilities.[1] This means that you can get a good idea of how secure your application is, based on how many bugs there are in your code.

Given that most software has somewhere between 15 and 50 bugs in every 1,000 lines of code (this is even after the code has been reviewed and tested), a small mobile application or web application with, say, 50,000 lines of code could easily have over 100 vulnerabilities.[2] Remember that almost all modern applications contain a lot of open source code, so even if you are doing everything right when it comes to writing secure code, you can't be sure that all the open source contributors were as careful, so you should lean toward an even higher number of vulnerabilities. Software quality problems—and security risk—increase significantly with the size of the code base. Large systems have much higher defect densities, which means these systems are increasingly more vulnerable.

Many high-profile security vulnerabilities, including Heartbleed and the Apple "goto fail" (EX1-A) SSL bugs, were caused by coding mistakes that could have and should have been caught in code reviews or through disciplined unit testing. No security wizardry required. Just solid defensive coding and close attention to testing.

Example 11-1. Apple Goto Fail…can you spot the bug?

```
static OSStatus
SSLVerifySignedServerKeyExchange(SSLContext *ctx, bool isRsa, SSLBuffer signedParams,
                                 uint8_t *signature, UInt16 signatureLen)
{
        OSStatus           err;
        ...

        if ((err = SSLHashSHA1.update(&hashCtx, &serverRandom)) != 0)
                goto fail;
        if ((err = SSLHashSHA1.update(&hashCtx, &signedParams)) != 0)
                goto fail;
                goto fail;
        if ((err = SSLHashSHA1.final(&hashCtx, &hashOut)) != 0)
                goto fail;
        ...

fail:
```

---

1 Carol Woody, Ph.D.; Robert Ellison, Ph.D.; and William Nichols, Ph.D.; "Predicting Software Assurance Using Quality and Reliability Measures" (*http://resources.sei.cmu.edu/asset_files/TechnicalNote/2014_004_001_428597.pdf*) Software Engineering Institute, Technical Note, December 2014.

2 Vinnie Murdico, "Bugs per lines of code" (*http://amartester.blogspot.com/2007/04/bugs-per-lines-of-code.html*), Tester's World, April 8, 2007.

```
        SSLFreeBuffer(&signedHashes);
        SSLFreeBuffer(&hashCtx);
        return err;
}
```

It's clear that your team's security program needs to build on its quality program, on the reviews and testing that are already in place, or that should be put into place. Let's look at the structure of how testing is done in Agile development, and where security needs to be considered.

The Agile Test Pyramid

We introduced the Agile Test Pyramid (*http://martinfowler.com/bliki/TestPyramid.html*) earlier in this book. Now let's drill down into how it actually works, as shown in Figure 11-1:

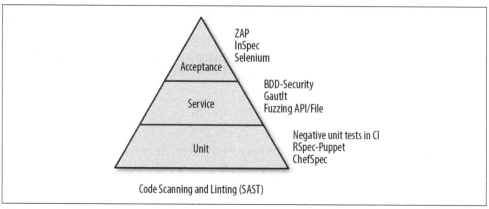

Figure 11-1. Security testing mapped to the Agile Test Pyramid

The test pyramid emphasizes lots (thousands, or tens of thousands) of low-level, automated unit tests at the base. These are white-box tests at the method or function level, written by developers to ensure that the code does what they expect it to do, using a test framework like xUnit (JUnit for Java) or TestNG.

Unit tests are the cheapest tests to write, the cheapest to run, and the easiest to change (which is good, because these are the tests that need to be changed most often).

Unit Test Doubles, Mocks, and Stubs

To create unit tests, developers write test code for each method or function, and create test fixtures or test doubles—mocks and stubs—to swap out dependencies with test implementations.

A *stub* simply replaces an existing dependency for the function being tested. It returns hardcoded responses, and might record what it receives from the function being tested. There may be more than one stub for each test.

A *mock* is a smart, fake object that decides whether the unit test passes or fails. It checks whether the function under test did what was expected and will fail the test if results don't meet expectations.

The middle of the pyramid is made up of black-box API and *integration tests*, "subcutaneous" tests that assert behavior at the service level and that test published APIs between services. These tests may be written using frameworks like FitNesse or Cucumber or JBehave.

Because tools like Cucumber can also drive higher-level acceptance tests through the user interface, the boundaries between layers can sometimes be blurred. The key thing to think about here is that this level of testing doesn't focus on the user experience, but rather on interaction between services and on testing service APIs and domain logic at higher levels of abstraction than unit tests.

At the top of the pyramid are UI-level *acceptance tests*: fat, high-value user-facing tests that check the important features and key use scenarios in the application. Acceptance tests are end-to-end tests that demonstrate to users and owners of the system that it is ready and working. These are the most expensive tests to write and run, and the most brittle (because they test so many different moving parts), so you want to keep the number of these tests to a minimum.

Some teams will script acceptance tests using a test tool like Selenium WebDriver, Sahi, or Watir. These scripts may be written by the Product Owner or a business analyst, or by a tester, and implemented by the development team. Acceptance tests may also be done manually, in demos with the customer, especially where the tests are expensive or inconvenient to automate.

The Agile Test Pyramid is a different way of thinking about where and how to focus your testing effort, as opposed to the traditional "Test Ice Cream Cone," which depends on a lot of manual or record/playback tests at the UI level executed by an independent test team, and few or no automated tests written by developers at lower levels.

Let's look at how to include security testing in each one of these layers.

Unit Testing and TDD

Starting at the base of the pyramid, we need to understand how and why developers write unit tests, and what this means to system security.

Developers write unit tests to prove to themselves that the code does what they thought it was supposed to do. They usually write these tests after they make coding changes, and run the tests before checking their code in. The tests are checked in along with the code so that they can be shared with the team—and run in continuous integration.

Many developers will write one or more unit tests as a first step in fixing a bug: write the test to duplicate the bug, run the test to prove that the test catches the bug, fix the bug, and run the test again to prove that the fix worked (and to catch the bug if comes back again by accident, as part of your regression testing going forward).

Some teams (especially XP teams) are "test obsessed" and take this approach further in what is called test-first, or test-driven development (TDD). Before writing any code, they write tests that specify what the code is supposed to do. They run the tests, prove that the tests fail, then write the code and run the tests again, filling in the code until the tests pass, switching back and forth between incrementally writing tests and writing code. The tests guide their thinking and their coding.

They can then rely on this testing safety harness to catch mistakes later as they refactor the code, restructure and clean it up, or make other changes.

Teams working this way naturally end up with higher levels of automated unit testing coverage than teams who work "test last," and there is evidence that test-first development can result in better quality code that is easier to understand and change.[3]

What Unit Testing Means to System Security

But even in test-obsessed environments, there are limits to what unit testing can do for security. This is because unit testing tests what the developer knows to look for: they assert, or reassert, expected behavior. Security problems, like the Spanish Inquisition, are rarely, if ever, expected.

There are some security vulnerabilities that can be caught in unit testing—if you take unit testing seriously enough.

For example, both the OpenSSL Heartbleed bug and Apple's Goto Fail vulnerabilities could have been caught by careful unit testing, as Mike Bland, a former Test Merce-

---

[3] Laurie Williams, Gunnar Kudrjavets, and Nachiappan Nagappan, "On the Effectiveness of Unit Test Automation at Microsoft" (*http://collaboration.csc.ncsu.edu/laurie/Papers/Unit_testing_cameraReady.pdf*), *2009 20th International Symposium on Software Reliability Engineering* (2009): 81-89.

nary at Google, explained in a post about testing culture (*http://martinfowler.com/arti cles/testing-culture.html*) on Martin Fowler's blog.

These high-profile vulnerabilities were caused by small, careless, low-level coding mistakes in security-sensitive code that got past smart developers, including the entire open source community. They were caused by not checking the length of a data parameter for Heartbleed, and a copy-and-paste or merge error in the case of Goto Fail. Bland wrote a set of straightforward but well-thought-out unit tests which showed how these problems could be caught, and that also helped to make the code simpler and easier to follow by refactoring the code to make it testable.

Unfortunately, as we'll see, unit testing is rarely done this thoroughly—and certainly wasn't done thoroughly at Apple or by the OpenSSL team.

Other security vulnerabilities are caused by fundamental oversights or ignorance. You missed implementing a control completely because you didn't know you were supposed to include it in the first place. Forgetting an access control check, trusting data when you shouldn't have, not parameterizing database queries to prevent SQL injection.

You can't find these mistakes through unit testing. Because if you don't know you are supposed to do something, you won't write a test to check for it. You will have to depend on somebody else who knows more about secure coding to find these mistakes in a code review, as we discussed in the previous chapter, or hope that they will get caught by a scanner or in pen testing.

Get Off the Happy Path

Most (if not all) tests that developers write are positive, "happy path" tests (*http:// www.sei.cmu.edu/library/assets/happy.pdf*), because developers want to prove to themselves, and to the user, that the code works. And the best way to do that is to write a test that shows just this.

QA (if there is QA) in most organizations often works the same way, spending most of their time writing and running through acceptance test checklists which prove to themselves, and the customer, that the features work as specified.

So we end up with a set of tests covering at least some of the main success scenarios through the application, and not much else.

The problem is that attackers don't stay on the happy path. They hack their way in by purposefully trying to step around, over, and into parts of the code in ways that developers did not expect.

It is *really, really hard* to get developers to think and work like attackers, because they aren't trained to do this, and they don't get paid to do this. Developers have enough of a challenge understanding and visualizing what the system is supposed to do and getting the code to do that. Unlike hackers, they don't—and can't afford to—spend hours thinking about how to abuse or break the system and look for small mistakes or inconsistencies. Most of the time, developers barely have time to write tests to prove that the code works.

This has serious consequences for security. Let's go back to Dr. David Wheeler's paper on "How to Prevent the Next Heartbleed" to look at unit testing from a security point of view:

> Many developers and organizations almost exclusively create tests for what should happen with correct input. This makes sense, when you think about it; normal users will complain if a program doesn't produce the correct output when given correct input, and most users do not probe what the program does with incorrect input. If your sole goal is to quickly identify problems that users would complain about in everyday use, mostly-positive testing works.

Even test-driven development or test-first development emphasizes writing tests that describe what the function should do—not what it should not do. With TDD, developers will end up writing a lot of tests, but almost all of these tests will be around success cases, and possibly some basic exception checking.

High levels of test coverage for positive tests aren't good enough to provide assurance. To meet security requirements, we also need to do negative testing (more from Wheeler):

> Mostly-positive testing is practically useless for secure software...You should include invalid values in your regression test suite to test each input field (in number fields at least try smaller, larger, zero, and negative), each state/protocol transition, each specification rule (what happens when this rule is not obeyed?), and so on.

As a security professional, or a developer or tester who cares about security, it's important to ensure that comprehensive negative testing like this is done for security libraries (such as crypto code), and other important platform code and high-risk features, if you want to have confidence in your tests.

Now let's move up the testing pyramid, and think about other places where security testing can and should be added in continuous integration or continuous delivery.

Service-Level Testing and BDD Tools

In addition to low-level unit tests, we want to have a set of meaningful integration tests and service-level tests that exercise the APIs of the system. These are black-box tests that check the important functions to ensure that they work under real-world conditions.

A common way to write these kinds of tests is using a behavior-driven development framework. Behavior-driven development (BDD) starts with specifications written in high-level English-like language: business stories that are understandable to the customer and testable.

There are a couple of BDD frameworks written specifically for security testing that can be run in CI or CD pipelines to execute automated tests and checks every time that a change to code or configuration is made.

Gauntlt ("Be Mean to Your Code")

Gauntlt (*http://gauntlt.org*) is a Ruby-based BDD test framework that makes it easy to write security tests and checks against your application and its configuration. It comes packaged with attack adaptors that wrap the details of using security pen testing tools, and several sample attack files:

- Checking your SSL configuration using sslyze
- Testing for SQL injection vulnerabilities using sqlmap
- Checking network configuration using nmap
- Running simple web app attacks using curl
- Scanning for common vulnerabilities using arachni and dirb and garmr
- Checking for specific serious vulnerabilities like Heartbleed

You can extend or customize these attacks, or use them as examples to build new attacks. Gauntlt also includes a generic attack adaptor that can be used to execute any command-line-driven tool that uses stdin/stdout. This makes it relatively easy to create new custom attacks of your own.

BDD-Security

BDD-Security (*https://github.com/continuumsecurity/bdd-security*) is another open source high-level automated security testing framework, written in Java. It includes a predefined set of tests for SSL checking (again using sslyze) and scanning for runtime infrastructure vulnerabilities using Nessus.

But one of the most powerful capabilities of BDD-Security is that it integrates nicely with Selenium WebDriver, a popular tool for automating functional tests. It includes templates and sample code that you can use to create your own automated tests for authentication and access control, and to automatically scan web applications using OWASP ZAP as part of your automated functional testing.

Let's Look Under the Covers

Both Gauntlt and BDD-Security use Cucumber (*https://cucumber.io*), an automated testing tool, under the covers. In Cucumber, you write tests in a Ruby DSL (Domain Specific Language) called Gherkin, following this syntax:

```
Given {preconditions}

When {execute test steps}

Then {results should/not be}
```

Each test returns a clear pass/fail result, which makes it easy to plug these tests into your CI or CD pipelines.

Now let's look at how Gauntlt attacks work in a bit more detail.

A Gauntlt attack file is any file with an *.attack* suffix. Each attack file contains one or more scenarios, each consisting of multiple Given/When/Then steps:

```
Feature: Attack/Check description

Background: set up tests for all scenarios

Scenario: specific attack logic in Given/When/Then format

Given "tool" is installed

When I launch a "tool" attack with:

    """"

    whatever steps

    """"

Then it should pass with/should contain/and should not contain:

    """"

    results

    """"
```

The command:

```
gauntlt --steps
```

lists the pre-built steps and attack aliases for common scenarios that you can use in your attacks:

```
launch a/an "xxxxx" attack with:
```

```
the file should (not) contain
```

Output parsing is done using regex to determine pass/fail status.

Gauntlt and BDD-Security help security teams and developers work together by providing a common and simple language to describe tests and easy-to-use tools. For teams that are already following behavior-driven development, these tools should be a natural fit.

Other teams that have already invested in their own tooling and test frameworks, or that don't buy in to the BDD approach and prefer to stay closer to the technical details, can write their own scripts to do the same kind of things. The goal should be to come up with a set of automated tests that probe and check security configurations and runtime system behavior for security features that will execute every time the system is built and every time it is deployed.

Acceptance Testing

Acceptance tests are generally done at the UI level by driving a browser or mobile client to execute a set of tests which exercise the key features of the application. Automated acceptance tests need to be written for security features such as authentication and user and password management, as well as for key functional workflows that handle money or private data. These are features that must work every time, which means that they need a high level of test coverage. They are also features which should rarely change, which makes them good candidates for automated acceptance testing.

This can be done with a test tool like Selenium WebDriver (*http://www.sele niumhq.org*), PhantomJS (*http://phantomjs.org*), or Sahi (*http://sahipro.com*). These tools allow you to programmatically launch and control a browser or web client, navigate to pages, locate elements on the UI, perform UI actions like entering data or clicking on buttons, and ask questions about the state of the UI objects or data.

Functional Security Testing and Scanning

Application pen testers use a variety of tools to understand and attack a system, including the following:

- Proxies to intercept traffic between a browser or mobile client and the application, letting them examine and tamper with the requests and responses
- Web spiders to crawl the application and search out all the links, mapping out the attack surface

- Application vulnerability scanners which use this information to attack the application by injecting malicious payloads against every parameter and field, trying out common attacks

Penetration testing tools like Arachni (*http://www.arachni-scanner.com*) or Burp (*https://portswigger.net/burp*), or on-demand scanning services from companies like WhiteHat or Qualys, are good at finding vulnerabilities like SQL injection or XSS, as well as other kinds of vulnerabilities that static code analysis scanners can't find. These include weaknesses in session management such as CSRF, serious runtime configuration mistakes, and access control violations.

You don't need to be a pen tester to take advantage of these tools as part of your own security testing program. But you will need to find tools that can be easily automated, that are simple to set up and use, and that will provide fast feedback to developers on security problems.

ZAP Tutorial

A good place to start with is the OWASP Zed Attack Proxy, aka ZAP (*https://www.owasp.org/index.php/OWASP_Zed_Attack_Proxy_Project*), a popular open source security testing tool.

Although ZAP is powerful enough to be used by professional pen testers, it was originally written for developers and testers who don't have security expertise. Which means that it is simple to understand and run—at least for a security tool.

We'll look at ZAP and how it fits into rapid testing cycles, because it will illustrate the challenges of trying to use scanning in continuous integration and continuous delivery, and because the patterns that we'll describe can be used with other tools.

The simplest way to try out ZAP and see how it works is its "Quick Start" mode. ZAP will ask for a URL, spider the application, and run basic canned attacks against what it finds. This will attack only the publicly-exposed attack surface of the system—it won't be able to attack any functions that require the user to be authenticated. The Quick Start will give you a taste of what ZAP can do. If it finds any serious vulnerabilities at this early stage of testing, you need to fix them immediately: if it was this easy for ZAP to find them, you can bet that an attacker can find them too, or already has.

If you want to get a better understanding of ZAP and do a better job of testing your application, you can configure ZAP as an intercepting proxy, and then run some functional tests against the application: log in to the application and navigate through some of the key forms and functions of the application.

ZAP will record what you do and build up a model of the application and how it works. While it is doing this, it will inspect responses from the application and look for common, simple mistakes—this is called *passive scanning*. Once you have finished your set of manual tests, you can tell ZAP to run an active scan against the pages that you've just tested. ZAP will try to inject malicious payloads into every field and parameter that it has seen, and observe how the system responds to these canned attacks.

As ZAP finds problems, it will report alerts, showing the request and response as proof of a successful attack, an explanation of the attack scenario, and other information to help you understand what happened and how to fix the problem.

The steps to do this are relatively straightforward:

1. Make sure that you have a recent version of ZAP so that you can take advantage of the latest capabilities and scanning rules—ZAP is updated weekly, so you can decide to take the weekly build (and try out the alpha or beta rules), or you can stick with the most recent official, stable release.
2. Start ZAP.
3. Fiddle a bit with the browser configuration to set up ZAP as a proxy (the ZAP user guide will help you with this).
4. Log in to the application and navigate to where you want to test, then walk through test scenarios for that form. If the feature that you want to test supports multiple user types, you will want to repeat these steps for each type of user.
5. Review the passive scanning results. ZAP will check HTTP headers, cookies, and parameter return values for common security mistakes.
6. Run an active scan and review the alerts. ZAP will execute a set of canned attacks against the fields and parameters that it has seen.
7. Compare the alerts against previous findings to identify anything new, and filter out false positives.
8. If you want to go further, you can try to spider the rest of the application, and run active scanning against those pages as well. You can also look at using some of the more advanced pen testing and fuzzing features in ZAP, to dig deeper.

But all of this takes time: time to set up ZAP and the browser configuration, time to run the manual scenarios, time to review the results and filter out the noise. This is time that developers, especially developers on Agile teams, do not have.

ZAP in Continuous Integration

A better way to run ZAP is automatically, in your continuous integration or continuous delivery pipeline.

Start with a simple set of smoke tests, using the ZAP Baseline Scan (*https://github.com/zaproxy/zaproxy/wiki/ZAP-Baseline-Scan*). The Baseline Scan is a Docker container that comes pre-packaged with the latest version of ZAP and the latest rules, set up to execute an abbreviated Quick Start test of your application. By default it spiders your app for one minute, runs passive scans, and reports back the results in a few minutes at most.

The Baseline Scan is designed to act as a health check that you can run frequently in your build and deployment pipeline (and even in production) to make sure that the application is configured safely, including HTTP headers and other security policies. This is how it is used at Mozilla, for example, where it was developed.

You can also include security checks as part of automated acceptance testing, following the same approach as you would in manual testing. Take a set of automated functional acceptance tests written using a tool like Selenium WebDriver, and proxy the test run through a ZAP instance running in headless mode.

This will give you confidence that at least the main user functions of your application don't have any obvious security problems.

All of these steps can be scripted and automatically executed by your CI/CD server.

You can use Javascript or ZAP's ZEST scripting language, its command-line interface, or its REST API to instruct ZAP to report passive scan findings, optionally spider the application and wait for the spider to finish, set scanning policies and alert thresholds, and run active attacks.

ZAP can report the results in HTML, XML, or JSON format, which means you can write scripts to examine the results, filter out false positives, and compare the results to previous runs to identify new findings.

If you are using Jenkins, for example, you can take advantage of ZAP's Official Jenkins plug-in (*https://wiki.jenkins-ci.org/display/JENKINS/zap+plugin*), which makes it easy to execute ZAP commands directly from Jenkins and to check the results in your build pipeline.

BDD-Security and ZAP Together

Or you can use a higher-level test framework like BDD-Security, which we have already looked at briefly. BDD-Security wraps execution of ZAP scans and Selenium tests inside a behavior-driven design framework. Using BDD-Security, you write security stories in Cucumber's high-level *Given/When/Then* format. The test framework takes care of the details of setting up and running the test tools, parsing the results, filtering results, and determining pass/fail status.

Example 11-2 is a sample story included with BDD-Security for executing a scan with ZAP and checking for SQL injection.

Example 11-2. BDD-Security Story

```
@app_scan
Feature: Automated Application Security Scanning
  Run automated application level tests against the application using OWASP ZAP

  Background:
    Given a new scanning session
    And a scanner with all policies disabled
    And all existing alerts are deleted
    And the application is navigated
    And the application is spidered

  @cwe-89
  Scenario: The application should not contain SQL injection vulnerabilities
    And the SQL-injection policy is enabled
    And the attack strength is set to High
    And the alert threshold is set to Low
    When the scanner is run
    And the following false positives are removed
      |url                    |parameter       |cweId       |wascId  |
    And the XML report is written to the file build/zap/sql_injection.xml
    Then no medium- or higher-risk vulnerabilities should be present
```

BDD-Security comes with stories for different kinds of scans as well as SQL injection, server-side include and server-side injection attacks, remote OS command injection, CRLF injection, external redirect, LDAP injection, xpath injection, and generic padding oracle attacks.

BDD-Security, together with Selenium, can be used to write and execute acceptance-level tests for authentication features to check that authentication is properly set up and to test negative error handling cases. It can also write access control checks to ensure that users can only see or do what they are authorized for. To do this you'll need to modify the sample Java code that comes packaged with BDD-Security.[4]

---

4 For more on how to use BDD-Security and ZAP together, watch Michael Brunton-Spall's presentation, "Building securely with agile" (*https://www.youtube.com/watch?v=jkxCLW0x650*).

Scanning APIs

OWASP ZAP and BDD-Security (with a bit of custom coding to extend some test plumbing classes) can also be used to scan REST APIs. The approach is roughly the same as testing a web app, using ZAP as an intercepting proxy while you exercise API functions with other tools, and running passive and active scans against the exposed surface of your APIs.

A more comprehensive and accurate approach to scanning APIs would be to take advantage of ZAP add-ons for SOAP and Open-API/Swagger (*https://zaproxy.blogspot.com/2017/04/exploring-apis-with-zap.html*) to import API definitions and help ZAP understand and explore your API.

Another option is to use use Tinfoil (*https://www.tinfoilsecurity.com*), a commercial application security scanner which automatically builds up a complete model of your REST APIs using Swagger or similar frameworks, and then does deep scanning and smart fuzzing of your APIs and authentication scheme to find security bugs and other runtime problems.

Challenges with Application Scanning

How much you get out of scanning depends on the following factors:

- How good the tool is, and whether you have set it up correctly
- How much of the application your automated acceptance tests cover, or how well the spider works (if you invoke it to crawl for other links)
- What rules you choose
- How much time that you have to run the tests

It can take a long time to crawl an application, trying to identify all the pages and parameters, and then more time to run attacks against the entry points that the scanner finds. It may not be practical or even possible to automatically spider and actively scan large web applications as part of your build pipeline. Automated tools can often lose their way, hang or time out, or even crash during long scans.

As we've already described, targeting scans against the key parts of the application that you've explored with automated functional testing is more efficient and probably more effective than brute-force spidering and scanning. But even these tests can take a long time to run.

There are some obvious steps that you can take to speed up scanning:

1. Scanning requires lots of CPU and memory. The more machine power you can throw behind the scanner and the system under test, the faster your scans will run.

2. Adjust the rule set. For example, by default, ZAP will run its full set of active scanning rules against every parameter, with medium strength. This may not always be necessary. For example, if your application does not use a SQL database, there's no reason to run SQL injection attacks.

3. Break scans down and run them in parallel. Take advantage of rapid provisioning to stand up multiple instances of the application and run scans using different rules or targeting different functions.

4. Run incremental scans only against new or changed URLs, rather than scanning code that hasn't been, or at least shouldn't have been, changed.

Another problem that you need to solve is accuracy. Black-box application scanners, like static analysis scanners, will often report hundreds or thousands of false positive findings and other warnings that you will need to review and filter out.

Some scanners still have problems today with complex Javascript code or other dynamic content in the UI, and get lost or don't find problems when they should.

You may need to try out a few different scanners before you find the tool and plug-ins that work best for your project. Spend time understanding the scanning tool and how it works, and make sure that it is set up correctly, before you try to wire it into your build pipeline.

Modern testing tools like ZAP are flexible and extensible through APIs, scripting languages, and plug-ins. Lots of people have taken advantage of this flexibility to implement automated scanning in different ways, which is reassuring, but also confusing. There is no "best practice" for scanning your apps. You'll need to Google for ideas and examples and run some experiments to see what works best for you.

 Get Your Pipeline Working First

Getting security scanning set up and working correctly in an automated pipeline isn't easy. You need success with setting up your CI/CD server and build workflows, and experience automating functional testing, before you should consider introducing security scanning.

Another tricky problem that you'll need to solve is getting the tool to automatically authenticate with your application, especially if you want to try and take advantage of spidering or if you want to test access controls. An unauthenticated scan will only hit the publicly exposed features or pages of your application, which are not usually the most interesting or valuable parts to you—or to attackers.

Most tools have different authentication modes to help with this. ZAP, for example, supports common authentication methods and a script-based method to support complex or custom authentication schemes and reauthentication steps. You can also manually walk through authentication steps in ZAP and save the resulting session information to your code repository to be reused in later automated scans.

Scanning Is Not the Same as Pen Testing

Understand that automated scanning like this is *not the same as pen testing*. Tools like ZAP run through a canned set of well-known attacks and look for well-known vulnerabilities and common mistakes.

This is just one of the first, and one of the easiest, things that a good pen tester will do.

But passing a set of automated scans should add to your level of confidence, and it will make pen testers—and attackers—work harder to find real problems in your system.

If you want to learn about pen testing, a good place to start is OWASP's Testing Guide (*https://www.owasp.org/index.php/ OWASP_Testing_Project*).

This guide explains how to set up and conduct a pen test. It provides checklists and techniques for reconnaissance, mapping the environment and the application, and fingerprinting the technology stack. It also offers tests for identity management, authentication functions, session management, authorization, different kinds of injection attacks, and how to find holes in business logic.

Testing Your Infrastructure

New tools such as Docker and Vagrant and Packer and Ansible make it fast and easy for developers to package up and provision their own development and test environments. Instead of waiting days or weeks for sys admins to build a system, developers can pull down community-built Chef cookbooks or Ansible playbooks or public Docker images, and spin up temporary instances in private or public clouds, with the complete runtime stack and all the tools that they need, ready to run, in minutes.

The advantages to an Agile development team of being able to self-provision development and test environments like this are obvious. They get control over how their environments are set up and when it gets done. They don't have to wait days or weeks to hear back from ops. They can try out new tools or platforms easily and cheaply, run technical experiments and iterate quickly. And they can eliminate the "works on my machine" problem by making sure that development and testing are done using the same runtime configurations.

But this also introduces a new set of risks that need to be managed:

- Like any other open source code, Docker images or other configuration recipes or templates, especially ones downloaded from community hubs, can contain mistakes, outdated packages, and other vulnerabilities, which developers can easily miss.

- To save time—and because they may not understand the technical details or don't care about them—developers will often take advantage of default configurations, which is almost never the safe thing to do.

- When developers self-provision their infrastructure, ops and security are taken out of the loop on purpose, which means that changes happen without their oversight or understanding.

- These insecure configurations can potentially become a target for attackers, and worse, can find their way into production.

The configuration specifications for these tools—Dockerfiles, Ansible playbooks, Chef recipes, and cloud templates—are code. Which means that infrastructure configuration can be automatically scanned and tested like any other code.

You can scan configuration code or images to look for common mistakes and vulnerabilities, and for compliance risks. There are a range of tools, for example, that you can use to statically scan Docker images and containers, including the following:

- Docker Bench for Security (*https://github.com/docker/docker-bench-security/*) scans Docker containers for compliance with the CIS Benchmark for Docker.

- Docker Security Scanning (*https://docs.docker.com/docker-cloud/builds/image-scan/*) is an add-on service from Docker to scan images in private repos for known vulnerabilities.

- Clair (*https://github.com/coreos/clair/*) is an open source vulnerability scanner for Docker images from CoreOS.

You can also write your own tests to do the following:

- Help guide your design in test-driven infrastructure: defining the end state of configuration in tests before writing the configuration code, in the same way that developers working in test-driven development write tests before they write code.

- Catch coding mistakes early: syntax checking and unit testing is important for configuration code with dynamic content, because many mistakes can't otherwise be caught until runtime.

- Catch regressions as engineers refactor (clean up and restructure) the code, update to new versions of tools, or move to new platforms.
- Check the health of system configurations, ensure consistency between systems and environments, and catch snowflakes (one-off setups).
- Act as documentation for the configuration.
- Enforce policies and guidelines: operational policies, compliance policies, security policies, and hardening guidelines.

And just like the application testing pyramid, there are tools and approaches for different levels of testing infrastructure code.

Linting

Linting tools perform syntax checking, and checking for formatting and good coding practices. These tools help ensure that your code runs correctly, and are particularly important for dynamic scripting languages:

- Puppet parser validate, Puppet-lint
- Foodcritic, Rubocop for Chef
- Ansible-lint

Code checking is of minimal value from a security perspective.

Unit Testing

By mocking or stubbing out the runtime environment in unit tests, you can check that the logic is consistent through fast dry runs. This helps to make code safer to change.

- RSpec-Puppet
- Chefspec

Like syntax checking, unit tests are not likely to catch any serious security problems.

Acceptance Testing

Acceptance tests are the best place to add security and compliance checks. Spin up a clean test environment, execute the recipe or playbook code, and compare the actual results to expected results. Like application acceptance tests, these tests are more expensive to run, providing slower, but more complete feedback:

- Bats—Bash Automated Testing System

- Beaker for Puppet
- Goss
- Serverspec
- InSpec—Tests which can explicitly trace back to compliance requirements
- RSpec—Roll your own test framework instead of using Serverspec's DSL

Let's look at some popular tools that can be used to test different configuration languages or specifications on a range of platforms. This is especially useful in larger enterprises where teams may use many different configuration management approaches, because they can all standardize on the same testing framework; and it also makes it easier to transition from one configuration management stack to another.

Test Kitchen

Test Kitchen (*http://kitchen.ci*) is a pluggable test management framework that you can use to set up and run tests for infrastructure code. From the "kitchen" name, it was obviously built to test Chef recipes, but it can be extended through plug-ins to test code for Puppet, Ansible, SaltStack, or other configuration management tools.

Test Kitchen allows you to write tests using different test frameworks, including Serverspec, RSpec, Bats, and Cucumber. It also allows you to run tests on Linux and Windows, supporting Vagrant, Docker, and most cloud platforms.

Serverspec

Serverspec (*http://serverspec.org*) is an extension of Ruby's RSpec testing framework, with specific support for testing infrastructure state. Using Serverspec you can write high-level acceptance tests which validate that the state of the system configuration (e.g., files, users, packages, services, and ports) match expectations. These tests can be run before or after changes are made.

Because Serverspec checks the end state, it doesn't matter what tool or tools you use to make configuration changes.

ServerSpec connects to each system using SSH, runs a set of passive checks on the configuration, and returns the results for comparison. This means that it can be safely run in test, as well as to audit production to help meet compliance requirements. Here is a simple example of Serverspec check:

```
describe package('httpd'), :if => os[:family] == 'redhat' do
  it { should be_installed }
end
```

There is a Serverspec variant called AWSpec (*https://github.com/k1LoW/awspec*) designed to execute similar tests on Amazon's AWS.

We'll look more at how to use tools like Serverspec to write security tests and runtime checks in Chapter 13, *Operations and OpSec*.

Creating an Automated Build and Test Pipeline

The velocity at which Agile and DevOps teams deliver keeps increasing. Scrum teams that used to work in one-month sprints now commonly deliver working code every week. DevOps teams following continuous deployment can make changes directly to production several times a day. At the extreme edge of this, at Amazon, thousands of developers working in small, "two pizza" teams continuously and automatically push out thousands of changes to their systems every day.

Working at this speed requires a different approach to designing systems and ways of building code and deploying changes that are optimized for rapid, incremental change. But all of this still builds on Agile and Lean ideas and fundamentals.

Let's look at the steps involved in moving toward rapid or continuous deployment, and what this means from a testing and security perspective.

Nightly Build

In order to move faster, teams will find that they need to build the system on a frequent basis: the longer between merges and builds, the more risk of conflicts and misunderstandings.

Back in the 1990s, Microsoft popularized the practice of a "nightly build." Developers were encouraged to check in changes each day, and each night a job would run to build the software so that the latest changes were available for everyone on the team to use the next morning. Over time, teams added tests after the build steps to catch common mistakes. Anyone who "broke the build" with a bad check-in would have to buy pizza or serve some other punishment, including babysitting the build until somebody else broke it.[5]

A lot of work can be required to get a system, especially a large legacy system, to build without mistakes. Being able to do this every day is a big step forward. A regular working build of the system provides a heartbeat for the team, increasing visibility into the state of development and confidence in the team's ability to deliver. And it gives everyone on the team a chance to catch mistakes and incorrect assumptions early.

---

5 Joel Spolsky, "The Joel Test: 12 Steps to Better Code" (*http://bit.ly/joel-test-12-steps*), Joel on Software, August 9, 2000.

Continuous Integration

The next step to improving visibility and velocity is continuous integration.

Developers learn to check in small changes frequently, often several times a day, to ensure that everyone on the team can always see and work with everyone else's changes. Each time that code is checked in, a continuous integration server (like Jenkins or Travis) is triggered and automatically builds the code and checks to make sure that the developer's change hasn't broken the build.

This is done by executing a suite of automated tests, mostly unit tests. These tests have to run quickly: the faster they run, the more often that developers will check in changes.

The following steps outline an example of a continuous integration workflow:

- Code inspections done inline in the developer's IDE
- Manual code review before check-in or merge to mainline
- Compile and check warnings
- Build checks
- Incremental static analysis checking executed by the CI server
- Unit testing
- Tag the build artifacts in an artifact repository such as Apache Archiva, Artifactory, or Sonatype Nexus

These steps should be enough to provide confidence that the changes are safe and the build is sound. Then we need to check that system is in a releasable state.

Continuous Delivery and Continuous Deployment

DevOps teams build on continuous integration practices and tools to implement continuous delivery, or continuous deployment, pipelines.

In continuous delivery, changes are pushed from development to testing and then finally to production in a sequence of automated steps, using a consistent set of tools and providing an end-to-end audit trail. At any point in time, the system is proven to be production ready.

Continuous deployment takes this all the way to production: developers check in a fix or a change, and if it passes the automated steps and checks in the pipeline, it is deployed immediately to production. This is how teams at Netflix, Amazon, and Etsy work.

Each change to code or configuration automatically kicks off continuous integration, building the code and running through the fast set of automated tests. If the build is good, the build artifacts are automatically packaged up and then deployed to a test environment for integration and acceptance testing.

If these tests pass, the code is promoted to staging to rehearse deployment in a production-like environment, and for system testing:

- Execute through the preceding continuous integration steps.
- Take the latest good build from the artifact repository, and package it.
- Provision a test environment (using an automated tool like Chef or Puppet, Vagrant, Docker or CloudFormation).
- Deploy to test (rehearse deployment steps).
- Start the application (check for errors).
- Run smoke tests and environment health checks.
- Run acceptance tests.
- Run integration tests.

If these steps all pass:

- Provision a staging environment.
- Deploy to staging (rehearse deployment and release steps in production-like environment).
- Repeat steps to start the application, smoke tests, acceptance tests, and integration tests.
- Load tests and operational tests.

This proves that the change is safe and that all the steps to deploy the change are working correctly.

Out-of-Band Testing and Reviews

Some tests and reviews have to be done outside of the continuous delivery pipeline because they take too long, or require manual handoffs, or both. The results of these tests and checks can be checked and fed back into the team's backlog. Some tests and reviews must be done outside of the continuous delivery pipeline because they take too long, or require manual handoffs, or both. Any findings need to be fed back into the team's backlog, creating another, larger feedback for the team. Out-of-band tests and reviews include:

- Manual exploratory testing and usability testing
- Deep scanning (static analysis or application scanning) will need to be done out of band for large systems, and the results reviewed and triaged manually

- Penetration testing
- Maybe API or file fuzzing

Fuzzing in CI/CD

Fuzz testing, or fuzzing, is a brute-force automated reliability testing technique. It takes negative testing to the extreme, automatically generating semi-random data values to test APIs or file import functions for problems in data validation, and to see what happens behind the code when bad data values get passed through (buffer overflows, integer overflows, memory corruption bugs, and so on).

Fuzzing is commonly done to test embedded software and network protocols. Fuzzing has also been an important part of the application security programs at Microsoft and Adobe and Google (especially in the Chrome team). Security researchers often use fuzzing to hunt for weaknesses in code, and fuzzers are used under the covers in the application vulnerability scanning tools that we've looked at.

To wire fuzz testing into an automated build pipeline, you'll need to limit how long the tests execute, and find a way to automatically feed results back. Fuzzing tools like Peach (*http://www.peachfuzzer.com*) provide options to time box or limit test runs, and plug in to popular continuous integration servers like Jenkins. Like ZAP, Peach can also be used as a proxy between your tests and the API being tested, to automatically fuzz data elements in the tests by running the same tests over and over.

But fuzzing has a number of downsides. To get confidence, you need to run through an awful lot of test cases, which could take several hours or even days. The system or service under test may crash, and will need to be restarted and reset. Fuzzing doesn't always provide clear feedback, especially when a crash happens—someone may need to manually review the tests and stack traces and error messages to confirm what failed, where, and why.

Because of these issues, fuzzing is unlikely to be a high-value starting point for test automation for most organizations.

Promoting to Production

Once the build, test, and deployment steps and checks pass, your latest changes are ready to be promoted to production. This step is done automatically in continuous deployment, or after manual approvals and other checks are completed if you are following continuous delivery.

Either way, you want to use the same artifacts, the same tools, and the same steps that you've used in the previous stages to deploy to production, because you have rehearsed them, debugged them, and proven that they work many times before you finally use them in production. This takes most of the pain and risk out of deployment.

Guidelines for Creating a Successful Automated Pipeline

Pipeline stages build on each other, moving progressively from simple tests and checks in simple environments to more real-world tests and checks done in more real-world environments.

You build and package a release candidate once early in the pipeline, store the build artifacts in a safe place, and promote this candidate through subsequent steps until you've overcome the objections to releasing it.

Even if you aren't ready for continuous integration or continuous delivery yet, you should design your testing program so that tests can be run automatically. This means that tests need to be repeatable and deterministic: they need to provide the same results each time that they are run. And they need to provide unambiguous pass/fail results that can be checked at runtime.

To save time, stack the sequence of tests so that you run the the most important tests as early as possible: tests that check important functions and tests that break often. If you have tests that are flakey or that have intermittent timing issues or other problems, isolate them so that they don't break the build.

As you add more tests and scanning steps, you'll need to start breaking them out into parallel streams and fan them out, taking advantage of public or private clouds to create test farms and scanning grids, so that you can execute a few hours worth of tests and checks in minutes of elapsed time.

Where Security Testing Fits Into Your Pipeline

We've already looked at how security testing can be automated. Once automated, these tests can be wired into different stages of your CI/CD pipeline.

Checks and tests to conduct before continuous integration:

- IDE static code inspections before code is checked in, using built-in code checkers or tool plug-ins
- Pre-merge check-in scanning for secrets
- Code reviews

Security tests and checks in continuous integration:

- Build checks, including detecting new components and components with known vulnerabilities (something we already looked at in Chapter 6, *Agile Vulnerability Management*).

- Unit testing, especially negative unit tests for key functions.
- Incremental static analysis, linting, and custom code checks for banned functions and other dangerous practices.
- Security smoke testing: fast, simple, security sanity checks, scripted using a tool like Gauntlt.

Security tests and checks in continuous delivery:

- Targeted application scanning (using ZAP, Arachni, or another DAST tool).
- Automated attacks with Gauntlt.
- Automated acceptance tests for security features (authentication, access control, identity management, auditing, and crypto) using BDD-Security and/or Selenium WebDriver.

Before adding security testing into your pipeline, make sure that the pipeline is set up correctly and that the team is using it correctly and consistently.

- All changes are checked into the code repository.
- Team members check in frequently.
- Automated tests run consistently and quickly.
- When tests fail, the team stops and fix problems immediately before making more changes.

 If the team isn't already relying on the automated build pipeline when it pushes changes out, and if it doesn't respond seriously to test failures in the pipeline, then adding security checks to the pipeline won't accomplish much.

As you automate security scans and tests, start by running them in a separate stream of the pipeline so that test failures won't cause the team's build to fail right away. Review the test results to set failure thresholds, and tune the tools so that they don't slow down the build too much and so that the team won't waste time chasing down false positive findings. Once this is working, then you can make these security checks a blocking factor to the main pipeline.

A Place for Manual Testing in Agile

Although Agile and especially DevOps emphasize automated testing because of the need for fast feedback and rapid cycling, there is still an important place for manual testing—and manual testers—in Agile development, especially when it comes to security.

Manual regression testing doesn't scale in high-velocity Agile environments and is a waste of people's time. In Agile development, waste is something that must be eliminated. But there are other cases where manual testing adds value. For example, usability testing needs to be done by real people: testers, or developers dog-fooding, or beta users in production.

Another kind of manual testing that can provide a lot of value is *exploratory testing*.

Exploratory testing is about learning how the application works and finding where its breaking points are. Exploratory testers try to push the system to its limits, to find bugs before users—or attackers—do.

It's not scripted, or perhaps only loosely scripted. Exploratory testers might start with walking through the acceptance criteria for a story, but then they will take off along paths that they think are interesting or important.

They may try to do steps out of order, push buttons that they maybe shouldn't push, fiddle with links and data, go backward and forward again to see what happens. Exploratory testers play and improvise as they test, and as they build up their understanding of how the system works. And all along the way they record what they did, what they found, and what went wrong so that they can report defects.

How to Break Software

To understand more about exploratory testing, it's worth reading James Bach's seminal essay, "Exploratory Testing Explained" (*http://www.satisfice.com/articles/et-article.pdf*).

James Whittaker's books *How to Break Software* (Pearson), *How to Break Web Software* (Addison-Wesley Professional), and *How to Break Software Security* (Addison Wesley) will teach you how to take an adversarial approach to testing your applications.

While some of the specific tools may be out of date, the approach and attack models that Whittaker describes are still relevant. URL jumping attacks in web apps, for example, are a simple way to test out controls in key workflows. Jump into, around, or over steps by browsing directly to a page. Try moving backward, skip over approval steps. If the application doesn't catch you, you've found an important bug that attackers or fraudsters can exploit.

Penetration testing is an extreme and specialized form of exploratory testing, where the tester takes on the role of an attacker. Pen testers use intercepting proxies and scanners and other tools to identify vulnerabilities, and then try to exploit them. This requires specific technical skills and experience to do effectively.

While most teams won't have good penetration testing skills in-house, they can still get a lot from adversarial exploratory testing. It can be done in an informal, lightweight way, with developers paired up with testers or with each other to explain the feature and to look into problems as they come up.

Exploratory testing should be done on security features like login and forgot password, and important business workflows like online shopping and online banking or payments handling.

And as we saw in the ZAP tutorial, manual exploratory testing is a useful and necessary first step in test automation, in order to understand the application and tools, and to identify important scenarios to be automated.

Adversarial exploratory testing, asking testers and developers to think out of the box, or trying to hack into your own systems, provides information that you can't get from structured, repetitive, automated testing. You can find serious usability and reliability and security bugs by testing this way. But what's more important is that it can tell you where you have weaknesses in the system and in your processes. When you find serious security and reliability bugs through exploratory testing, you need to look closer at the code and the design, and at the rest of your reviews and testing work to understand what else you could be missing, and what else might need to be fixed.

This kind of testing is expensive and can't scale. It takes time to do right, and it is highly dependent on the individual skills, experience, and instincts of the testers. Take advantage of it as much as you can, but recognize that you can't depend on manual testing to keep your system safe and secure.

How Do You Make Security Testing Work in Agile and DevOps?

To make security testing work, you need to recognize the limitations and constraints that Agile development and continuous delivery force on you.

There's not enough time to do exhaustive gate-based testing and audits. You need to break testing down into small steps that can be automated so that they can be run every time a change is made. Focus on tests that will catch common and important mistakes early.

Test automation is hard to do right. You need to understand the domain and the design of the system and the runtime platform, and how to build and configure them correctly in order to stand up the system for security testing. You need to understand testing tools and continuous integration, and how to code and script tests, work out how to respond to test failures when they happen, and how to rule out false positives.

All of this has to be done at high velocity to keep up with the team members and with the changes that they are continuously making.

You need a strong combination of technical and testing and security skills to do this, which requires bringing the security team, developers, and testers together in the following ways:

- The security team can help developers write acceptance criteria and test scenarios for security stories.

- Security can review unit tests for high-risk code and automated tests for infrastructure playbooks.

- Try a test-driven security approach: have security engineers write tests for the team before they write the code, and make these tests part of the team's acceptance goals.

- Security can help the team to implement black-box application scanning and infrastructure scanning in the build pipeline.

- Security can participate in exploratory testing, especially on security features, and show the team how to turn an exploratory testing session into a security test, by introducing an attack proxy like ZAP into the test.

Look for ways to simplify and share tests. Take advantage of templates provided by tools like Gauntlt and BDD-Security to create standard tests that can be shared across teams and across systems.

Look for ways to get developers involved in writing security tests and owning the outcome. Make security testing self-service, something simple that developers can spin up and run on their own. Nothing flakey, no warnings that need an expert to decide whether there is a real problem or not.

Review and improve as you go. Fill in gaps in your testing as you need to: when you find vulnerabilities; when the team makes a change in direction, arrives at a new design, or upgrades the technology; or when the threat landscape changes.

Key Takeaways

In Agile teams, developers are effectively responsible for testing their own work, and rely heavily on test automation and continuous integration to catch problems quickly:

- Most developer testing is done along "happy path" success scenarios to demonstrate that features work. However, adversaries step off of this path to find edge cases and weaknesses in design and coding that can be exploited.

  Developers need to understand the importance of negative testing, especially for security libraries and other high-risk code.

- Black-box dynamic scanning using tools like OWASP ZAP can be wired into continuous delivery pipelines to catch common security vulnerabilities in web applications and mobile apps. But this is not easy.
- Start small. Run some experiments. Learn how your tools work inside out before you push them onto a development team.
- Test-driven development (writing automated tests before writing the code) can be followed by security teams to start injecting security into testing for the application and for infrastructure.
- Automated security test frameworks like Gauntlt and BDD-Security provide test templates that can be used to build security smoke tests, and shared across multiple teams and systems.
- Test your infrastructure as well as your application. Tools like Serverspec and InSpec can be used to check that infrastructure is set up properly and safely.
- Automated tests, including scanning, have to be implemented so that the tests run quickly and provide clear pass/fail feedback to developers.
- Manual acceptance testing won't scale in Agile environments. But manual exploratory testing and pen testing can find important problems that automated tests may miss, and provide valuable information to the team members about weaknesses and risks in the system and in their processes.

Security testing needs to be part of the team's Definition of Done: the contract that the team has with one another and with the organization to deliver working software in each release. The team needs to understand its compliance and security obligations, and agree on what testing needs to be done to meet these obligations. What kinds of security tests and scans need to be run, and how often? What kind of findings will break the build? What level of automated test coverage is needed for security libraries and other high-risk code?

CHAPTER 12

External Reviews, Testing, and Advice

There is a global shortage of information security skills, especially in application security. This means that you may have to go outside for help in setting up your security program and keeping it on track.

Pen tests, bug bounties, vulnerability assessments, and other external reviews can provide your organization with access to a wide community and its experience, creativity, expertise, and energy.

As your security capabilities grow, your reliance on external consultants may diminish; but you should not plan for it to ever disappear entirely. Even if you have strong technical security capabilities in-house, there is still value in bringing in external expertise to backstop your organization—and to keep you honest.

Many common regulations that your operating environment may be subject to include requirements for external security testing or audits of some kind to provide an independent verification that you have shown due diligence in protecting your systems, customers, and data.

For example, PCI DSS mandates that the systems and applications that comprise the environment covered by the standard are reviewed by certified testers (called Qualified Security Assessors or QSAs in the case of PCI) both annually and any time that you make a significant change to the environment. These testers must follow recognized industry standards and methodologies, and produce a detailed report of their findings. You, as the party being assessed, must take action to rectify any significant findings.

There is an entire section of the security industry dedicated to providing compliance assessment services and to supporting your organization in navigating the different aspects of regulatory compliance. This is an example of where security support from external parties is not only beneficial but actually required.

Getting external reviews can be a daunting process. Getting good value from these reviews can be even more challenging. This chapter aims to help you understand how to go about engaging with external security practitioners and, perhaps more importantly, how to ensure you get the most out of the investments you make in them.

Disclaimer

All opinions and guidance in this section are intended to set direction and should not be taken as endorsement of any approach, company, or technique for external assurance.

To put it simply, we're not trying to sell you anything, or telling you to spend money on consultants. But in our experience, there can be real value in getting expert help from outside of your organization, and we believe that external reviews play an important part in mature application security programs.

Why Do We Need External Reviews?

External security reviews serve a number of different purposes besides compliance:

Independence

Outsiders don't have a stake in making your team or organization look good. In fact, their interest is opposed to this: they want to find serious problems so that you will bring them in again, or so that you will ask for their help in fixing these problems. From a penetration tester's perspective, the worst engagement imaginable is one where they don't find any meaningful issues, and they are incentivized to work hard to avoid that situation!

Expertise

Hiring specialist security testers and auditors is not only challenging but expensive. There is a global skills shortage, and many tests need specific or niche skills that suit the technology or context. Keeping these on the team may not be an option for your organization, and therefore seeking such expertise from outside parties can make the most practical and financial sense.

Management support and escalation

Spending real money on external reviews can be an effective tool for ensuring that management and the executive team understand the risks faced by the organization. Problems identified by an outside party will often be given more visibility than issues found during internal reviews, and can be easier to escalate. Your organization's leadership has an obligation to steer the company safely and reduce risk—external reviews can be a valuable tool to help them meet this obligation as well as helping them demonstrate that they have taken that responsibility seriously.

Learning and improvement

In order to understand if your approach to security is working, you need some way to measure its effectiveness. External reviews cannot provide a perfectly complete assessment of all aspects of your security program, but do provide both quantitative and qualitative data that you can feed back into your program to identify strengths and weaknesses and use to improve over time.

Objectivity

Outsiders will never understand your environment as well as you do. While this lack of contextual knowledge can sometimes provide challenges when engaging external parties, the objectivity they provide can be invaluable. They will not have the same biases, assumptions, and predispositions as an internal team, and can be considered to be in the truest sense *fresh eyes*. These eyes may see issues that you would not consider or expect, despite the outside party's lack of familiarity with your business and systems.

Customer expectations

Finally, if you are building a product or service for others to use (and probably pay you for), your customers may well have the expectation that you have sought outside expertise in assessing the security of the thing itself and the environment it operates in. It is increasingly common during a procurement process for customers to ask for access to the full or executive summary of third-party assessment reports, along with the remediation actions you took to any findings. If you are not able to provide customers with such evidence, there is a very real chance you will lose out on business due to a diminished trust in your solution.

Proving a Negative

Something worth being completely comfortable with before investing in any form of security testing (either internal or external) is that no matter how much money you decide to throw at the testing process, you're not going to be able to *prove* it is secure, only that the process and testers you had look at it could find no more issues. Proving a negative, that your application is *not* insecure, is not possible outside of some very specific cases using formal proofs and specially designed languages (which are all very much beyond the scope of this book!).

It is also worth recognizing that your applications and the environment in which they operate are dynamic, and so any assessment of their security may only be valid for a period, or even point, in time. This goes even more so in Agile environments where the code base may be being updated continually, and perhaps even being deployed continuously.

Don't let this discourage you! Assessing the security of any application or environment is about doing your best to validate the design and implementation against your threat model and getting outside perspectives and expertise to challenge your own.

> The goal is rarely to prove the target is 100% secure; rather, it's to prove that you have done your due diligence to see whether it is secure enough.

There are a range of security assurance services available, and it's important to choose the services that will meet your needs. This means balancing the aim of the exercise, the cost, and the depth of the evaluation.

Let's look at the common types of assessment and reviews available and their aims, as well as their limitations and common misunderstandings of what they can provide you.

Vulnerability Assessment

Vulnerability assessment is usually the cheapest of the external assessment options at your disposal, and as such tends to give you a broad view of your environment's security, but one that lacks the depth of other approaches. In these assessments you hire an outside party to run a series of tools such as vulnerability scanners that look for common mistakes in configuration, unpatched software with known problems, default credentials, and other known security risks. Once the scans are complete, they will summarize the results in a report that you can give to your auditors, which should include an overall assessment of risk and a high-level remediation plan.

Even if you do have access to a set of tools that can perform automated security scans and you are running them on your own, there can still be value in having someone with broader experience running scans and evaluating the results. Vulnerability assessment tools in themselves are rarely complicated to run, but someone who does this for a living can make sure that they are configured correctly for a given environment, and help your organization understand the results and how best to remediate them.

Vulnerability Assessment Tools and Scanners

There are a number of vulnerability assessment tools available that you can use to check different layers of your technology stack. These range from open source tools to commercial scanners and testing platforms.

We look at vulnerability scanning and compliance scanning tools in more detail in Chapter 13, *Operations and OpSec*.

A professional who has used these tools many times before should know how to make sure that the tools and scans are set up and configured to run properly, and what policies and plug-ins will provide the most value, instead of relying on defaults.

A common downside of automated security scanning tools is the volume of results they produce, the lack of context surrounding the results, and the number of false positives. With this in mind, having someone familiar with vulnerability scanning and their tooling can pay dividends in terms of having the results analyzed to reduce excess volume, remove false positives, and provide environment-specific context that the tooling is just unable to.

One of your key expectations when employing an outside expert to run a vulnerability assessment for you is that the expert will filter and prioritize the results correctly, so you can maximize your ROI when you remediate the findings. Your own system administrators and operations engineers may be too dismissive of findings ("that will never happen"), but an objective outsider can help you to understand what risks actually need to be addressed.

Furthermore, some vulnerabilities on their own may appear to be low risk and easily dismissed. But a skilled professional who is familiar with chaining vulnerabilities together to achieve complex compromises might recognize when low severity vulnerabilities, aggregated with other risks in your environment, could pose a higher risk to your organization.

It's important to make a distinction between vulnerability assessments and other forms of more involved assessment. By its very design, a vulnerability assessment will only be able to provide you with a list of (potential) vulnerabilities and misconfigurations. It is a great way to identify low-hanging fruit and get a general perspective as to the overall security health of your environment, but it is not going to be either exhaustive or imaginative in the way in which an environment's security posture is exercised. Getting a clean bill of health from a vulnerability assessment is certainly a positive, but don't mistake this for a declaration that the environment is therefore free of defects and is *secure*.

Penetration Testing

We looked briefly at penetration testing and what's involved in having a skilled white-hat security tester try to hack his way into your network or your application. Penetration testing is one of the most common security assessments, and unfortunately one of the least understood.

Good penetration testing combines a range of factors:

- A disciplined and structured approach to scoping and managing the testing itself.
- Testers with access to appropriate tooling that supports efficient and deep assessment.
- Experience and expertise with the systems and languages being assessed.

- The ability to build on first principles and adapt to novel environments quickly and creatively.

It may sound clichéd, but you get what you pay for with penetration testing, and cutting corners or going with inexperienced or low-skilled testers may result in an assessment that is little more than a vulnerability assessment.

Penetration Testing Is About Scope

Penetration testing is a scoped review. This means that typically you have engaged a team to test a certain component or level of your technology stack, and given them a fixed time period in which to do it.

Penetration testing can be scoped to any aspect of your application deployment, and it's important that you check this scope in when you are purchasing.

Tests can be scoped to:

Network
> The deployed infrastructure for your application, including the exposed software and services.

Application
> The complete application and its deployed components, excluding the operating system and host level.

Mobile app
> The testing of mobile application components, normally separated by target operating system.

Integration
> Testing the integration points between deployed components, sometimes including third-party systems and crossing trust boundaries in the architecture.

API
> Testing exposed APIs separately from the user interface components. This may or may not include testing the configuration of any API gateway or orchestration components.

Scoping also comes into play when you are considering the length of time that will be allocated to the assessment, as well as the focus that will be given to the underlying design and architecture versus the implementation.

Penetration testing is most often done as a final security check before pushing a major new release of a system to the final production environment. Most organizations hire a recognized penetration testing firm, let them hack for a couple of weeks, get the report, and because they left the test to so late in their project, try to fix whatever they can before they run out of time. In many cases the shipping date has already been set in stone, so fixes and mitigations may not even make it into the initial release itself.

These organizations miss the real value of a penetration test: to learn about how attackers think and work and use this information to improve their systems and the way that they design, build, and test their systems. A good term to keep in mind that captures this value well is *attack-driven defense*, the use of an attacker's perspective on your environment or application to drive a continual prioritization and improvement of the defense you choose to put in place.

Your goal shouldn't be to "pass the test." Organizations that look at penetration testing this way may stack the deck against the pen testers, containing their work and feeding them limited information so that the number of problems they can find is minimized. They often justify this by stating that black-box tests are more realistic, because the pen tester and an outside attacker both start with the same limited information.

But the more information that you provide to pen testers, the better job they can do, and the more that you can learn. *Gray-box* testing, where the tester knows how the system works, just not as well as your team does, beats black-box testing hands down. White-box testing is the next step in terms of making information available to the pen testers by giving them full source code access and allowing them to combine code analysis, architectural review, and dynamic hands-on testing during their assessment.

A number of different attack scenarios can be built around the constraints and allowances provided to an external pen testing team. The reality is that it takes a fairly mature security organization to be able to actually make real use of those differing perspectives. Far more common is the situation where the external assessment is the first time the solution in question will have been through an offensive security assessment, and it will be conducted on a limited budget. In these cases, one of your primary motivations should be to get out of the way of the testers and to allow them to put their experience to best use in identifying the parts of the solution that raise the most flags for them so that they can dig in and demonstrate successful attack scenarios and their impact.

In this regard, a white-box assessment will allow the testers to avoid wasting time understanding the limitations of the system and any security controls it may have, and go directly to the source to answer those questions. Typically for a one-to-two week assessment, a white-box test will return you far more coverage, as well as more fully exercised attack pathways, than a gray- or black-box test. It will often also provide more specific guidance in terms of remediation, as the testers will have seen the code and may well be able to identify the exact deficiency behind any finding. This makes it much easier for the team responsible for working with the results to get remediations in place in a timely fashion.

As we looked at in detail in Chapter 11, manual testing, including penetration testing, can't keep up with rapid Agile development or continuous delivery in DevOps. To meet compliance requirements (like PCI DSS) and governance, you may still need to schedule penetration testing activities on a regular basis, typically at least once per year. But instead of treating pen testing as a gate, think of it more as a validation and valuable learning experience for the entire team.

Red Teaming

Red Teaming is running an active attack against your operations to test not only the security of your environment as it actually works together in the day-to-day, but more importantly your incident detection and response and other defensive capabilities.

The goals and approach are different than a pen test. Instead of trying to uncover and prioritize vulnerabilities for you to fix, Red Teams actively exploit a vulnerability (or a chain of vulnerabilities) or use social engineering techniques to infiltrate the network and see how long it takes for your operations or security teams to discover what they are doing and react to them. Such an approach where you invite an external team to target your environment as a real group of attackers is also known as an *attack simulation* or a *goal-oriented attack*. The scope of Red Team engagements is very broad by definition or even *no holds barred*, with everything on the table.

Time and Scope Versus Goal-Oriented Testing

It's important to understand when you are scoping your external testing or review activities that you can choose how to structure the engagement.

Typically, penetration testing is a time-bounded exercise where the team will spend x number of days or weeks testing the in-scope systems and deliver its analysis.

Alternatively, Red Team testing can be objective focused instead of time or system scoped. In an objective-focused test, you set the team a challenge, such as *Alter a transaction* or *Gain root access on the production environment*. There are significantly fewer restrictions about how the team will get there, and this can yield more representative results.

In terms of time frame, Red Team engagements that the authors of this book have been involved with have lasted anywhere from six weeks to six months, with open-ended engagements where *it takes as long as it takes* not being unheard of.

Red Teams will find important vulnerabilities in systems. It is not uncommon for such engagements to produce zero-day vulnerabilities in both internal applications as well as commercial applications in use at an organization.

But their real value is helping your security and operations teams to learn and improve how to deal with real-world attack scenarios, conducted by highly motivated and skilled adversaries.

The deliverables that result from Red Team exercises are generally quite different from what you get from a pen test. Red Team reports often present findings in the form of attacker diaries, attack trees containing the pathways taken through an environment that led to a realized goal, and detailed descriptions of custom tools and exploits written specifically for the engagement. This offers more insight into the attacker mindset, with discussions covering the *why* as much as the *what*.

Failed attack pathways, things the testers tried and didn't succeed, are also incredibly important, as they provide a measure of effectiveness of security controls that may be in place and offer some qualitative measures of the defensive investments you have made.

Red Team engagements are not cheap, and to get the most from them, the security posture of an organization needs to be fairly mature. Early on in an organization's security journey, money may be better spent on a larger or more frequent set of penetration tests rather than opting for the much sexier goal-oriented-attack approach.

However, when you do feel you are in a position to benefit from working with a Red Team, then it can be one of the most enlightening and humbling experiences you, and your security program, can undergo. It can provide you some very insightful qualitative data that can answers questions that the more quantitative pen test and vulnerability assessment approaches cannot.

Again, the focus on learning should be paramount. Gaining a deep and nuanced insight into how a group of skilled and motivated adversaries traversed your environment should be used to inform your approaches to both defensive and detection measures.

Some organizations, especially large financial services and cloud services providers, have standing Red Teams that continuously run tests and attack simulations as a feedback loop back to security and incident response. We'll look at this approach some more in Chapter 13, *Operations and OpSec*.

Bug Bounties

If there's one type of external assessment that has ridden the hype-train over the 18–24 months that preceded the writing of this book, it's bug bounties. Inevitably, and unfortunately, with the hype have come misconceptions, misunderstandings, as well as plain-and-simple misinformation. Rest assured that despite what the internet may tell you, you're not grossly negligent if you don't currently run a bug bounty. In fact, you're more likely to be considered negligent if you enter into the world of bug bounties and your security program overall isn't in a mature enough place to be able to handle it. If you don't have a solid AppSec program in place, then you should invest in getting that up to scratch before even thinking *bug bounties*, if you don't, you will find things accelerating off ahead of you and quickly be in a place where it will be hard to cope.

With all of that said, bug bounties are definitely an option as your security program progresses. What follows is an effort to help you cut through the hype and view the value you may get back from a bug bounty.

How Bug Bounties Work

First, before we jump into all the ways in which bug bounties can support your security program, as well as the ways it can't, let's define what a bug bounty really is.

Bug bounties stem from the reality check that every internet-facing system or application is constantly under attack, whether you like that idea or not. Some of those attacks will be automated in nature and be the result of all sorts of scans and probes that constantly sweep the internet, and some of them will be more targeted in nature and have an actual human in the driver's seat. Regardless of the source, get comfortable with the fact that active attempts are being made to find vulnerabilities in your systems even as you read these words.

Bug bounties are the rational extension of this acceptance, where you are taking the next step from accepting this reality and actually encouraging people to probe your production systems, and most importantly to invite them to let you know what they find.

Furthermore, you make a public commitment that for issues brought to you that you can validate (or that meet some stated criteria), you will reward the submitter in some way. While this seems an entirely logical and rational approach to take when written out like this, it wasn't that long ago that a majority of organizations defaulted to sending the lawyers after anyone who brought to their attention issues that had been found. Unfortunately, there are still organizations that *lawyer up* when someone makes them aware of a security vulnerability rather than engaging, understanding, and rewarding them. It would be fair to say that this is increasingly considered an antiquated view and one that if you're reading this book, we hope you do not subscribe to.

The range of people running a bug bounty has grown considerably in a short time, with now everyone from big players like the Googles, Facebooks, and Microsofts of the world running them, to atypical candidates like the US Army, alongside a multitude of other players from all across the web. Bug bounties can clearly provide value even to those organizations with highly skilled internal teams staffed by the best and brightest.

Setting Up a Bug Bounty Program

With all that being said, deciding to run a bug bounty and engage with the vibrant communities that have built up around them is not a decision to be taken without due consideration.

First and foremost, you must understand that above all else, running a bug bounty is about engaging with a community, and such engagement requires the investment of time and money in some way, shape, or form. Viewing bug bounties as cheap pen tests is missing the point: you are building relationships between your organization's brand, the security practitioners you employ, and the wider security community. Seeing that community as a way to sidestep the costs involved with engaging with a dedicated pen testing team, or as a way to tick a box that shows you really *do* care about security, is going to inevitably backfire.

What follows is a list of quickfire tips, tricks, and things to keep in mind as you think about establishing a bug bounty program, derived from learning the hard way about this relatively new player in the assessment space:

In-house or outsource?
> One of the first decisions you will need to make is whether you are going to run your own bug bounty or use a third-party service to help run one for you. In-house programs give you ultimate control of your bounty, allowing you to design it exactly as you need. If you already have an established technical security team, it may work out cheaper than paying a third party to do what your internal security team is already being paid to do in terms of bug qualification and analysis.
>
> Third-party programs, however, have established communities of researchers ready to tap into, can act as a filtering function to reduce the noise you see compared to the signal of submissions, and will enable you to get up and running with a bounty in a short space of time. At the time of writing, the two most popular bug bounty services are Hackerone (*https://hackerone.com*) and Bugcrowd (*https://bugcrowd.com*). Third parties can't do everything, and there will always be a point at which people familiar with the application will have to determine the validity of a submission against your threat model as well as the way in which it needs to be addressed.

Rules of engagement
> While the real attacks against your systems follow no set of rules, it's reasonable (and expected) that a bug bounty will have some ground rules for participation. Typically, things covered in rules of engagements will be domains or applications that are considered to be in-scope, types of vulnerabilities that rewards will be given for as well as types of vulnerabilities that will not be rewarded, types of attacks that are off-limits (e.g., anything to do with denial of service is typically excluded). There may also be some legalease in these rules to satisfy your compa-

ny's or geography's legal requirements. It's definitely worth checking in with your legal eagles on what they need to see in any bug bounty rules page.

The internet has plenty of examples of bug bounty rules of engagement to use as inspiration for your own, but a good starting place would be to look at "Google Vulnerability Reward Program (VRP) Rules" (*https://www.google.com/about/appsecurity/reward-program/index.html*), as they have a well established and respected bounty program.

Rewards

Stating up front the rewards that researchers can expect if they were to find a vulnerability is also a good practice to follow. Setting expectations clearly starts off the relationship with the community in an open and honest way. Rewards can be hard cash, swag such as t-shirts and stickers (if a successful bounty submission is the only way to get that swag, all the better, exclusivity carries value), or public recognition of the finding itself.

Many programs will have scales associated with the rewards given, depending on the severity of the issues found. Some programs also increase the reward if the submitter has successfully found a vulnerability previously, in an effort to keep those people engaged with finding bugs in their apps and to become more deeply familiar with them. While most bug bounty programs will offer a range of rewards, it is worth noting that your program will be taken more seriously if you are paying in hard cash rather than just t-shirts and stickers (though you should definitely send t-shirts and stickers!).

Bounty pool size

Most companies will not have an open-ended budget for bug bounties, so you need to decide how much will be available to pay the participating researchers in the coming quarter or year. Different organizations will have different requirements and constraints, but a rule of thumb from one of the authors of this book was to allocate the cost of one single penetration test as the yearly bug bounty pool. In this way, the cost of the bug bounty becomes simple to budget for and can easily be justified as an extension of the existing pen test program.

Hall of fame

While it may seem trivial, a hall of fame or some other way of recognizing the people who have contributed to your bug bounty program and help make your application more secure is a very important aspect to the community you engage with. Names, twitter handles, or website links, along with the date and type of finding, are all typical aspects of a bug bounty hall of fame. Some programs go further and gamify the hall of fame, with repeat submitters being given special ranking or denotations. A great example of a fun and engaging hall of fame is the one put together by Github (*https://bounty.github.com*). Get inventive with the way you recognize the contributions from researchers, and it will pay you back in terms of participation and kudos.

Provide some structure for submissions

Free-form submissions to a bug bounty program bring with them a few niggles that can be best to iron out at the very beginning. Providing some kind of form or way for your bountiers to make you aware of the issue they have found in a structured manner can be really helpful in making sure that you are getting all the information you need from the outset to be able to do timely and efficient analysis and triage. Not all of your submitters will be seasoned security researchers, and asking them clearly for the information you need will help them get all the relevant information across to you. This isn't to say you should deny free-form input altogether, just that you should attempt to provide some guardrails to your submitters.

An example of one such submission form can be seen on Etsy's bug bounty page (*https://www.etsy.com/bounty*). There are many advantages to this approach, beyond reducing some of the manual back-and-forth communication with a submitter as you try and get the details about the issue you actually want. One big advantage is the ability to more accurately track metrics relating to your program in terms of the kind of issues you are seeing, their frequency, and how the trends are evolving over time. Another advantage is that it helps keep one issue per submission rather than multiple issues being discussed at once, which is ripe for confusion. Single issues can be assigned tickets and responders and their time to resolution tracked.

Timely response, open, and respectful communication

As has already been said, fostering relationships with the community of researchers who engage in bug bounties is key to the success of your program. Often the first step in that is responding in a timely manner to people providing you with candidate vulnerabilities and keeping them in the loop as to where in the validation or fixing process their submission is.

It's also important to recognize that your first language, or English as the lingua franca of the internet, may not be the submitter's mother tongue, which may mean a few rounds of communication have to take place to establish exactly what is being discussed. This can sometimes be frustrating for everyone involved, but polite clarification, along with the assumption of best intent, will go a long way to building trust and respect with your community.

On a related note, politely saying, "thanks, but no thanks" for those submissions that are incorrect or that show a lack of understanding for the topic at hand (or computers in general!) is a skill that must be developed, as you are sure to get some plain crazy things sent your way.

Pay on time

This is pretty self-explanatory, but once a submission has been validated as a real issue that meets the rules, getting payment to the researcher in a timely fashion is very important. Planning ahead of time the mechanism by which you are going to make payment of any monetary reward is something you need to do. Different programs take different approaches here. Some send pre-paid credit cards (some even using cards with a custom design printed on them). Others send funds electronically using PayPal or wire transfers.

Payment can sometimes be challenging with the combination of different countries and tax laws. For example, at the time of writing, PayPal cannot be used to send funds to either India or Turkey, two countries from which you will likely see a good volume of submissions. Finding good methods to pay researchers from these and other countries is something you should look into up front so as to not have unexpected delays when trying to pay out your bountiers. Payment is one of the areas using a third-party bug bounty service will help take off of your plate, as it will be the one interfacing with the researchers and getting them their money, so don't underestimate the value that adds.

It's kind of a one-way door

Once you start a public bug bounty, it is going to be pretty hard to roll it back at a future date. So if you're moving forward, realize that this is a lifestyle choice you expect to stick to, not a fad that you can walk away from when it's not as cool any more.

Don't underestimate the initial surge

When you start your bounty, realize you're in some senses opening the flood gates. Be prepared to meet the initial demand, as this is when you are building your relationship with the community. First impressions count. The first two weeks will likely see a dramatically higher volume of submissions than your program will see on average, so ensure you set aside time and resources to validate, investigate, and triage the flow of submissions as they come in. Depending on the size of the team that will be fielding the submissions, it may get little else done for a couple of weeks. Make sure you time your program to open at a point in your calendar when this makes sense.

There will be duplicate, cookie-cutter, and just plain terrible submissions

Accept from the outset that there will always be some people looking to game the system and to get paid for doing as little as possible, or even to make money off nonissues. Be comfortable with the fact that out of the total number of submissions your program will receive, a majority of them will not result in a bounty and will just be noise.

Also realize that as soon as a new general vulnerability or issue is discovered and made public, the bug bounty community will hunt across every site trying to find instances of it that they can claim a bounty for. Have a clear plan of how you handle duplicate submissions of a valid vulnerability (often the first submission *wins* and is the only person who will receive a reward), as well as how you handle submissions that focus on a risk that you have accepted or that is an intended feature of the system itself.

Using Bug Bounties to Get More from Pen Testers

As useful as bug bounties may be, they will never replace an experienced penetration testing team. They can, however, be used to make penetration tests more effective. The rationale is that if you're paying testers to pen test your environment, they will want to have some results to show. If they return to you empty-handed, their chances of being asked back will likely be reduced. If critical findings are hard to come by, pen testers will often resort to padding out a report with lower-impact or trivial issues just so they have something so show to you. This isn't a good use of your money or their time.

If you are running a bug bounty, your apps will be undergoing a constant sweep for the lower-hanging fruit, with smaller bounties being paid out for these less critical issues when they are found. This leaves little to no easy pickings for pen testers to pad out their reports with. In these cases, the pen testing company is likely to throw additional testers or more senior testers at the engagement as they start to near the completion date, so that they can have something to show you. Desperate pen testers often get mighty inventive and can discover some of the more obscure bugs when pressed.

In this way, bug bounties can give you not only the continual assessment and discovery of vulnerabilities, but also make the more expensive external engagements you invest in work harder for you and return better value.

Are You Sure You Want to Run a Bug Bounty?

The whirlwind tour of the world of bug bounties is almost complete, so why might you not want to run one when all you hear about them is that they are the greatest thing ever? Well, first consider who might be telling you about them. A lot of the promotion is coming from people with vested interests in the widest adoption of bug bounties, hopefully on their platform. Outside the marketing side of the hype cycle, there are aspects of bounties that may result in you deciding they are not the right thing for you:

You need to have a fairly well-established response capability.
> While your systems are being attacked all the time, opening your window to the internet and shouting, "Come at me, bro" takes things to the next level. You need to be confident in your ability to evaluate, respond, and fix issues that are raised

to you in a timely manner. If you are not able to perform these functions, then a bounty program can do more harm than good.

The always-on nature of a bug bounty is both a strength and a weakness. Scheduled engagements allow you to set aside time for triage and response. New bounties still come in at any time day or night and may require immediate response (even to nonissues). This leads into the potential danger of burnout for your team, the cost of which can manifest in multiple ways, none of which are good.

The signal to noise is low.

If you think that once you have a bug bounty program you will be receiving round-the-clock, high-quality pen testing, then think again. Most of the submissions will be false positives. For those that are real issues, a majority will be low-value, low-impact vulnerabilities. All will require investigation, follow up, and communication, none of which is free. You can partner with a bug bounty provider to help, but that leads to the next point.

Outsourcing your bug bounty program means others will be representing your security brand.

Partnering with a third-party bounty platform provider means that you are also outsourcing your security brand, which, as discussed in Chapter 15, *Security Culture*, is something that is hard fought and easily lost. Having a third party represent the security of your applications and environments means that you are placing them in a position where they can directly impact the trust that your customers and the wider public have with your products and organization. This is not something to do lightly.

The line between bounty and incident is a fuzzy one.

When does a bounty attempt blur into becoming a real security incident? This is a question that's hard to answer in an absolute sense, and is likely one that you don't have much control over aside from publishing a set of rules. Bountiers are incentivized to maximize the severity and impact of their findings, as they get paid more the *worse* something is (unlike a pen testing contract that normally pays a set rate regardless of findings).

This has resulted in situations where an *overeager* (to put it politely) bountier trying to demonstrate the severity of his finding, or one who is dissatisfied with the response or bounty you gave him, crosses the line into actually causing a security incident that impacts real customer data and that needs to be responded to in a formal and complete way. The cost of managing and responding to just one such incident, alongside the PR fallout, will dwarf the cost of the bug bounty program.

Bug bounties can result in bad PR.

Be comfortable that some of the folks in the community you are engaging with will not be happy with how you classify, respond, or pay out for an issue, and will seek leverage by going public with their side of the story. Threats of *publishing this on my blog* or *I will tweet about this* will be a regular occurrence and may now and again result in PR that is not overly positive. An additional word of caution will be that you should assume that all communications with the bug bounty community will appear publicly at some point, and so author them accordingly, however troublesome or annoying the submitter may be.

The return will likely diminish over time, and the cost will increase.
The uncomfortable truth is that as the number of bug bounty programs grow, the community of researchers fueling these programs' success will not grow in proportion. This means that to continue to attract the interest of the community, you will have to make your program more attractive than the one next door. This means increasing the payouts, resulting in a program that will continue to increase in cost.

You also need to take into account that you are going to see the biggest ROI in the early days of the program, when there is the most low-hanging fruit to be found, and that the volume of real, impactful issues found will likely diminish over time. Taken to the extreme, this means there will be a point reached where bug bounties are economically not the best investment you can make.

Ultimately, the decision about whether to run a big bounty is not a simple one, and is one that only you can determine if/when is the right time to jump in. Just be cautious of jumping on the bandwagon before you have a good handle on what the pros and cons mean for your organization.

ISO 29147 Vulnerability Disclosure

The International Standards Organization has deemed that vulnerability disclosure is a key security process and worthy of an ISO standard. ISO 29147 (*http://bit.ly/iso-publicly-available-standards*) outlines the process and requirements for managing vulnerability disclosure, and is now available free of charge.

Whether you are planning to use a third party to manage your bug bounty program, or manage this on your own, this standard can guide you on how to handle vulnerability findings from outside researchers, and your obligations to report and remediate these findings.

Configuration Review

A *configuration review* is a manual or scanning-based review of a system configuration against hardening best practices, or one of the standards like the CIS Benchmarks that we will look at in Chapter 13, *Operations and OpSec*.

This can be a good health check for the runtime platform, the OS or VMs or containers, and runtime software like Apache or Oracle that can be difficult to set up correctly.

As much as possible, this kind of checking should be replaced by running automated compliance scans on your own, on a regular basis.

Secure Code Audit

Even if your team is trained in secure coding and consistently using automated code review tools, there are cases where you should consider bringing in a security specialist to audit your code. This is especially valuable in the early stages of a project, when you are selecting and building out your frameworks, and want to validate your approach. You may also need to bring in outside reviewers in response to a security breach, or to meet compliance obligations.

Most auditors start by running an automated code review tool to look for obvious security mistakes and other low-hanging fruit. Then they will focus in on security features and security controls, and data privacy protection. But good reviewers will also find and report other kinds of logic bugs, runtime configuration problems, and design concerns as they go.

Code audits can be expensive, because they require a lot of manual attention and specialized skills. You need to find someone with security knowledge and strong coding skills who understands your development environment and can come up to speed quickly with the design and the team's coding conventions.

Code auditors face the same challenges as other code reviewers. They can get hung up on style issues and misled by code that is poorly structured or too complex. And code auditing is exhausting work. It can take at least a couple of days for the reviewers to understand the code well enough to find important problems, and within a few more days they will reach a plateau.

So it makes sense to aggressively time-box these reviews, and you should be prepared to help the auditors as much as possible during this time, explaining the code and design, and answering any questions that come up. Assigning experienced developers to work with the auditors will help to ensure that you get good value, and it should provide a valuable opportunity for your team to learn more about how to do its own security code reviews.

Crypto Audit

Crypto audits have been broken out as a separate class of assessment from the more generic code audits for one simple reason: they are really hard and need a distinctly specialist skillset to do. Of all the areas of external assessment, crypto audits have the fewest experienced practitioners available and will be the hardest to source expertise on. It's not uncommon to have to go on a waiting list and have your test scheduled far out into the future due to the lack of available people qualified in the art. Don't, however, let this this tempt you to cut corners and substitute a true crypto auditor for someone who has more availability.

The reasons behind needing a specialist crypto audit fall into two main categories:

1. You want to validate your use of cryptography in a wider system. The questions you're asking here center around *Am I getting the properties I think I am from my use of cryptography?* and *Have I inadvertently undermined the guarantees a particular set of crypto primitives offers somehow?*

2. You are designing and/or implementing your own cryptography primitives, and you want to validate that the design and implementation of your algorithms actually do what you want them to.

If you fall into the second category, stop. Go for a walk, probably a drink, and then revisit whether designing and implementing new or novel crypto primitives is actually the best solution to the problem you are trying to solve. Crypto is hard, like mind-bogglingly hard, and the most seemingly innocuous slip-up can bring everything tumbling down around you.

For most situations you will find yourself in, there are well-established, off-the-shelf components and patterns that will solve your problem, and there is no need to get inventive and roll your own. If, despite the walking and drinking, you're convinced that you need to design some new algorithm, or alter an existing one, or that there is no implementation of an existing algorithm in the form or language you need, then the best advice we can give is ensure you have in-house expertise from the inception of the project, or reach out to an external specialist for help. Even after doing that, you will want a separate set of eyes to review whatever is produced to perform additional validation.

If your needs fall into the first category, then still realize crypto is hard and that gaining an external perspective on both the use and application of cryptography is something that can carry huge value. The findings and results that come back from your first crypto review will likely be surprising to you. Even for usages you thought were simple, there can be level of nuance, right down to the compiler being used to generate the binaries, so that you may start to question your own understanding of computers and numbers in general. This is good. This is what you're paying for.

If your solution is making heavy use of crypto, then hopefully this helps stress the importance of getting some specialist eyes on it. The only remaining thing to say would be that once your crypto has undergone validation, it should be a part of your code base that isn't touched outside of the rarest of circumstances, and should hopefully only be interfaced through well-defined APIs.

Choosing an External Firm

There are a number of factors that go in to choosing an external partner or consultant.

Why are you getting help?

- To meet a compliance mandate?
- As a proactive health check?
- Reactive response to a failed audit or a breach?

How much commitment will it require from your team to ensure that it is successful?

A configuration review or a standardized vulnerability assessment can be done without too much involvement from your team, at least until it comes time to review the report. You care about cost and availability and evidence of capability.

But a code audit or a Red Team exercise requires both parties to work much closer together, which means that you need to know more about the people involved, and how well you will work together.

What kind of security assessor are you working with?

There are different types of external providers that offer different value:

Security testing factories
  IT security firms with highly structured offerings designed to meet compliance requirements. Often highly automated, methodology-driven, scalable, and repeatable.

Expert consultants and boutique shops
  Individuals or small specialist teams relying heavily on expert skills and experience rather than methodologies, customized offerings, and custom-built tools. You get what you pay for in these cases: the people who present at Black Hat or Defcon or OWASP conferences, or who teach security classes, can be expensive (depending on their reputation and availability), and there aren't that many of them around.

Enterprise service providers
  Security services provided as part of a larger, more comprehensive IT services program that includes other consulting, training, and tools across multiple programs and projects. Highly scalable, repeatable, and expensive.

Auditor or assessor

> Services from a recognized auditing firm, such as a CA firm, or from another qualified assessor (like a PCI QSA). Checklist-driven, assesses systems against specific regulatory requirements or some other standard.

It's relatively straightforward to evaluate a security testing factory, by looking at its methodology. It can be harder to choose a boutique or an individual consultant, because you need to have a high level of confidence in their skills and expertise and working approach. And you must be able to trust them to maintain confidentiality and to work carefully, especially if you are allowing them inside your production network.

Experience with Products and Organizations Like Yours

How important is it to get reviewers or testers with experience in your specific industry? Or with specific technologies? Again, this depends on the type of assessment. Vulnerability scanning is industry-agnostic, and so is network pen testing. For code audits or application pen tests, you'll obviously need someone who understands the language(s) and application platform. Familiarity with your problem domain or industry would make her job—and yours—much easier, but it's usually not a deal breaker.

Actively Researching or Updating Skills

Do you care if the testers or reviewers have certifications?

A CISSP or Certified Ethical Hacker or a SANS certification is a baseline of capability. But it's obviously much better to get an expert who has helped to define the field than someone without much real experience who passed a test.

Certifications are not the be-all and end-all, and our advice would not be to over-index on them.

Meet the Technical People

If you are working with a boutique or contractors, it's important to meet with the people who will be doing the work, and build a relationship, especially if you expect to work with them for a while. This isn't required, or practical, if you are working with a testing factory or an enterprise supplier: what's important here is how comprehensive their methodology is and how comfortable you are with their engagement model.

It also depends on what kind of work you need done. It's not important to get to know the engineer or analyst who is doing a vulnerability scan. All that you care about are the results. But it's important to build trust with a consultant who is auditing your code, and to make sure that you're comfortable with his expertise as well as his working style, so that he doesn't have a negative impact on the team.

Finally, be on the lookout for the *bait-and-switch*. It's not unheard of for companies to introduce you to their most senior, experienced, or famous consultants while they are trying to get your business and then give the work to more junior consultants. Take the time to get the names of who exactly will be working on an engagement and, depending on the job, establish ways that you can stay in communication with them while the assessment progresses (email, phone calls, IRC, or Slack are all channels often used).

Getting Your Money's Worth

Make sure that you understand what you are getting for your money.

Are you paying for someone with a certificate to run a scanning tool and provide an "official" report? Or are you paying for high-touch experts, who may take extra time to build custom tools and custom exploits to assess your system?

Race to the Bottom

As the security industry has grown and the need for engaging with external players has become more widely recognized, the money that stands to be made has grown significantly and has driven ever-increasing competition between service providers.

Using price as a differentiator quickly became the norm, which has forced service providers to find ways to reduce the cost of conducting assessments. Most often this is done by replacing skilled people with automated tools. What was once by definition the contracting of individuals skilled in the art of system compromise has increasingly given way to the selling of highly automated services that aim to reduce the elements of human insight and skill.

While this is not to say that contracting highly skilled attackers is no longer possible, it is merely a warning that you should do your homework on the services you are procuring and understand what it is you are actually getting. As with many things in life, you get what you pay for; and if the price seems too good to be true, it probably is.

Don't Waste Their Time

Most security assessments (except bug bounties and goal-focused Red Team engagements) are done on a tight time budget. Make sure that you don't waste any of this time. Get everything set up and ready for the pen testers or auditors in advance. Give them the credentials and other access needed to do their jobs. Make sure that someone is available to help them, answer questions, review results, and otherwise keep them from getting blocked.

Challenge the Findings

Make sure that your team clearly understands the findings and what to do about them. Each finding should state what the problem was, the risk level, where and how the problem was found, what steps you need to take to reproduce the problem on your own, and how to fix it, all in language that you can follow.

If you don't understand or don't agree with findings, challenge them. Get rid of unimportant noise and false positives, and work through misunderstandings (there will always be misunderstandings). Make sure that you understand and agree with the risk levels assigned so that you can triage and prioritize the work appropriately.

Having said all of this, commit to yourself that you will never commit the cardinal sin of engaging in an external assessment, asking the assessors to change their report, severities, or remove findings because they make you or your team look bad. It's surprisingly common for the recipients of tests to ask for "severe" or "high" findings to be classified to a lower level so that their bosses don't see them. If that is the situation you are in, there are more fundamental problems with you or your organization. The whole purpose of external assessments is to find problems and for you to remediate and learn from them. Don't be tempted to undermine this process and the value it can bring to the security of your organization and customers.

Insist on Results That Work for You

Don't just accept a PDF report. Insist that results are provided in a format that you can easily upload directly into your vulnerability manager or your backlog system, using XML upload functions or taking advantage of API support between tools.

Put Results into Context

Assessors will often provide you lists of vulnerabilities classified by the OWASP Top 10 or some other compliance-oriented scheme. Organize the results in a way that makes sense for you to work with so that it is clear what the priorities are and who needs to deal with them.

Include the Engineering Team

It should not just be the responsibility of the security team to work with outsiders. You should get the team involved, including developers and operations and the Product Owner, so that they understand the process and take it seriously.

Measure Improvement Over Time

Once you have entered findings from assessments into a vulnerability manager or a project management tool like Jira, you can collect and report on metrics over time:

- How many vulnerabilities are found
- How serious are they
- How long are they taking to remediate

Where are your risks? Are assessments effective in finding real problems? Is your security program improving?

It's easy to understand this once you have the raw information.

Hold Review/Retrospective/Sharing Events and Share the Results

Use Agile retrospectives or a DevOps postmortem structure to discuss serious findings. Treat them as "near misses": an incident that could have happened but luckily was caught in time.

As we will see in Chapter 13, *Operations and OpSec*, a postmortem review can be a powerful tool to understand and solve problems, and to strengthen the team by bringing them together to deal with important issues. This can also help to build a sense of ownership within the team, ensuring that problems will get fixed.

Spread Remediation Across Teams to Maximize Knowledge Transfer

In larger organizations, it's important to share results across teams so that people can learn from each other's experience. Look for lessons that can be applied to more than one team or one system so that you can get more leverage from each assessment. Invite members from other teams to your postmortem reviews so that they can learn about the problems you found and to get their perspectives on how to solve them.

Rotate Firms or Swap Testers over Time

As we've discussed, some of the key benefits of external reviews are to get new and different perspectives, and to learn from experts who have unique experience. Therefore it's useful to get more than one external reviewer involved, and rotate between them, or switch to different vendors over time:

- In the first year, it takes time and effort to select a vendor, get contracts and NDAs and other paperwork in place, understand their engagement model and the way that they think and talk, and for them to understand how you work and talk.

- In the second year you get better value, because it's faster and easier to set up each engagement, and it's easier for you to understand and work with the results.
- Once it becomes too easy and too predictable, it's time to switch to another vendor.

Obviously this may not be possible to do if you are locked in with an enterprise services partner on a strategic level, but you could look for other ways to change the rules of the game and get new value out of them, such as asking for different kinds of assessments.

Key Takeaways

External reviews can be daunting, even for the most experienced teams. Choosing the right vendors and the right services, and learning how to get the most from these events, can really increase their value:

- There are a range of services that an external firm can offer: choose the right one on a per system and project basis.
- External reviews can provide objectivity and specialist skills that may not be naturally available inside your organization.
- It takes effort to get the most of your testing results. Work with your testing firm to make sure you understand the results and that they are fed into pipelines and systems.
- Choose your firm well, and don't forget this is a big marketplace: you can ask questions and shop around.
- Take advantage first of simpler, cheaper assessments like vulnerability assessments to catch obvious problems before you go on to pay for more expensive engagements. Don't pay expensive consultants to find problems that you can find for less, or find on your own.
- Don't try to narrow the scope and set up tests or audits so you that you know you will "pass." Give pen testers and other reviewers access and information so that they can do a thorough job, giving them a better chance to find real problems for you.
- Bug bounties can be an effective way to find security holes in your systems. But keep in mind that setting up and running a bug bounty program is an expensive and serious commitment. If you go in thinking that this is a way to get pen testing done on the cheap, you're going to be unpleasantly surprised. An effective bug bounty program won't be cheap to run, and it's hard to back out of once you've started.

Bug bounty programs are about community management more than about testing. Be prepared to treat all security researchers patiently and politely, respond to their findings in a meaningful way, and reward them fairly. Otherwise you can damage your organization's brand, disrupt operations, and even encourage malicious behavior. Someone in your organization will have to spend a lot of time reviewing and understanding what they find, and often a lot more time politely explaining to someone who put a lot of their own time into finding, duplicating, and writing up a problem, why what he found (and expects to be paid for) was not, in fact, a bug, or at least not a bug that you are prepared to fix.

- If you are not taking advantage of external reviews to learn as much as you can from these experts, you are wasting their time and your money.

CHAPTER 13

Operations and OpSec

Agile teams often come up against a wall with operations, because they can deliver changes much faster than ops can handle. But the walls between dev and ops are coming down, as operations functions move to the cloud, and as operations teams start their own Agile transformations.

This is what the DevOps movement is all about: applying ideas and engineering practices and tools from Agile development and Agile values to operations, and finding ways to bring operations and developers closer together. These development teams don't hand off work to operations and sustaining engineering, and then go on to the next project. Instead, developers and operations share responsibility for getting the system into production and making sure that the system is running correctly, for the life of the system.

Developers are getting directly involved in packaging and provisioning, runtime configuration and deployment, monitoring and incident response, and other operations functions. As operations moves infrastructure into code, they are adopting the same engineering practices and tools as developers, learning about refactoring and test-driven development and continuous integration. We are starting to see more demand for hybrid roles like site reliability engineers (SREs) patterned after Google: engineers who have a strong background in operations as well as strong software development skills.

But whether developers are working in DevOps teams or not, they need to understand how to deploy and set up their systems correctly and safely, how the system works under real-world load conditions and in failure situations, and what information and tools operations needs to effectively run and monitor and troubleshoot the system. And they should do everything that they can to reduce friction with ops and to improve feedback from production.

In this chapter we'll look at the natural intersections between dev and ops and security, and how Agile development creates new challenges—and opportunities—for operations and security.

System Hardening: Setting Up Secure Systems

While much of the popular focus of security discussion is around the discovery of application-level bugs and flaws that can be used in subtle ways to gain advantage, the reality is that the correct configuration and setup of the operating environment is imperative to being secure. Designing and building your application to be secure is important, but it isn't enough.

One of the first things that a pen tester—or an attacker—will do is to enumerate your environment to see the options that may be available in terms of attack. The combination of systems, applications, their interrelations, and the people who used them are often referred to as the *attack surface*, and it is these building blocks that will be used to map out potential routes to compromise.

An important point to note is that from an attacker's perspective, people are just as important, and potentially vulnerable, as technology. So from a defender's perspective, system hardening needs to be done with a clear understanding of how those systems will get used by people in reality and not just in an idealized scenario.

Firewalls that aren't configured properly, ports that shouldn't have been left open, default admin passwords, out-of-date operating systems, software packages with known exploits, passwords being shared on an internal wiki page or in a git repo, and other common and easily avoided mistakes all present opportunities that can be used to pick apart an environment in furtherance of an attacker's goal.

Many of the tools discussed in this book that developers rely on to build software are designed to make it as easy as possible for people like them to pick up and start using right away. As we'll see in this chapter, as teams continue their Agile development journey and deploy code both more frequently and in a more automated fashion, this can create a serious set of security risks.

Runtime software is no better. Databases, web servers, and even the operating system and security tools are also packaged so that they are simple to set up and get running using their default configs. Attackers know this, and know how to take advantage of it.

This means that after you have provisioned a system and installed the necessary software packages and finally have things working correctly, you'll need to go through extra steps to harden the system against attack. This applies to your production systems, and, as we'll see, even extends into your build and test environments. Of course, any systems that have internet-facing components will require even greater levels of scrutiny.

System-hardening steps focus on reducing your attack surface. As Justin Schuh of Google stated succinctly on Twitter: "Security at its core is about reducing attack surface. You cover 90% of the job just by focusing on that. The other 10% is luck."

Common hardening techniques include things like the following:

- Disabling or deleting default accounts and changing default credentials
- Creating effective role separation between human and system principals (i.e., don't run * as root!)
- Stripping down the installation and removing software packages, or disabling daemons from auto-starting that are not needed for the system's role
- Disabling services and closing network ports that are not absolutely required
- Making sure that the packages that you do need are up to date and patched
- Locking down file and directory permissions
- Setting system auditing and logging levels properly
- Turning on host-based firewall rules as a defense-in-depth protection
- Enabling file integrity monitoring such as OSSEC or Tripwire to catch unauthorized changes to software, configuration, or data
- Ensuring the built-in security mechanisms for each platform, such as full disk encryption, or SIP (System Integrity Protection) (*https://en.wikipedia.org/wiki/ System_Integrity_Protection*) on macOS, or ALSR/DEP on Windows, are enabled and functioning correctly.

As we'll see, this is not a complete list—just a good starting point.

 For a quick introduction on how to harden a Linux server, check out this excerpt from *The Defensive Security Handbook* (O'Reilly) by Lee Brotherston and Amanda Berlin.

You will need to go through similar steps for all the layers that your application depends on: the network, the OS, VMs, containers, databases, web servers, and so on.

Detailed discussions of each of these areas are books in and of themselves, and continue to evolve over time as the software and systems you use change and have new features added. Ensuring you stay familiar with the best practices for hardening the technologies that make up your runtime stack is one of the key aspects of operational security overall, and is worth investing in as deeply as you are able.

Regulatory Requirements for Hardening

Some regulations such as PCI DSS lay out specific requirements for hardening systems. In Requirement 2.2, PCI DSS requires that you have documented policies for configuring systems that include procedures for:

- Changing vendor-supplied defaults and removing unnecessary default accounts
- Isolating the function of each server (using physical isolation, VM partitioning, and/or containers) so that you don't have applications or services with different security requirements running together
- Enabling only those processes and services that are required, and removing scripts, drivers, subsystems, and filesystems that aren't needed
- Configuring system parameters to prevent misuse

Understanding the specific hardening requirements of whatever regulations you are required to comply with is quite obviously a key aspect of being compliant with those regulations and something you will need to demonstrate during the auditing process.

Hardening Standards and Guidelines

Outside of regulations, there are hardening standards and guidelines for different platforms and technologies that explain what to do and how to do it. Some of the more detailed, standardized guidelines include:

- US DoD STIGs (Security Technical Implementation Guides) (*http://iase.disa.mil/stigs/Pages/index.aspx*) for hardening platforms for use on US Department of Defense projects
- United States Government Configuration Baseline (USGCB) guides (*https://usgcb.nist.gov/*)
- CIS (Center for Internet Security) Benchmarks (*https://benchmarks.cisecurity.org/*)

There are also product-specific hardening guides published by vendors such as Red Hat, Cisco, Oracle, and others, as well as guides made freely available by practitioners in various parts of the security space.

The Center for Internet Security (*https://www.cisecurity.org*) is a cross-industry organization that promotes best practices for securing systems. It publishes the Critical Controls (*https://www.cisecurity.org/critical-controls.cfm*), a list of 20 key practices for running a secure IT organization, and the CIS benchmarks, a set of consensus-based security hardening guidelines for Unix/Linux and Windows OS, mobile devices, network devices, cloud platforms, and common software packages. These guidelines are designed to meet the requirements of a range of different regulations.

The CIS checklists are provided free in PDF form. Each guide can run to hundreds of pages, with specific instructions on what to do and why. They are also available in XML format for members to use with automated tools that support the SCAP XCCDF specification (*https://scap.nist.gov/specifications/xccdf/*).

Hardening guides like the CIS specifications are intended to be used as targets to aim for, not checklists that you must comply with. You don't necessarily need to implement all of the steps that they describe, and you may not be able to, because removing a package or locking down access to files or user permissions could stop some software from working. But by using a reference like this you can at least make informed risk trade-offs.

Challenges with Hardening

System hardening is not an activity that occurs once and is then forgotten about. Hardening requirements continuously change as new software and features are released, as new attacks are discovered, and as new regulations are issued or updated.

Because many of these requirements tend to be driven by governments and regulators that inevitably involve committees and review boards, the process of publishing approved guidelines is bureaucratic, confusing, and s l o w. It can take months or years to get agreement on what should and shouldn't be included in any given hardening specifications before being able to get them published in forms that people can use. The unfortunate reality is that many such official guides are for releases of software that are already out of date and contain known vulnerabilities.

It's a sad irony that you can find clear and approved guidance on how to harden software which has already been replaced with something newer that should be safer to use, if you only knew how to configure it safely. This means that you will often have to start off hardening new software on your own, falling back to first principles of the reduction of attack surface.

As mentioned, many hardening steps can cause things to break, from runtime errors in a particular circumstance, to preventing an application from starting altogether. Hardening changes need to be made iteratively and in small steps, testing across a range of cases along the way to see what breaks.

The problem of balancing hardening against functionality can feel as much an art as a science. This can be even more challenging on legacy systems that are no longer being directly supported by the vendor or author.

Even when using systems that are brand new and supported by their vendor, the process of hardening can leave you feeling very much alone. For example, one of us recently had to harden an enterprise video conferencing system. This required countless emails and phone calls with the vendor trying to get definitive information on the function of the various network ports that the documentation stated needed to be open. The end result: the customer had to explain to the vendor which subset of specific ports was actually needed for operation, in place of the large ranges that the vendor had requested. Regrettably, this is not an uncommon situation, so be prepared to have to put in some groundwork to get your attack surface as small as possible, even with commercial solutions.

Another trend that is making hardening more challenging still is the blurring of the boundary between operating system and online services. All the major general-purpose operating systems now come with a range of features that make use of online services and APIs out of the box. Depending on your environment, this *cloudification* of the OS can pose significant worries in terms of both security and privacy; and it makes the task of building trust boundaries around endpoints increasingly difficult.

Frustratingly, system and application updates can also undermine your hardening effort, with some updates changing configuration settings to new or default values. As such, your hardening approach needs to include testing and qualification of any new updates that will be applied to those systems being hardened.

Hardening is highly technical and detailed oriented, which means that it is expensive and hard to do right. But all the details matter. Attackers can take advantage of small mistakes in configuration to penetrate your system, and automated scanners (which are a common part of any attacker's toolbox) can pick many of them up easily. You will need to be careful, and review closely to make sure that you didn't miss anything important.

Automated Compliance Scanning

Most people learned a long time ago that you can't effectively do all of this by hand: just like attackers, the people who build systems need good tools.

There are several automated auditing tools that can scan infrastructure configuration and report where they do not meet hardening guides:

- CIS members can download and use a tool called CIS-CAT, which will scan and check for compliance with the CIS benchmarks.
- OpenSCAP (*https://www.open-scap.org*) scans specific Linux platforms and other software against hardening policies based on PCI DSS, STIG, and USGCB, and helps with automatically correcting any deficiencies that are found.
- Lynis (*https://cisofy.com/lynis/*) is an open source scanner for Linux and Unix systems that will check configurations against CIS, NIST, and NSA hardening specs, as well as vendor-supplied guidelines and general best practices.

- Freely contributed system checkers for specific systems can also be found on the internet, examples being osx-config-check (*https://github.com/kristovatlas/osx-config-check*) and Secure-Host-Baseline (*https://github.com/iadgov/Secure-Host-Baseline*)

- Some commercial vulnerability scanners, like Nessus and Nexpose and Qualys, have compliance modules that check against CIS benchmarks for different OSes, database platforms, and network gear.

> Compliance scanning is not the same as vulnerability scanning. Compliance scanners check against predefined rules and guidelines (good practices). Vulnerability scanners look for known vulnerabilities such as default credentials and missing patches (bad practices). Of course there are overlaps here, because known vulnerabilities are caused by people not following good practices.
>
> Scanners like Nessus and Nexpose scan for vulnerabilities as well as compliance with specific guidelines, using different policy rules or plug-ins. On Red Hat Linux only, OpenSCAP will scan for compliance violations, as well as for vulnerabilities.
>
> Other scanners, like the OpenVAS project, only check for vulnerabilities. OpenVAS is a fork of Nessus from more than 10 years ago, before Nessus became closed source. It scans systems against a database of thousands of known weaknesses and exploits, although it has built up a bit of reputation for flagging false positives, so be prepared to validate its results rather than taking them as truth.

If you are not scanning your systems on a regular basis as part of your build and deployment pipelines—and correcting problems as soon as the scanners pick them up—then your systems are not secure.

Approaches for Building Hardened Systems

Automation can also be used to build hardened system configurations from the start. There are two basic strategies for doing this:

Golden image

Bake a hardened base template or "golden image" that you will use to stand up your systems. Download a standardized operating system distribution, install it on a stripped-down machine, load the packages and patches that you need, and walk through hardening steps carefully until you are happy. Test it, then push this image out to your production systems.

These runtime system configurations should be considered immutable: once installed, they must not be changed. If you need to apply updates or patches or make runtime configuration changes, you must create a new base image, tear the machines down, and push a completely new runtime out, rebuilding the machines from scratch each time. Organizations like Amazon and Netflix manage their deployments this way because it ensures control at massive scale.

Tools like Netflix's Aminator (*https://github.com/Netflix/aminator*) and Hashi-Corp's Packer (*https://www.packer.io*) can be used to bake machine images. With Packer, you can configure a single system image and use the same template on multiple different platforms: Docker, VMware, and cloud platforms like EC2 or Azure or Google Compute Engine. This allows you to have your development, test, and production on different runtime platforms, and at the same time keep all of these environments in sync.

Automated configuration management

Take a stripped-down OS image, use it to boot up each device, and then build up the runtime following steps programmed into a configuration management tool like Ansible, Chef, Puppet, or Salt. The instructions to install packages and apply patches, and configure the runtime including the hardening steps, are checked in to repos like any other code, and can be tested before being applied.

Most of these tools will automatically synchronize the runtime configuration of each managed system with the rules that you have checked in: every 30 minutes or so, they compare these details and report variances or automatically correct them.

However, this approach is only reliable if all configuration changes are made in code and pushed out in the same way. If engineers or DBAs make ad hoc runtime configuration changes to files or packages or users that are not under configuration management, these changes won't be picked up and synchronized. Over time, configurations can drift, creating the risk that operational inconsistencies and vulnerabilities will go undetected, and unresolved.

Both of these approaches make system provisioning and configuration faster, safer, and more transparent. They enable you to respond to problems by pushing out patches quickly and with confidence, and, if necessary, to tear down, scratch, and completely rebuild your infrastructure after a breach.

Automated Hardening Templates

With modern configuration management tools like Chef and Puppet, you can take advantage of hardening guidelines that are captured directly into code.

One of the best examples is DevSec (*https://github.com/dev-sec*), a set of open source hardening templates originally created at Deutsche Telekom, and now maintained by contributors from many organizations.

This framework implements practical hardening steps for common Linux base OS distributions and common runtime components including ssh, Apache, nginx, mysql, and Postgres. A full set of hardening templates are provided for Chef and Puppet, as well as several playbooks for Ansible. All the templates contain configurable rules that you can extend or customize as required.

The hardening rules are based on recognized best practices, including Deutsche Telekom's internal standards, BetterCrypto.org's Applied Crypto Hardening guide (*https://bettercrypto.org/static/applied-crypto-hardening.pdf*), which explains how to safely use encryption, and various hardening guides.

Hardening specifications like these are self-documenting (at least for technical people) and testable. You can use automated testing tools like Serverspec, which we looked at in Chapter 12, to ensure that the configuration rules are applied correctly.

DevSec comes with automated compliance tests written using InSpec (*https://github.com/chef/inspec*), an open source Ruby DSL. These tests ensure that the hardening rules written in Chef, Puppet, and Ansible all meet the same guidelines. The DevSec project also includes an InSpec compliance profile for the Docker CIS benchmark (*https://github.com/dev-sec/cis-docker-benchmark*) and a SSL benchmark test (*https://github.com/dev-sec/ssl-benchmark*).

InSpec works like Serverspec in that it checks the configuration of a machine against expected results and fails when the results don't match. You can use it for test-driven compliance, by writing hardening assertions that will fail until the hardening steps are applied, and you can also use these tests to verify that new systems are set up correctly.

InSpec tests are specifically designed to be shared between engineers and compliance auditors. Tests are written in simple English, and you can annotate each scenario to make the intention explicit to an auditor. For each testing rule, you can define the severity or risk level, and add descriptions that match up to compliance checklists or regulatory requirements. This makes it easy to walk through the test code with an auditor and then demonstrate the results.

Here are a couple of examples of compliance tests from the InSpec GitHub:

```
Only accept requests on secure ports - This test ensures that a web server is
only listening on well-secured ports.

describe port(80) do
  it { should_not be_listening }
end

describe port(443) do
  it { should be_listening }
  its('protocols') {should include 'tcp'}
end
```

Use approved strong ciphers - This test ensures that only enterprise-compliant ciphers are used for SSH servers.

```
describe sshd_config do
    its('Ciphers') ↵
    { should eq('chacha20-poly1305@openssh.com,aes256-ctr,aes192-ctr,aes128-ctr') }
end
```

InSpec is also the basis of Chef's Compliance Server product. Developers at Chef are working on translating automated hardening profiles like CIS from SCAP XML into InSpec, so that these rules can be automatically checked against your complete infrastructure.

Network as Code

In traditional systems development, network security and application security are mostly done independently of each other. Developers may need a firewall ACL opened or a routing change, or they might need know how to deal with proxies in a DMZ. But otherwise these worlds don't touch each other much.

This is changing as applications are moved to the cloud, where more network rules and management capabilities are exposed to developers—and where developers can no longer rely on perimeter defenses like network firewalls to protect their applications.

Network appliances such as firewalls, intrusion detection or prevention systems, routers, and switches are still often set up and configured (and hardened) by hand, using custom scripts or device consoles. But over the last few years, network vendors have added REST APIs and other programmable interfaces to support software-defined networking; and tools like Ansible, Chef, and Puppet have added support for programmatically configuring network devices, including switches and firewalls from providers like Cisco Systems, Juniper Networks, F5 Networks, and Arista Networks.

Taking advantage of this tooling, "network as code" could become the same kind of game changer as "infrastructure as code" has been for managing servers and storage and cloud service platforms. All the same advantages apply:

- Network device configurations can be versioned and managed in source control, providing an audit trail for change management and for forensics.

- Configuration rules for network devices can be expressed using high-level languages and standardized templates, making changes simpler and more transparent to everyone involved.

- Network configuration changes can be reviewed and tested in advance, using some of the same tools and practices that we've described, instead of relying on ping and traceroute after the fact.
- Changes can be automatically applied across many different devices to ensure consistency.
- Network configuration changes can be coordinated with application changes and other infrastructure changes, and deployed together, reducing risk and friction.

In many organizations the network operations group is a completely separate team that may well predate the systems operations team, which means embracing concepts like those above will require the same kind of cultural and engineering changes that are taking place in the way that server infrastructure is managed in DevOps teams. But it holds open the promise of making network configuration and management more open to collaboration, simpler to understand, and simpler and safer to change. All of which is good for security.

Monitoring and Intrusion Detection

It is a fact of modern life that you cannot bring up a computer or network device on the internet without it being port scanned within minutes. Your detection systems must be able to tell the difference between the background noise of failing attempts by bots scanning your system perimeter and successful breaches, as well as distinguishing between normal and attacker behavior: is that low and slow data exfiltration, or the periodic update of a stock ticker?

In large organizations, security monitoring is usually done by a specialized security operations center (SOC), staffed by analysts sifting through attack data, intrusion alerts, and threat feeds. In smaller organizations, security monitoring might be outsourced to a managed security services provider (MSSP) like SecureWorks or Symantec—or it might not be done at all. This kind of monitoring is mostly focused at the network level, examining network traffic for known bad signatures or unusual patterns in activity.

Operations engineers monitor servers, networks, storage, databases, and running applications using tools like Nagios or services like Zabbix or New Relic to check on system status and to watch out for indications of slowdowns or runtime problems: hardware failures, disks filling up, or services crashing.

Applications monitoring is done to check on the health of the application, and to capture metrics on use. How many transactions were executed today? Where is most of the traffic coming from? How much money did we make? How many new users tried out the system? And so on.

Monitoring to Drive Feedback Loops

Agile, and especially DevOps and Lean startup teams, use information about how the system is running and how it is being used to shape design, making data-driven decisions about which features are more usable or more useful, and what parts of the system have reliability or quality problems. They build feedback loops from testing and from production to understand where they need to focus, and where they need to improve. This is quite different than many traditional approaches to security where the security goals are defined in advance and delivered in the forms of edicts that must be met.

DevOps teams can be metrics-obsessed, in the same way that many Agile teams are test-obsessed. Monitoring technologies like Etsy's statsd+carbon+graphite stack (*https://github.com/etsy/statsd*), Prometheus (*https://prometheus.io*), Graylog (*https://www.graylog.org*), or Elastic Stack (*https://github.com/elastic*), or cloud-based monitoring platforms like Datadog or Stackify, make it relatively cheap to create, collect, correlate, visualize, and analyze runtime metrics.

DevOps leaders like Etsy, Netflix, and PayPal track thousands of individual metrics across their systems and capture hundreds of thousands of metrics events every second. If someone thinks that a piece of information might be interesting, they make it a metric. Then they track it and graph it to see if anything interesting or useful jumps out from the rest of the background noise. At Etsy, they call this: "If it moves, graph it," and are the first to admit that they "worship at the church of graph."

Using Application Monitoring for Security

The same tools and patterns can also be used to detect security attacks and to understand better how to defend your system.

Runtime errors like HTTP 400/500 errors could indicate network errors or other operations problems—or they could be signs of an attacker trying to probe and spider the application to find a way in. SQL errors at the database level could be caused by programming bugs or a database problem, or by SQL injection attempts. Out of memory errors could be caused by configuration problems or coding mistakes—or by buffer overflow attacks. Login failures could be caused by forgetful users, or by bots trying to break in.

Developers can help operations and the security team by designing transparency and visibility into their applications, adding sensors to make operational and security-related information available to be analyzed and acted on.

Developers can also help to establish baselines of "normal" system behavior. Because they have insight into the rules of the application and how it was designed to be used, they should be able to see exceptions where other people may just see noise in logs or charts. Developers can help to set thresholds for alerts, and they will jump when an "impossible" exception happens, because they wrote the assert which said that this could never happen. For example, if a server-side validation fails and they know that the same check was also implemented at the client, this means that someone is attacking the system using an intercepting proxy.

Alerting and Analytics Tools

There are some cool alerting frameworks and toolsets available to help you implement real-time application operations and security alerting.

If you are using the Elasticsearch-Logstash-Kibana (ELK) stack as your monitoring stack, you might want to look at using Yelp's Elastalert (*https://github.com/Yelp/elastalert*), which is built on top of Elastic Search.

Etsy's 411 alert management system (*https://github.com/etsy/411*) is also based on ELK, and helps with setting up alert rules and handling alert workflows.

AirBnB has open sourced StreamAlert (*https://github.com/airbnb/streamalert*), a comprehensive serverless real-time data analysis framework.

You can use this information not only to catch attackers—hopefully before they get too far—but also to help you to prioritize your security work. Zane Lackey at Signal Sciences, and former head of Etsy's security engineering team, calls this *attack-driven defense*. Watch what attackers are doing, learn how they work, and identify the attacks that they are trying. Then make sure that you protect your system against these attacks. A vulnerability found by a code scanner or in a threat modeling review might be important. But a vulnerability that you can see attackers actively trying to exploit in production is critical. This is where you need to immediately focus your testing and patching efforts.

Detection systems for compromise should be set up on isolated networks and devices, otherwise compromise of a machine can enable the attackers to disable the detection systems themselves (although a good security system will notice a machine that does not check-in as well). Network taps and parallel monitoring and detection tools work particularly well in this regard.

It is also worth recognizing ahead of time that the use of SSL/TLS within your environment not only increases the cost and challenge posed to adversaries intercepting traffic, but also to your security and network operations team who are trying to do the same—albeit with different intent. If you are switching from a non-SSL'd network setup internally to one that includes encryption on the internal links, enter the new architecture with an idea of the places in which you will require monitoring and design accordingly.

To protect from insider attacks, make sure that you set up monitoring tools and services so that they are are administered separately from your production systems, to prevent local system administrators from being able to tamper with the security devices or policies, or disable logging. You should also pay special attention to any staff who can or do rotate between security and systems administration teams.

Auditing and Logging

Auditing and logging are fundamental to security monitoring, and are important for compliance, for fraud analysis, for forensics, and for nonrepudiation and attack attribution: defending against claims when a user denies responsibility for an action, or helping to make a case against an attacker.

Auditing is about maintaining a record of activity by system principals: everything that they did, when they did it, in what order. Audit records are intended for compliance and security analysts and fraud investigators. These records must be complete in order for them to be useful as evidence, so auditing code needs to be reviewed for gaps in coverage, and audit records need to be sequenced to detect when records are missing.

When designing an auditing system, you will have to carefully balance requirements to record enough information to provide a clear and complete audit trail against transactional overheads and the risk of overloading the backend auditing and analytics systems, especially if you are feeding this information into a SIEM or other security analytics platform.

But the guiding principle should be that as long as you can afford it, you should try to audit everything that a user does, every command or transaction, and especially every action taken by administrators and operations. With the cost of storage on a seemingly never-ending decline, the decision on how much audit data should be kept can be made based on privacy and data retention regulations, rather than budget.

In distributed systems, such as microservices architectures, audit logs should ideally be pooled from as many systems as possible to make it easy for auditors to join information together into a single coherent story.

Application logging is a more general-purpose tool. For operations, logging helps in tracking what is happening in a system, and identifying errors and exceptions. As a developer, logging is your friend in diagnosing and debugging problems, and your fallback when something fails, or when somebody asks, "How did this happen?" Logs can also be mined for business analytics information, and to drive alerting systems. And for security, logs are critical for event monitoring, incident response, and forensics.

One important decision to make in designing your logging system is whether the logs should be written first for people to read them, or for programs to parse them. Do you want to make log records friendlier and more verbose for a human reader, or more structured and efficient so that they can be more easily interpreted by a tool to drive alerting functions and IDS tools or dashboards?

With either approach, ensure that logging is done consistently within the system, and if possible, across all systems. Every record should have common header information, clearly identifying the following:

- Who (userid and source IP, request ID).

- Where (node, service ID, and version—version information is especially important when you are updating code frequently).

- What type of event (INFO, WARN, ERROR, SECURITY).

- When (in a synchronized time format).

Teams should agree on using a logging framework to take care of this by default, such as Apache Logging Services (*https://logging.apache.org/*), which include extensible logging libraries for Java, .NET, C++, and PHP.

As we outlined in Chapter 5, some regulations such as PCI DSS dictate what information must be, and should not be, logged, and how long certain logs need to be retained.

At a minimum, be sure to log:

- System and service startup and shutdown events.

- All calls to security functions (authentication, session management, access control, and crypto functions), and any errors or exceptions encountered in these functions.

- Data validation errors at the server.

- Runtime exceptions and failures.

- Log management events (including rotation), and any errors or exceptions in logging.

Be careful with secrets and sensitive data. Passwords, authentication tokens, and session IDs should never be written to logs. If you put personally identifiable information (PII) or other sensitive data into your logs, you may be forcing your log files and log backup system into scope for data protection under regulations such as PCI DSS, GLBA, or HIPAA.

For more information about how and what to log, and what not to log, from an application security perspective, check out OWASP's Logging Cheat Sheet (*https://www.owasp.org/index.php/Logging_Cheat_Sheet*). Also make sure to read "How to do Application Logging Right" (*http://arctecgroup.net/pdf/howtoapplogging.pdf*) by Dr. Anton Chuvakin and Gunnar Peterson.

Another important consideration is log management.

Logging should be done to a secure central logging system so that if any individual host is compromised, the logs can't be destroyed or tampered with, and so that attackers can't read the logs to identify weaknesses or gaps in your monitoring controls. You can consolidate logs from different applications and nodes using a log shipper like rsyslog (*http://www.rsyslog.com/*), logstash (*https://github.com/elastic/logstash*), or fluentd (*http://www.fluentd.org/*), or cloud-based logging services like loggly (*https://www.loggly.com/*) or papertrail (*https://www.papertrail.io/uk/*).

Log rotation and retention has to be done properly to ensure that logs are kept for long enough to be useful for operations and security forensic investigation, and to meet compliance requirements: months or even years, not hours or days.

Proactive Versus Reactive Detection

You won't be able to find all security problems in near real time using immediate runtime detection or online analytics (despite what many vendors may claim!). Finding a needle in a haystack of background noise often requires sifting through big data to establish correlations and discover connections, especially in problems like fraud analysis, where you need to go back in time and build up models of behavior that account for multiple different variables.

When thinking about detection, many people only consider the ability to identify and respond to events as they happen, or how to catch and block a specific attack payload at runtime. But when you see a problem, how can you tell if it is an isolated incident, or something that has been going on for a while before you finally noticed it?

Many security breaches aren't identified until several weeks or months after the system was actually compromised. Will your monitoring and detection systems help you to look back and find what happened, when it happened, who did it, and what you need to fix?

You also need to make cost and time trade-off decisions in monitoring. Flooding ops or security analysts with alerts in order to try to detect problems immediately isn't effective or efficient. Taking extra time to sum up and filter out events can save people wasted time and prevent, or at least reduce, alert fatigue.

Catching Mistakes at Runtime

The more changes that you make to systems, the more chances that there are to make mistakes. This is why Agile developers write unit tests: to create a safety net to catch mistakes. Agile teams, and especially DevOps teams that want to deploy changes to test and production more often, will need to do the same thing for operations, by writing and running runtime checks to ensure that the application is always deployed correctly, configured correctly, and is running safely.

Netflix and its famous "Simian Army" (*https://github.com/Netflix/SimianArmy*) show how this can be done. This is a set of tools which run automatically and continuously in production to make sure that their systems are always configured and running correctly:

- Security Monkey (*https://github.com/Netflix/security_monkey*) automatically checks for insecure policies, and records the history of policy changes.
- Conformity Monkey (*https://github.com/Netflix/SimianArmy/wiki/Conformity-Home*) automatically checks configuration of a runtime instance against predefined rules and alerts the owner (and security team) of any violations.
- Chaos Monkey (*https://github.com/netflix/chaosmonkey*) and her bigger sisters Chaos Gorilla and Chaos Kong are famous for randomly injecting failures into production environments to make sure that the system recovers correctly.

Netflix's monkeys were originally designed to work on Amazon AWS, and some of them (Chaos Monkey, and more recently, Security Monkey) run on other platforms today. You can extend them by implementing your own rules, or you can use the same ideas to create your own set of runtime checkers, using an automated test framework like Gauntlt, which we looked at in Chapter 12, or InSpec, or even with simpler test frameworks like JUnit or BATS (*https://github.com/sstephenson/bats*).

These tests and checks can become part of your continuous compliance program, proving to auditors that your security policies are continuously being enforced. Besides preventing honest mistakes, they can also help to catch attacks in progress, or even discourage attackers.

An often overlooked benefit of having an environment that is in constant and unpredictable state of flux (often referred to as embracing chaos engineering), is that it presents a moving target to an adversary, making it harder to enumerate the operational environment, as well as making it harder for the adversary to gain a persistent foothold. Neither is made impossible, but the cost of the attack is increased.

When writing these checks, you need to decide what to do when an assert fails:

- Isolate the box so that you can investigate.

- Immediately terminate the service or system instance.

- Try to self-repair, if the steps to do so are clear and straightforward: enabling logging or a firewall rule, or disabling an unsafe default.

- Alert the development team, operations, or security.

Safe SSL/TLS

Setting up SSL/TLS correctly is something that most people who build or operate systems today need to understand—and something that almost everybody gets wrong.

Ivan Ristic at Qualys SSL Labs (*https://www.ssllabs.com*) provides detailed and up-to-date guidelines on how to correctly configure SSL/TLS (*http://bit.ly/github-configure-ssl-tls*).

SSL Labs also provides a free service (*https://www.ssllabs.com/ssltest/*) which you can use to check out the configuration of your website against the guidelines provided, and give you a report card. A big fat red F will force people to pick up the guidelines and figure out how to do things properly.

Making sure that SSL is set up correctly should be a standard part of your tests and operational checks. This is why both Gauntlt and BDD-Security include tests using sslyze (*https://github.com/nabla-c0d3/sslyze*), a standalone security tool. This is something that you need to do continuously: the cryptography underpinning SSL and TLS is under constant attack, and what got you an A last week might be only a D today.

Runtime Defense

In addition to monitoring for attacks and checking to make sure that the system is configured safely, you may want to—or need to—add additional protection at runtime.

Traditional network IPS solutions and signature-based Web Application Firewalls (WAFs) that sit somewhere in front of your application aren't designed to keep up with rapid application and technology changes in Agile and DevOps. This is especially true for systems running in the cloud, where there is no clear network perimeter to firewall off, and where developers may be continuously deploying changes to hundreds or thousands of ephemeral runtime instances across public, private, and hybrid cloud environments.

Cloud Security Protection

Recognizing the risks that come with the newer operational approaches, there are a number of security startups offering different runtime protection services for applications in the cloud, including automated attack analysis, centralized account management and policy enforcement, continuous file integrity monitoring and intrusion detection, automated vulnerability scanning, or micro-segmentation:

- Alert Logic (*https://www.alertlogic.com*)
- CloudPassage Halo (*https://www.cloudpassage.com/products/*)
- Dome9 SecOps (*https://dome9.com*)
- Evident.io (*http://evident.io*)
- Illumio (*https://www.illumio.com/home*)
- Palerra LORIC (*http://palerra.com/platform/*) (Acquired by Oracle and now known as Oracle CASB Cloud Service)
- tCell (*https://www.tcell.io*)
- Threat Stack (*https://www.threatstack.com*)

These services hook into cloud platform APIs and leverage their own analytics and threat detection capabilities to replace yesterday's enterprise security "black boxes."

Other startups like Signal Sciences (*https://www.signalsciences.com*) now offer smarter next-generation web application firewalls (NGWAFs) that can be deployed with cloud apps. They use transparent anomaly detection, language dissection, continuous attack data analysis, and machine learning, instead of signature-based rules, to identify and block attack payloads.

A word of caution for all things machine learning! Big data and machine learning are the hottest topics in tech right now; they are irresistible for vendors to include in their products with wild proclamations of them being the silver bullet security has been waiting for. As with all vendor claims, approach from the point of skepticism and inquire for details as to exactly what machine learning techniques are being employed, and for data to back up the relevance to solving the problem at hand rather than just having another buzzword bingo box ticked. False positives can often be a killer and the tuning periods required to train the models to the actual production environment have undermined more than one deployment of the next great security-panacea-in-a-box.

RASP

Another kind of defensive technology is *runtime application self-protection* (RASP), which instruments the application runtime environment to catch security problems as they occur. Like application firewalls, RASP can automatically identify and block attacks as they happen. And like application firewalls, you can use RASP to protect legacy apps or third-party apps for which you don't have source code.

But unlike a firewall, RASP is not a perimeter-based defense. RASP directly instruments and monitors your application runtime code, and can identify and block attacks directly at the point of execution. RASP tools have visibility into application code and runtime context, and examine data variables and statements using data flow, control flow, and lexical analysis techniques to detect attacks while the code is running. They don't just tell you about problems that could happen—they catch problems as they happen. This means that RASP tools generally have a much lower false positive (and false negative) rate than application firewalls or static code analysis tools.

Most of these tools can catch common attacks like SQL injection and some kinds of XSS, and include protection against specific vulnerabilities like Heartbleed using signature-based rules. You can use RASP as a runtime defense solution in blocking mode, or to automatically inject logging and auditing into legacy code, and provide insight into the running application and attacks against it.

There are only a handful of RASP solutions available today, mostly from small start-ups, and they have been limited to applications that run in the Java JVM and .NET CLR, although support for other platforms like Node.js, PHP, Python, and Ruby are now starting to emerge:

- Contrast Security (*https://www.contrastsecurity.com/rasp*)
- HPE Application Defender (*http://bit.ly/hpe-application-defender*)
- Immunio (*https://www.immun.io*)
- Prevoty (*https://www.prevoty.com*)
- Waratek (*http://www.waratek.com*)

RASP can be a hard sell to a development team—and an even harder sell to the operations team. You have to convince team members to place their trust in the solution's ability to accurately find and block attacks, and to accept the runtime overhead that it imposes. RASP also introduces new points of failure and operational challenges: who is responsible for setting it up, making sure that it is working correctly, and dealing with the results?

OWASP AppSensor: Roll Your Own RASP

OWASP's AppSensor project (*http://appsensor.org*) provides a set of patterns and sample Java code to help you to implement application-layer intrusion detection and response directly inside your app.

AppSensor maps out common detection points in web applications: entry points in the code where you can add checks for conditions that should not happen under normal operations. Then it defines options for how to deal with these exceptions, when to log information and when you should consider blocking an attack and how to do it. It shows you how to automatically detect—and protect against—many common attacks.

But RASP could provide a compelling "quick fix" for teams under pressure, especially teams trying to support insecure legacy or third-party systems, or that are using Web Application Firewalls to protect their apps and are fighting with the limitations of this technology.

Incident Response: Preparing for Breaches

Even if you do everything already discussed, you still need to be prepared to deal with a system failure or security breach if and when it happens. Create playbooks, call trees, and escalation ladders so that people know who has to be involved. Map out scenarios in advance so that when bad things happen, and everyone is under pressure, they know what to do and how to do it without panicking.

Security Breaches and Outages: Same, but Different

Operations teams and security incident response teams both need to act quickly and effectively when something goes wrong. They need to know how and when to escalate, and how to communicate with stakeholders. And they need to learn from what happened so that they can do a better job next time.

But their priorities are different. When you are dealing with an operational outage or serious performance problem, the team's goal is to restore service as quickly as possible. Security incident response teams need to make sure that they understand the scope of the attack and contain its impact before they recover—and get snapshot runtime images and collect logs for forensic analysis before making changes.

Operational and security concerns can cross over, for example, in the case of a DDOS attack. The organization needs to decide which is more important, or more urgent: restore service, or find the source of the attack and contain it?

Get Your Exercise: Game Days and Red Teaming

Planning and writing playbooks isn't enough. The only way to have confidence that you can successfully respond to an incident is to practice doing it.

Game Days

Amazon, Google, Etsy, and other online businesses regularly run game days, where they run through real-life, large-scale failures, such as shutting down an entire data center to make sure that their failover procedures will work correctly—and that they are prepared for exceptions that could come up.

These exercises can involve (at Google, for example) hundreds of engineers working around the clock for several days, to test out disaster recovery cases and to assess how stress and exhaustion could impact the organization's ability to deal with real accidents.

At Etsy, game days are run in production, even involving core functions such as payments handling. Of course, this begs the question, "Why not simulate this in a QA or staging environment?" Etsy's response is, first, the existence of any differences in those environments brings uncertainty to the exercise; second, the risk of not recovering has no consequences during testing, which can bring hidden assumptions into the fault tolerance design and into recovery. The goal is to reduce uncertainty, not increase it.

These exercises are carefully tested and planned in advance. The team brainstorms failure scenarios and prepares for them, running through failures first in test, and fixing any problems that come up. Then, it's time to execute scenarios in production, with developers and operators watching closely, and ready to jump in and recover, especially if something goes unexpectedly wrong.

Less grand approaches to game days can also be pursued on a regular basis, with scenarios like those shared by the Tabletop Scenarios Twitter stream (*https://twitter.com/badthingsdaily*) being a great source of *what if* conversations to promote brainstorming among team members over coffee.

Red Team/Blue Team

You can take many of the ideas from game days, which are intended to test the resilience of the system and the readiness of the DevOps team to handle system failures, and apply them to security attack scenarios through *Red Teaming*.

Organizations like Microsoft, Intuit, Salesforce, and several big banks have standing Red Teams that continuously attack their live production systems. Other organizations periodically run unannounced Red Team exercises, using internal teams or consultants, to test their operations teams and security defenses, as we outlined in Chapter 12.

Red Teaming is based on military Capture the Flag exercises. The Red Team—a small group of attackers—tries to break into the system (without breaking the system), while a Blue Team (developers and operations and security engineers) tries to catch them and stop them. Red Team exercises try to follow real-world attack examples so that the organization can learn how attacks actually happen and how to deal with them.

Some of these exercises may only run for a few hours, while others can go on for days or weeks to simulate an advanced, persistent threat attack.

The Red Team's success is measured by how many serious problems it finds, how fast it can exploit them (mean time to exploit), and how long it can stay undetected.

The Blue Team may know that an attack is scheduled and what systems will be targeted, but it won't know the details of the attack scenarios. Blue Teams are measured by MTTD and MTTR: how fast they detected and identified the attack, and how quickly they stopped it, or contained and recovered from it.

Red Teaming gives you the chance to see how your system and your ops team behave and respond when under attack. You learn what attacks look like, to train your team how to recognize and respond to attacks, and, by exercising regularly, to get better and faster at doing this. And you get a chance to change how people think, from attacks being something abstract and hypothetical, to being something tangible and immediate.

Over time, as the Blue Team gains experience and improves, as it learns to identify and defend against attacks, the Red Team will be forced to work harder, to look deeper for problems, to be more subtle and creative. As this competition escalates, your system—and your security capability—will get stronger.

Intuit, for example, runs Red Team exercises the first day of every week (they call this Red Team Mondays (*https://www.acast.com/eyeonsecurity/red-blue-and-intuit*)). The Red Team identifies target systems and builds up its attack plans throughout the week, and publishes its targets internally each Friday. The Blue Teams for those systems will often work over the weekend to prepare, and to find and fix vulnerabilities on their own, to make the Red Team's job harder. After the Red Team Monday exercises are over, the teams get together to debrief, review the results, and build action plans. And then it starts again.

Most organizations won't be able to build this kind of capability in-house. It takes a serious commitment and serious skills. As we discussed in Chapter 12, you may need to pull in outside help to help run Red Team exercises.

Blameless Postmortems: Learning from Security Failures

Game days and Red Team exercises are important learning opportunities. But it's even more important to learn as much as you can when something actually goes wrong in production, when you have an operational failure or security breach. When this happens, bring the team together and walk through a postmortem exercise to understand what happened, why, and how to prevent problems like this from happening again.

Postmortems build on some of the ideas of Agile retrospectives, where the team meets to look at what it's done, what went well, and how it can get better. In a postmortem, the team starts by going over the facts of an event: what happened, when it happened, how people reacted, and then what happened next. Included are dates and times, information available at the time, decisions that were made based on that information, and the results of those decisions.

By focusing calmly and objectively on understanding the facts and on the problems that came up, the team members can learn more about the system and about themselves and how they work, and they can begin to understand what they need to change.

There are several sources of information that you can use to build up a picture of what happened, why, and when, in your postmortem analysis. This includes logs, emails, records of chat activity, and bug reports. Etsy has open-sourced Morgue (*https://github.com/etsy/morgue*), an online postmortem analysis tool which has plug-ins to pull information from sources like IRC and Jira, as well as logs and monitor snapshots, to help create postmortem reports.

Facts are concrete, understandable, and safe. Once the facts are on the table, the team can start to ask why errors happened and why people made the decisions that they made, and then explore alternatives and find better ways of working:

- How can we improve the design of the system to make it safer or simpler?
- What problems can we catch in testing or reviews?
- How can we help people to identify problems earlier?
- How can we make it easier for people to respond to problems, to simplify decision making, and reduce stress—through better information and tools, or training or playbooks?

For this to work, the people involved need to be convinced that the real goals of the postmortem review are to learn—and not to find a scapegoat to fire. They need to feel safe to share information, be honest and truthful and transparent, and to think critically without being criticized or blamed. We'll talk more about how to create a blameless and trusting working environment, and look more at issues around trust and learning in postmortems, in Chapter 15, *Security Culture*.

Operations failures are in many ways easier to deal with than security breaches. They are more visible, easier to understand and to come up with solutions. Engineers can see the chain of events, or they can at least see where they have gaps and where they can improve procedures or the system itself.

Security breaches can take longer to understand, and the chain of causality is not always that clear. You may need to involve forensics analysts to sift through logs and fill in the story enough for the team to understand what the vulnerabilities were and how they were exploited, and there is often a significant time lag between when the breach occurred and when it was detected. Skilled attackers will often try to destroy or tamper with evidence needed to reconstruct the breach, which is why it is so important to protect and archive your logs.

Securing Your Build Pipeline

Automating your build, integration, and testing processes to pull from your repositories upon commit into a beautifully automated pipeline is a key milestone in the Agile life cycle. It does, however, come with a new set of responsibilities—you now have to secure the thing!

Given the tasks you delegate to your build pipeline and the privileges it will inevitably require, it rapidly becomes a critical piece of infrastructure and therefore a very attractive target of attack.

This attractiveness increases again if you are fully embracing continuous deployment, where each change is automatically deployed into production after it passes through testing.

Build and deployment automation effectively extends the attack surface of your production system to now include your build environment and toolchains. If your repositories, build servers, or configuration management systems are compromised, things get very serious, very quickly.

If such a compromise provides read access, then data, source code, and secrets such as passwords and API keys are all open to being stolen. If the compromise provides write or execution privileges, then the gloves really come off, with the possibility for backdooring applications, injection of malware, redirection or interception of production traffic, or the destruction of your production systems.

Even if a test system is compromised, it could provide an attacker with enough of a path back into the automated pipeline to cause damage.

If you lose control of the build pipeline itself, you also lose your capability to respond to an attack, preventing you from pushing out patches or hot fixes.

In addition to protecting your pipeline from outside attackers, you need to protect it from being compromised by insiders, by ensuring that all changes are fully authorized and transparent and traceable from end to end so that a malicious and informed insider cannot bypass controls and make changes without being detected.

Do a threat model of your build pipeline. Look for weaknesses in the setup and controls, and gaps in auditing or logging. Then, take these steps to secure your configuration management environment and build pipeline:

1. Harden the runtime for your configuration management, build, and test environments.

2. Understand and control what steps are done in the cloud.

3. Harden your build, continuous integration, and continuous delivery toolchains.

4. Lock down access to your configuration management tools.

5. Protect keys and secrets.

6. Lock down source and binary repos.

7. Secure chat platforms (especially if you are following ChatOps).

8. Regularly review logs for your configuration management, build, and test environments.

9. Use Phoenix Servers for build slaves and testing—create these environments from scratch each time you need them, and tear them down when you are done.

10. Monitor your build pipelines the same way that you do production.

That's a lot. Let's explore each of these steps in more detail.

Harden Your Build infrastructure

Harden the systems that host your source and build artifact repositories, the continuous integration and continuous delivery server(s), and the systems that host configuration management, build, deployment, and release tools. Treat them the same way that you treat your most sensitive production systems.

Review firewall rules and network segmentation to ensure that these systems, as well as your development and test systems, are not accidentally exposed to the public internet, and that development and production environments are strictly separated. Take advantage of containers and virtual machines to provide additional runtime isolation.

Understand What's in the Cloud

Scaling build and testing using cloud services is easy and attractive. Ensure that you clearly understand—and control—what parts of your build and test pipelines are done on-premises and what is performed in the cloud. The use of services in the cloud has many advantages, but can introduce trust issues and significantly expand the attack surface that you need to manage.

Holding your code repos in the cloud using GitHub, Gitlab, or BitBucket makes perfect sense for open source projects (of course), and for startups and small teams. These services provide a lot of value for little or no investment. But they are also juicy targets for attackers, increasing the risk that your code, and whatever you store in your code (like secrets), could be compromised in a targeted attack, or scooped up in a widespread breach.

Cloud-based code repository managers like GitHub are under constant threat. This is because attackers know where to look, and what to look out for. They know that developers aren't always as careful as they should be about using strong passwords, and resist using multifactor authentication and other protections, and they also know that developers sometimes mistakenly store proprietary code in public repos. These mistakes, and coding or operational mistakes by the service providers, have led to a number of high-profile breaches over the past few years.

If your developers are going to store proprietary code in the cloud, take appropriate steps to protect the code:

1. Ensure that developers use strong authentication (including multifactor authentication).
2. Carefully check that private repos are, in fact, private.
3. Monitor your GitHub repos using a tool like GitMonitor (*https://gitmonitor.com*).
4. Regularly scan or review code to make sure that it does not contain credentials, before it gets committed.

The potential impact here extends beyond just your organization's repositories and into the personal repositories of your developers. The propensity for developers to share their *dotfiles* with the world has been the initial entry point for many an internet to internal network compromise.

If you are using hosted continuous integration and build services like Travis CI or Codeship, check to make sure that access is set up correctly, and make sure that you understand their security and privacy policies.

Finally, as with any SaaS solution, it becomes imperative that you control access to those systems tightly and revoke access permissions when people switch roles or leave the company. If your investment in cloud-based services is nontrivial, then you should consider using a single-sign-on (SSO) solution to control access to those applications via a single identity. Maintaining multiple, distinct accounts across different systems is an invitation for things to slip through the cracks during off-boarding. Given the global accessibility (by design) of cloud based applications, the use of multifactor authentication (MFA) to help protect against the risks of credential theft becomes a baseline requirement.

Harden Your CI/CD Tools

Harden your automated build toolchain. Most of these tools are designed to be easy for developers to get set up and running quickly, which means that they are not secure by default—and it may be difficult to make them safe at all.

Jenkins, one of the most popular automated build tools, is a good example. Although the latest version includes more security capabilities, most of them are turned off out of the box, including basic authentication and access control, as the website explains:[1]

> In the default configuration, Jenkins does not perform any security checks. This means the ability of Jenkins to launch processes and access local files are available to anyone who can access Jenkins web UI and some more.

Take time to understand the tool's authorization model and what you can do to lock down access. Set up trust relationships between build masters and servers, and enable whatever other security protection is available. Then logically separate build pipelines for different teams so that if one is compromised, all of them won't be breached.

After you finish locking down access to the tools and enabling security controls, you also need to keep up with fixes and updates to the tools and any required plug-ins. Security advisories for some of these tools, even the most popular, can't always be relied on. Watch out for new patches and install them when they are made available. But always test first to make sure that the patch is stable and that you don't have dependency problems: build chains can become highly customized and fragile over time.

Continuous Integration Tools Are a Hacker's Best Friend

"Running a poorly configured CI tool is like providing a ready-to-use botnet for anyone to exploit."

Check out security researcher Adrian Mittal's presentation from Black Hat 2015, where he walks through serious vulnerabilities that he found in different CI/CD tools, including Jenkins, Go, and TeamCity.[2]

Lock Down Configuration Managers

If you are using configuration management tools like Chef or Puppet, you must lock them down. Anyone with access to these tools can add accounts, change file permissions or auditing policies, install compromised software, and alter firewall rules. Absent controls, it's like granting someone root on all boxes under configuration control. Who needs the root password when someone else will kindly type in all the commands for you?

---

1 Jenkins, "Securing Jenkins" (*https://wiki.jenkins-ci.org/display/JENKINS/Securing+Jenkins*), Apr 15, 2016.

2 Nikhil Mittal, "Continuous Intrusion: Why CI tools are an attacker's best friend" (*https://www.blackhat.com/docs/eu-15/materials/eu-15-Mittal-Continuous-Intrusion-Why-CI-Tools-Are-An-Attackers-Best-Friend.pdf*), presentation at Black Hat Europe 2015.

Configure the tools safely, and restrict access to only a small, trusted group of people —and audit everything that they do. For an example, see the article from Learn Chef Rally, "How to be a secure Chef" (*https://learn.chef.io/modules/securing-chef/be-a-secure-chef#/*).

Protect Keys and Secrets

A continuous delivery pipeline needs keys and other credentials to automatically provision servers and deploy code. And the system itself needs credentials in order to start up and run. Make sure that these secrets aren't hardcoded in scripts or plain-text config files or in code. We'll look at how to manage secrets safely in the next section.

Lock Down Repos

Lock down source and binary repos, and audit access to them. Prevent unauthenticated or anonymous or shared user access to repos, and implement access control rules.

Source repos hold your application code, your tests and sample test data, your configuration recipes, and if you are not careful, credentials and other things that you don't want to share with attackers. Read access to source repos should be limited to people on the team, and to other teams who work with them.

Anybody with write access to your code repos can check-in a malicious change. Make sure that this access is controlled and that check-ins are continuously monitored.

Binary repos hold a cache of third-party libraries downloaded from public repos or vendors, and the latest builds of your code in the pipeline. Anybody with write access to these repos can inject malcode into your build environment—and eventually into production.

You should verify signatures for any third-party components that you cache for internal use, both at the time of download, and when the components are bundled into the build. And change the build steps to sign binaries and other build artifacts to prevent tampering.

Secure Chat

If you are using collaborative ChatOps tools like Slack or Mattermost and GitHub's Hubot (*https://github.com/github/hubot*) to help automate build, test, release, and deployment functions, you could be opening up another set of security risks and issues.

Collaborative chat tools like Slack and HipChat provide a simple, natural way for development and operations teams and other people to share information. Chatbots can automatically monitor and report the status of a system, or track build and deployment pipelines, and post information back to message rooms or channels.

They can also be used to automatically set up and manage build, test, release, and deployment tasks and other operations functions, through simple commands entered into chat conversations.

What rooms are channels and are public or private? Who has access to these channels? Are any of them open to customers, or to other third parties, or to the public? What information is available in them?

What are bots set up to do? Who has access to them? Where do the bots run? Where are the scripts?

You'll need to take appropriate steps to secure and lock down the chain of tools involved: the chat tool or chat platform, the bots, and the scripts and plug-ins that team members want to use. Treat chat automation scripts like other operations code: make sure that it is reviewed and checked in to a repo.

Many of these collaboration tools are now in the cloud, which means that information that team members post is hosted by someone outside of your organization. You must review the chat service provider's security controls, and security and privacy policies. Make sure that you track the provider's security announcements and that you are prepared to deal with outages and breaches.

And make sure that teams understand what information should and should not be posted to message rooms or channels. Sharing passwords or other confidential information in messages should not be allowed.

Control and audit access to chat tools, including using MFA if it is supported. If your team is big enough, you may also need to set up permission schemes for working with bots, using something like hubot-auth (*https://github.com/hubot-scripts/hubot-auth*).

Remember that bots need credentials—to the chat system and to whatever other systems or tools that they interact with. These secrets need to be protected, as we will see later in this chapter.

Review the Logs

Your build system logs need to be part of the same operations workflows as your production systems. Periodically review the logs for the tools involved to ensure that they are complete and that you can trace a change through from check-in to deployment. Ensure that the logs are immutable, that they cannot be erased or forged. And make sure that they are regularly rotated and backed up.

Use Phoenix Servers for Build and Test

Use automated configuration management and provisioning tools like Chef or Puppet, Docker (especially), Vagrant, and Terraform to automatically stand up, set up, patch, and tear down build slaves and test servers as and when you need them.

Try to treat your build and test boxes as disposable, ephemeral "Phoenix Servers" (*http://martinfowler.com/bliki/PhoenixServer.html*) that only exist for the life of the test run. This reduces your attack surface, regularly tests your configuration management workflows, and gives you more confidence when you deploy to a hardened production environment.

Don't Let Your Test Data Get You into Trouble

Because it is difficult to create good synthetic test data, many shops take a snapshot or a subset of production data and then anonymize or mask certain fields. If this isn't done properly, it can lead to data breaches or other violations of privacy laws and compliance regulations.

You need strong controls over how the snapshots are handled, and reliable (and carefully reviewed) methods to ensure that identifying information like names, addresses, phone numbers, email IDs, as well as any passwords or other credentials, and other sensitive information are removed and replaced with random data, or otherwise scrubbed before this data can be used in test.

Make sure that all the steps involved are audited and reviewed, so that you can prove to customers and compliance auditors that this information was protected.

Monitor Your Build and Test Systems

Ensure that all of these systems are monitored as part of the production environment. Operational security needs to be extended to the tools and the infrastructure that they run on, including vulnerability scanning, IDS/IPS, and runtime monitoring. Use file integrity checking to watch for unexpected or unauthorized changes to configurations and data.

Shh…Keeping Secrets Secret

Keeping secrets secret is a problem in every system. The application needs keys, passwords and user IDs, connection strings, AWS keys, code signing keys, API tokens, and other secrets that need to be protected. Operations engineers and administrators need access to these secrets—and so do their tools.

As you automate more of the work of configuring, testing, deploying, and managing systems, the problems of managing secrets gets harder. You can't just share secrets between a handful of people. And you don't want to store secrets in scripts or plaintext configuration files—or in source code.

Storing secrets in code is a bad idea. Code is widely accessible, especially if you are using a DVCS like Git, where every developer has her own copy, which means that every developer has access to the system secrets. If you need to change secrets, you will have to make a code change and re-deploy. And code has a way of getting out, exposing your secrets to the outside.

You Can't Keep Secrets Secret on GitHub

There have been several cases where people in high-profile organizations have been found posting passwords, security keys, and other secrets in searchable, public repos on GitHub.[3]

This includes several well-intentioned people who uploaded Slackbot code up to public GitHub repos, accidentally including their private Slack API tokens, which can be harvested and used to eavesdrop on Slack communications or impersonate Slack users.

In a famous recent example, Uber confirmed that an attacker compromised its driver database using a database key which had been accidentally posted on GitHub.[4]

Regularly scan GitHub using Gitrob (*https://github.com/michenriksen/gitrob*) or Truffle Hog (*https://github.com/dxa4481/truffleHog*) to check for files in public repos that could contain sensitive information from your organization.

You could use tools like git-secret (*https://github.com/sobolevn/git-secret*) or StackExchange's BlackBox (*https://github.com/StackExchange/blackbox*) or git-crypt (*https://github.com/AGWA/git-crypt*) to transparently encrypt secrets and other configuration information and confidential code, as you check them into a repo.

But this still exposes you to risks. What if someone forgets to encrypt a sensitive file?

You need to scan or review code to make sure that credentials aren't checked in to repos, or take advantage of pre-commit hooks to add checks for passwords and keys. Talisman (*https://github.com/thoughtworks/talisman*), an open source project from ThoughtWorks, Git Hound (*https://github.com/ezekg/git-hound*), and git-secrets

---

3 Dan Goodin, "PSA: Don't upload your important passwords to GitHub" (*http://bit.ly/goodin-passwords-to-github*), *Ars Technica*, 1/24/2013.

4 Dan Goodin, "In major goof, Uber stored sensitive database key on public GitHub page" (*http://bit.ly/goodin-database-key-on-github*), *Ars Technica*, 3/2/2015.

(*https://github.com/awslabs/git-secrets*) are tools that can be used to automatically check for secrets in code and block them from being checked in.

Continuous integration and continuous delivery servers need access to secrets. Deployment scripts and release automation tools need secrets. Your configuration management tools like Ansible, Chef, or Puppet need credentials in order to set up other credentials. You can use the following to manage secrets for these tools:

- Ansible Vault (*http://docs.ansible.com/ansible/playbooks_vault.html*)
- Chef Vault (*https://github.com/chef/chef-vault*)
- hiera-eyaml for Puppet (*https://github.com/TomPoulton/hiera-eyaml*)

But this only solves one piece of the problem.

A much better approach is to use a general-purpose secrets manager across all of your tools as well as for your applications. Secrets managers do the following:

1. Safely store and encrypt passwords, keys, and other credentials at rest.
2. Restrict and audit access to secrets, enforcing authentication and fine-grained access control rules.
3. Provide secure access through APIs.
4. Handle failover so that secrets are always available to system users.

Some open source secrets managers include the following:

1. Keywhiz from Square (*https://github.com/square/keywhiz*).
2. Knox (*https://github.com/pinterest/knox*) the secrets keeper used at Pinterest.
3. Confidant (*https://github.com/lyft/confidant*) from Lyft, to manage secrets on AWS.
4. CredStash (*https://github.com/fugue/credstash*) a simple secret keeper on AWS.
5. HashiCorp Vault (*https://www.vaultproject.io*), arguably the most complete and operationally ready of the open source secrets management tools.

Key Takeaways

Secure and reliable system operations presents challenging problems, and there is a bewildering choice of tools and new engineering techniques that you could consider using to try to solve them.

Where should you start? Where can you get the best ROI, the most bang for your buck?

- Your people are a key component of your build pipeline and should be considered as part of its attack surface in addition to the technology.

- In rapidly changing environments, vulnerability scanning needs to be done on an almost continuous basis. Scanning once a year or once a quarter won't cut it.

- Security hardening must be built into system provisioning and configuration processes—not done as an afterthought.

- Automating system provisioning and configuration management using programmable tools like Ansible or Chef, containers such as Docker, imaging tools like Packer, and cloud templating technologies, should be a foundation of your operations and security strategy.

  With these technologies you can ensure that every system is set up correctly and consistently across development, test, and production. You can make changes quickly and consistently across hundreds or even thousands of systems in a safe and testable way, with full transparency and traceability into every change. You can automatically define and enforce hardening and compliance policies.

- Getting operations configuration into code, and getting operations and development using the same tools and build pipelines, makes it possible to apply the same security controls and checks to all changes, including code reviews, static analysis checks, and automated testing.

- Your automated build pipeline presents a dangerous attack surface. It should be treated as part of your production environment, and managed in the same way as your most security-sensitive systems.

- Secrets have to be kept secret. Private keys, API tokens, and other credentials are needed by tools and often need to be used across trust boundaries. Don't store these secrets in scripts, config files, or source code. Get them into a secure secrets manager.

- Security that is built into application monitoring feedback loops, makes security issues more transparent to developers as well as to operations.

- Prepare for incidents—for serious operational and security problems. Bad things will happen. Make sure that operations and developers understand what they need to do and how they can help.

  Practice, practice, practice. Run regular game days, or Red Team/Blue Team games or other exercises to work out problems and build organizational muscles.

- Postmortem reviews after operational problems and security incidents provide the team with an opportunity to learn, and, if done properly, in an open and sincere and blameless way, to build connections and trust between teams.

CHAPTER 14

Compliance

Regulatory compliance is a major driver for security. In some organizations, compliance is *the* main driver for the security program, defining how changes are made, what reviews and testing are done and when, which vulnerabilities are fixed and which ones are not, and how developers, testers, operations, and security people work together.

Regulations such as PCI DSS, HIPAA and HITECH, SOX, GLBA, SEC regulations and MiFID, 23 NYCRR 500, FDA safety regulations for software validation, FERC and NERC, FERPA, FedRAMP, FFIEC and FISMA, and COBIT and HiTRUST and ISO/IEC 27001 and the NIST and CIS standards that organizations follow to meet these regulations, all define requirements and rules, guidelines and constraints on system design and assurance, staff training and awareness, risk management and vulnerability management, change control and release management, auditing and data retention, network and system monitoring, and IT operations.

If you work in a regulated environment, you must understand how compliance impacts your security program and how to include compliance in development and operations. In other parts of this book we try to help you to think like an attacker, to focus on threats and vulnerabilities and forensics. In this chapter, we will help you to think like an auditor, and understand how to look at your system from an auditor's point of view, to focus on risks and controls and evidence.

Compliance and Security

Now, before we get onto what compliance means at a practical level, it's important to draw attention to the difference between compliance and security for a moment.

Security is the process of putting in place physical, technical, and administrative controls to protect the confidentiality, integrity, and availability of information. It means taking steps to ensure that only the people who are authorized to access our systems and data can do so, that the data we store is accurate and remains that way, and that customers can use a system as and when they need to.

Compliance is a bit different—it's about showing that we understand and are committed to security, and meeting requirements so that we're allowed to keep operating. Security is the policies and processes that protect all of our information and systems. Compliance allows us to operate in certain fields or store certain types of information by showing that we can do so safely.

Compliance standards and regulations like PCI and HIPAA and GLBA, and government privacy laws such as California state privacy laws and German and Italian national privacy laws, Canada's PIPEDA, and the EU's new General Data Protection Regulation (GDPR), lay out legal requirements and specific obligations for protecting personal and private information, where this information can and cannot be kept, and what you have to do in the event that these obligations are violated.

PHI and PII

Throughout this chapter, and in other chapters, we'll refer to different categories of personal or private information. Some of this information is important enough to have their own acronyms: PHI and PII.

PHI

Personal (or Protected) Health Information: any information that relates to the physical or mental health of an individual, including the patient's condition, provision of health care, or payment for health care.

PII

Personally Identifiable Information: any information used to identify a person's identity, including name, date of birth, biometric records, SSN, IP address, and credit card records.

The point of regulatory compliance is to achieve the following:

1. Make sure that you understand how to do things responsibly by defining a minimum set of requirements for security and privacy, generally requiring you to follow recognized standards or best practices for risk management, change management, software development, vulnerability management, identity and access management, data encryption, and IT operations.

2. Force you to prove that you are doing things responsibly by requiring you to establish and maintain top-down policies, track all changes, regularly scan and

test for vulnerabilities, and undergo periodic assessments and audits to check that your controls are effective.

3. Punish your organization if you fail to meet these requirements through fines and other sanctions. These fines could run to tens or hundreds of thousands of dollars per month for banks that do not comply with PCI DSS, and to several million dollars for health care organizations in the event of a data breach under HIPAA.

In this chapter, we'll look at compliance to understand how it impacts:

- Design and requirements management (regulatory auditing and reporting requirements, and traceability).
- Testing and reviews (assurance and assessments, validation, and verification).
- Delivering software changes into production (change control and release management).
- Oversight of developers especially in production (separation of duties).
- Protection of data (privacy, access control and encryption, and data retention).
- Documentation (how to get by with the least amount of paperwork necessary).

Disclaimer

We'll examine different compliance frameworks, including PCI DSS, throughout this book, to show how they work and what they mean at a technical level. And we'll explore ways to meet compliance requirements effectively and efficiently in Agile environments.

But we won't be providing exhaustive coverage of any regulation. We aren't offering legal advice. You need to take time to understand and confirm your compliance obligations, what systems and data and activities are in scope, and work with your compliance and risk and security officers, your auditors, and management to come up with an approach that works for you and for them.

Compliance may be enforced on your organization directly, or, if you are a service provider, by your customers. Some organizations operate under multiple regulations, with overlapping and varying requirements. For example, if you are a public company offering an online medical service, you could be subject to SOX, HIPAA, PCI DSS (if your customers can pay using credit/debit cards), and different data privacy regulations. You will need to come up with an approach that satisfies their requirements together, and independently.

Different Regulatory Approaches

Some regulations give you a pretty clear idea of what you need to do. Others? Not so much. This is because there are two very different approaches that regulators can take when framing regulations:

Prescriptive: Rules-based

> A set of specific guidelines on what you must or can, and what you must not or cannot, do. Prescriptive, rules-based regulations lay out a set of specific controls and procedures, highlight risks, and tell you—and auditors—what you must do, when or how often, and what evidence you need to keep. These are regulations that can be mostly captured in checklists.

> Examples of rules-based regulations include PCI DSS, FedRAMP, FISMA, and various safety regulations.

Descriptive: Outcome-based

> These regulations describe security or risk management or operational objectives, or legal obligations, that you must meet, but they don't specify how you need to do this. There are usually a few detailed rules around regulatory reporting and assessments, but otherwise your organization is free to choose its own approach, provided that your controls are deemed to be "adequate," "effective," and "reasonable."

> In theory, this allows you to be more efficient and more innovative in meeting regulatory requirements. But this also means that compliance is less certain. Auditors have more leeway to judge if your programs and controls are sufficient or satisfactory, and penalties are assessed by how inadequate, ineffective, or unreasonable the auditors found them to be. You will need to defend your approach and clearly show how it supports the regulations.

> This is why so many organizations fall back on heavyweight control frameworks like COBIT (*http://www.isaca.org/cobit/pages/default.aspx*) and ITIL (*https://en.wikipedia.org/wiki/ITIL*). Following a standardized, widely accepted, and comprehensive governance model adds costs and delays, but reduces the risk that your program will be found inadequate by auditors or investigators, which should help minimize penalties or liability when something goes wrong.

> Examples of outcome-based regulations are HIPAA, FDA QSR, SOX 404, and SEC Regulation SCI.

Let's take a quick look at a couple of examples to show how fundamentally different these regulatory approaches are.

PCI DSS: Rules-Based

The Payment Card Industry Data Security Standard (PCI DSS (*https://www.pcisecuritystandards.org/*)) is a cross-industry standard of practice that many teams will end up having to deal with, as it applies to any system that deals with credit or debit card payments, either directly, or through a third-party service.

Rather than vague legal statements that you must demonstrate appropriate due care, PCI DSS lays out specific, mostly concrete requirements and obligations: you must do this, you must not do that, and this is how you must prove it. It sets reasonably clear expectations about what risks need to be managed and how, about what data needs to be protected and how, what testing or reviews you need to do, and when you need to do them.

PCI DSS is described in a number of guides, supplementary documents, notices, checklists, and FAQs; but the core of the regulation is relatively small. While it isn't fun (regulations are never fun), it's not that difficult to follow. There's even a Quick Reference Guide (*http://bit.ly/pci-dss-quick-reference-guide*), only about 40 pages long, that does a decent job of outlining what you need to do.

There are 12 sections in a PCI-compliant security program. While people can—and do—argue about the effectiveness or completeness of the specific controls, PCI DSS is a reasonably good model for a security program, whether or not you deal with credit card information. It anticipates many of the risks and security issues that you need to deal with in any online system that holds important data, and lays out a structured approach to manage them. Just substitute "cardholder data" with whatever sensitive or private data that you need to manage:

Secure network design
> Use of firewalls and network segmentation. Ensure that configurations are periodically reviewed and that all configuration changes are tested. Map all connections and data flows.

Configuration hardening
> Identifying all of the systems involved, and making sure that they are configured safely to "industry-accepted definitions" (eg., CIS), specifically making sure to change vendor-supplied default credentials.

Protect sensitive data (cardholder data) at rest
> Limit/restrict storage. Use one-way hashing, strong encryption, tokenization, masking, or truncation. Specific restrictions on what data can/cannot be stored.

Secure communications
> Using strong encryption and security protocols when transmitting sensitive data over open networks.

Protecting systems against malware
  Use of antivirus systems.

Develop and maintain secure systems and applications
  We'll look at this section in more detail below.

Restrict access to cardholder data
  Access control restricted based on business need-to-know.

User identification and authentication guidelines
  Including when multifactor authentication is required.

Physical security
  Restricting and tracking physical access to data centers and sensitive areas, and to backup media.

Track and monitor all access to network and cardholder data
  Auditing, logging. Specific requirements for auditing of activities, access to restricted data, and retention of audit trails.

Regular security testing and scanning
  Scanning for wireless access points, internal and external network vulnerability scanning, penetration testing, intrustion detection/prevention, and detective change control.

Paperwork
  Governance, risk assessment, and information security policies to prove that management and everyone else understands the requirements and how they are being met, in addition to insisting that operational procedures and policies for each of the previous requirements are "documented, in use, and known to all affected parties."

  This includes regular security and compliance awareness training for developers and operations.

In order to be compliant, your organization must meet all of these requirements, and undergo regular assessments.

Requirement 6 is the section that applies most directly to software development. It addresses requirements, design, coding, testing, reviews, and implementation.

6.1 vulnerability management
  Identify vulnerabilities, determine priority based on risk, and deal with them. We looked at vulnerability management in more detail in Chapter 6, *Agile Vulnerability Management*.

6.2 patching

Make sure that patches to third-party software are up to date. Critical patches must be installed within one month.

6.3 secure coding practices to ensure that software is built "based on industry best practices"

This includes specific requirements such as ensuring that all test accounts and credentials are removed before applications are put into production, reviewing code changes (manually or using automated tools) for security vulnerabilities, and making sure that code review results are reviewed and approved by management before the code changes are released.

6.4 change control

Including clear separation of duties between production and development/test, evidence of security testing, impact analysis and backout planning, and documented change approval by authorized parties.

6.5 train the development team in secure coding

At least annually, and provide them with secure coding guidelines.

6.6 protect web applications

Requires an application vulnerability assessment review at least once per year, or before rolling out major changes. Alternatively, you can protect your system by implementing a runtime defense solution that blocks attacks (such as a Web Application Firewall).

6.7 paperwork

To prove all of this.

That's "all there is" to PCI compliance from a development perspective, beyond correctly implementing controls over credit cardholder data in Requirement 3 and access restrictions to cardholder data in Requirement 7. The devil, of course, is in the details.

Reg SCI: Outcome-Based

Contrast this with Reg SCI (Systems Compliance and Integrity), which is one of a number of regulations that stock exchanges and other financial services organizations in the US need to meet. It is concerned with ensuring the capacity, integrity, resiliency, availability, and security of financial systems.

Reg SCI is 743 pages of legalese, much of it describing the process followed to draft the regulation. The core of the regulation is captured in about 20 pages starting somewhere after page 700. It requires that organizations develop and maintain "written policies and procedures reasonably designed" to ensure that systems are developed and operated safely and that they meet all necessary legal requirements.

These policies and procedures must cover system design and development, testing, capacity planning and testing, continuity planning and testing, change management, network design and management, system operations, monitoring, incident response, physical security, and information security, as well as outsourcing any of these responsibilities. Reg SCI also lays out obligations for reporting to the SEC, and for annual audits.

Policies and procedures may be considered to be "reasonably designed" if they comply with "information technology practices that are widely available to information professionals in the financial sector and issued by a recognized organization" such as the US government.

The list of recognized best practices includes, for almost every area, NIST SP 800-53r4 (*http://nvlpubs.nist.gov/nistpubs/SpecialPublications/NIST.SP.800-53r4.pdf*), which is a 462-page document describing 218 specific risk management, security, and privacy controls and how to apply them for US federal information systems (based on the risk profile of the system). Controls that apply to software development are described under a number of different control areas, such as System Acquisition (mostly), Configuration Management, Risk Assessment, System and Information Integrity, Awareness and Training, Privacy, Security Assessment and Authorization, and so on. Each of these controls reference other controls or other NIST documents, and other publications and standards.

The overall effect is, well, overwhelming. Determining what you need to do, what you should do, what you can afford to do, and how to prove it, is left up to each organization—and to its auditors.

NIST SP 800-53r4 doesn't say you can't build and deliver systems using Agile and Lean methods, but it is a shining example of everything that Agile and Lean is against: legal policies and shelf-loads of paper that are designed to make a bureaucrat happy, but that don't translate to specific, measurable requirements that can be satisfied.

The SEC makes it clear that the list of standards is offered as guidance. Your controls and programs would be assessed against these standards. If you don't choose to follow them, the burden is on you to prove that your system of controls is "reasonably designed."

Which Approach Is Better?

While Reg SCI's outcome-based approach allows an organization some flexibility and freedom to make risk-based decisions on how to meet requirements, PCI's prescriptive checklists are much clearer: you know what you have to do, and what you will be measured against. If you fail to meet PCI's requirements, you should have a pretty good idea why, and what to do about it. On the other hand, it's difficult to get auditors and assessors to look up from their detailed checklists at what you are doing, to help you understand whether your program is actually making your organization secure.

Risk Management and Compliance

Regulations and governance frameworks are risk driven: they are intended to help protect the organization, and more important, customers and society, against security and privacy risks.

Risk management in Agile development was covered in Chapter 7, *Risk for Agile Teams*. For now, let's look at how risk management drives compliance-related decisions and the application of controls from a compliance perspective.

Regulators require your organization to have an active risk management program to address security-related and privacy-related risks, and related operational and technical risks. This ensures that you're not only trying to meet the basics of a compliance checklist, but that management and everyone working on projects and in operations are proactively working to identify, understand, and deal with rapidly changing risks and threats.

Auditors will look for a formal policy statement explaining why risk management is important to the organization, and outlining people's responsibilities for managing risks. They will also look for evidence of your risk management program in operation, and test that your operational and security controls and procedures are being regularly reviewed and updated to deal with changing risks.

For example, PCI DSS 12.1.2 requires organizations to perform a formal risk assessment, at least annually, to review threats and vulnerabilities, as well as any changes to the environment, and to ensure that controls and programs are in place to effectively address these risks.

On a day-to-day level, your risk management program should include doing the following:

- Using threat information to prioritize patching, testing, reviews, and security awareness training—we explored this in Chapter 8, *Threat Assessments and Understanding Attacks*
- Taking advantage of regular Agile retrospectives and reviews, and include reviewing new security risks or operational risks or compliance risks and how they need to be dealt with
- Conducting postmortem analysis after operational problems, including outages and security breaches, as well as after pen tests and other assessments, to identify weaknesses in controls and opportunities for improvement

- Ensuring that team members are aware of common risks and have taken appropriate steps to deal with them—risks such as the OWASP Top 10

OWASP Top 10 Risk List

The Open Web Application Security Project (OWASP), a community of application security experts, regularly publishes a set of the top 10 risks that web applications face: the OWASP Top 10 (*https://www.owasp.org/index.php/Category:OWASP_Top_Ten_Project*).

This is a list of the 10 most critical web application security risks. For each risk, the OWASP Top 10 provides examples of vulnerabilities and attacks, and guidance on how to test for these problems and how to prevent them.

The OWASP Top 10 is widely referenced in regulations such as PCI DSS, as a key risk management tool. Security training for developers is expected to cover the OWASP Top 10 risks. Security scanning tools map findings to the OWASP Top 10, and application pen testers will report if their findings map into the OWASP Top 10.

Traceability of Changes

A fundamental requirement of compliance and governance frameworks is the ability to prove that all changes are properly authorized and tracked—and that unauthorized changes have been prevented. This involves tracing changes from when they were requested, to when they were delivered, and proving that the necessary checks and tests were performed:

- When was a change made?
- Who made the change?
- Who authorized it?
- Who reviewed it?
- Was the change tested?
- Did the tests pass?
- How and when was the change deployed to production?

This could require a lot of paperwork. Or, as we'll explain in this chapter, it could be done without any paperwork at all, by relying on your existing workflows and toolchains.

Data Privacy

HIPAA, PCI DSS, and GLBA are examples of regulations that address protecting private or confidential information: health records, credit cardholder details, and customer personal financial data, respectively.

These regulations, and government privacy laws as we mentioned earlier, identify information which must be classified as private or sensitive, and lay out rules and restrictions for protecting this data, and what you need to do to prove that you are protecting it (including assurance, auditing, and data retention).

Don't Try to Do This without Legal Advice

We are only providing general guidance here. Consult your data privacy officer or compliance officer or legal counsel to understand your organization's data privacy obligations.

The basic steps to dealing with data privacy include:

1. Provide clear, vetted guidelines and rules up front to the Product Owner and the rest of the team, as well as training if necessary, so that everyone appreciates and understands data privacy risks, rules, and constraints.

   Work with the team to ensure that compliance requirements are included in the team's Definition of Done. This includes any documentation or other evidence that needs to be created or recorded for auditors.

2. Create a matrix of all information that is private or sensitive, who in the organization owns the data, and who is allowed to access (create, change, read, delete) it. Make this easily available to the team, and keep it up to date.

3. Understand and confirm data residency constraints, especially if you are running a system in the cloud. Some privacy laws may dictate that protected data cannot be shared or stored outside of specific legal jurisdictions.

4. Map out where protected data is collected, stored, updated, deleted, shared, and referenced, using the same kind of data flow diagrams that you created in threat modeling. Include temporary copies and working copies, caches, reports, spreadsheets, and backups.

5. Ensure that protected data is encrypted at rest and in transit using a recognized standard encryption algorithm, masked or pseudonymized, or substituted with a secure token.

6. Write stories to handle requirements for privacy consent and opt-out, right to be forgotten and notice provisions, as well as mandatory auditing, logging, data retention, and regulatory reporting.

7. For any story that collects, stores, updates, deletes, references, or shares protected data, carefully review the acceptance criteria against your compliance requirements, and mark these stories for additional legal reviews or compliance testing before they can be considered done.

8. Regularly scan content and databases and files, including logs, test data, and operations working directories, for protected data that is not encrypted, masked, or tokenized.

9. Scan code for references to protected data and calls to crypto, masking, or tokenization functions, and alert when this code is changed so that it can be reviewed.

10. Write compliance stories for audits, external reviews, pen tests, and other mandated checks so that they will be scheduled and planned for.

11. Create an incident response plan to deal with data breaches and disclosure, and regularly test your incident response capability (as we outline in Chapter 13).

12. Record evidence that you did all of this properly, including code review comments, acceptance tests, change control records, system access logs, and audit results.

13. Regularly review with the team to make sure that these practices and guidelines are being followed consistently.

OWASP Crypto Cheat Sheets

To help you to follow good practices for crypto, experts at OWASP have put together these cheat sheets:

1. For an explanation on how to store data safely, use the Cryptographic Storage Cheat Sheet (*https://www.owasp.org/index.php/Cryptographic_Storage_Cheat_Sheet*).

2. Because safely working with passwords is a separate, specific problem, there is a separate, specific Password Storage Cheat Sheet (*https://www.owasp.org/index.php/Password_Storage_Cheat_Sheet*).

3. For safely communicating data, use the Transport Layer Protection Cheat Sheet (*https://www.owasp.org/index.php/Transport_Layer_Protection_Cheat_Sheet*).

To reiterate: do not implement your own encryption algorithm. If you have questions about how to handle crypto, get expert help.

How to Meet Compliance and Stay Agile

How can you adapt your Agile or DevOps approach to the constraints of highly regulated environments?

Start by confronting compliance head-on. Don't take a passive approach to compliance, and wait for someone to tell you what to do and how to do it—or worse, to tell you when you have failed to do something that you should have. Try to understand the intent and goals of regulatory directives, list out any clearly defined hard rules that they state, and look for ways to wire compliance into your workflows, and especially into automation.

Consider how you can leverage good technical practices and automation to meet compliance as well as your own support needs. If you can ensure—and prove—that every change is made through automated pipelines after it has been reviewed and checked in to version control, you have a powerful response to auditors as well as a powerful tool for investigating, and even preventing, operational problems.

You can do all this in a way that doesn't slow teams down, that puts them in charge, and makes them accountable for meeting compliance requirements.

Compliance Sometimes Means Having to Say "No"

Throughout this book we emphasize how important it is that the security team find ways to be an enabler rather than a blocker: ways to help development and operations get their jobs done safely rather than getting in their way.

But sometimes in order to stay onside of compliance, you have to stand up and say, "No, we can't do that," and reject a change or block a deployment. Each time this has to happen, go back to the team and to management and find a way to prevent the situation from coming up again, by building compliance into the design or into the team's workflows.

Compliance Stories and Compliance in Stories

Mandatory compliance testing, reviews, and other items in compliance checklists need to be considered in the team's Definition of Done, for stories, sprints, and releases:

- What reviews need to be done and who needs to do them
- What testing needs to be done
- What documentation needs to be updated

- What evidence needs to be provided that all of this was done

In Chapter 5 we looked at how to write *security stories* to help in implementing security requirements or security controls. In the same way, you may want to write *compliance stories* to describe explicit steps that need to be done and proven, separate from compliance criteria that might be part of specific user stories.

Compliance stories can act as reminders or schedule placeholders for controls that need to be put into place up front, including compulsory training for team members, and for assessments such as audits and pen tests.

Use tools like osquery (*https://osquery.io*) and InSpec (*http://inspec.io*) to write automated online compliance checks, and to provide traceability back to specific regulations or rule areas or governance controls.

More Code, Less Paperwork

Agile and Lean teams look for ways to minimize waste by keeping documentation to a minimum: working code over documentation.

But when it comes to compliance, some paperwork is unavoidable.

So what is the minimum amount of documentation that you need to satisfy your compliance and governance obligations? And what can you leverage from artifacts that you are already creating?

You will need documented security and risk management policies and guidelines, directional stuff establishing management accountability and clearly communicating responsibilities. And legal protection, such as confidentiality and nondisclosure agreements. All of this will need to be handed out to all staff, signed off, filed, and regularly reviewed and updated.

Don't Write It Down if You Don't Mean It

If you write something down in a policy, you must be prepared for everyone to follow it—and to prove that they followed it correctly.

Don't copy and paste from a policy template that you find on the web (such as at *https://www.sans.org/security-resources/policies*) without making sure that it is practical for your organization, or write something down because you think it sounds like a good idea. If your organization fails to meet its own policies, auditors could use this as evidence of a material failure of controls, especially if you are in an outcome-based regulatory environment. People can be fired for this, and executives can be held personally liable.

Policies must be taken seriously. Treat them like promises—and you always keep your promises, right?

You will also need to keep a record of requirements so that they can be audited, and to trace changes: you won't be able to just write stories on index cards or sticky notes pasted on a wall, and then throw them out as they are implemented.

But most compliance procedures and detailed checklists can be, and should be, taken out of documents and pushed into team workflows for developers and operations, and, wherever possible, into code. These should be enforced through rules in your automated build and deployment pipelines, in automated tests and checks, and by taking advantage of the audit trails that are automatically created.

To do this you will need to bring management, compliance, internal audit, the PMO, and the security team together with development and operations.

Compliance rules and control workflows need to be defined up front by all of these stakeholders working together—and any changes to the rules or workflows should be formally approved by management and documented, for example, in a change advisory board (CAB) meeting. Developers and operations need to walk through procedures and checklists with compliance and security and the PMO, map out key controls, and agree on simple ways to automate them. Management needs to understand how operational risks, security risks, and other risks will be controlled and managed through these automated workflows, tests, and pipelines.

Let's look at how to solve some specific compliance concerns, in code.

Traceability and Assurance in Continuous Delivery

In Chapter 11, we explained how an automated build pipeline works, and how to use continuous integration and continuous delivery tools and workflows to test and deploy changes quickly and safely.

Now you get to use all of this for compliance, tracing each change from when it was requested to when it was delivered, to show that changes are handled properly and consistently. These are the steps that an Agile team could take to prove traceability and assurance in a regulatory environment:

1. As we've seen, instead of working from detailed requirements specifications, Agile teams like to write up requirements in simple, concrete *user stories* on index cards or sticky notes that are thrown away once the story is implemented. But to satisfy compliance, you'll need to keep a record of each feature and change, who asked for it, who approved it, and the acceptance criteria (i.e., conditions of satisfaction) that were agreed to.

   While you could try to do this using a spreadsheet, for example, teams today can take advantage of Agile project management tools or story trackers like Rally,

Version One, or Jira to provide insight into what the team is doing, and what it has already done from an auditing perspective.

2. The team works with compliance to agree on its Definition of Done, including the evidence needed to prove compliance for stories, sprints, and releases.

3. Everything—application code, configuration recipes and templates, tests, policies, and documentation (everything, that is, except for secrets)—is committed to version control, with a tie back to the specific requirement or change request or bug report (using a story ID, ticket number, or some other unique identifying tag that can be referenced as a comment on check-in), so that you have a detailed history of everything associated with each change.

4. Commit filters automatically scan for secrets and unsafe calls before code can be merged in to the mainline.

5. Changes to code and configuration are reviewed—before commit if possible—and the results of reviews are visible to the team, using Git pull requests or a collaborative code review tool like Gerrit or Review Board.

   Reviewers follow checklists to ensure that all code meets the team's standards and guidelines, and to watch out for unsafe coding practices. Management periodically audits to make sure that reviews are done consistently, and that engineers aren't rubber-stamping each other's work.

6. Every change (to application code and to configuration) is tested through continuous integration or continuous delivery: TDD, static code analysis, and other scanning, and automated acceptance testing as described in Chapter 11. Test coverage is automatically measured. Any serious problems cause the build to fail.

   Because tests are checked into a source repo, you can review the tests and match them up against the acceptance criteria for each story, to see if the requirements were implemented correctly.

7. Code (including code dependencies) and infrastructure are regularly scanned for vulnerabilities as part of your automated pipelines, and vulnerabilities found are recorded and pushed into the team's backlog to be fixed.

8. Changes are deployed automatically to acceptance test, then staging, and, if all tests and checks pass, to production, so that you can show when a change was promoted to each environment, and how this was done.

9. Systems are regularly scanned for unauthorized changes using detective change controls (like Tripwire or OSSEC).

This is a beautiful thing for operations and support. You can tell when changes are made or vulnerabilities are patched, and, if something goes wrong, you can trace exactly what was changed so that you can fix it quickly. It's a beautiful thing for governance, because you can follow each change and ensure that the changes were made consistently and responsibly. And it's a beautiful thing for compliance, because you can prove all of this to your auditors.

Managing Changes in Continuous Delivery

Change control is fundamental to compliance regulations, and to governance frameworks like ITIL (the IT Infrastructure Library) and COBIT. This comprises:

- Making sure that all changes are authorized—SOX, insider threats, fraud, Reg SCI
- Minimizing the operational risk of change—making sure that changes are understood, tested, and safe
- Ensuring that changes are auditable, which builds on traceability

Most governance frameworks deal with change management in a bureaucratic, paperwork-heavy way, with forward planning, and formal approvals at change advisory board (CAB) meetings where a committee meets to assess the risks and impact of a change, determine preparedness, and agree to scheduling.

This is in essential conflict with Agile and Lean development, and especially with DevOps and continuous deployment which are predicated on frequent, iterative change, including running A/B experiments in production to get feedback. This could mean making changes several times a week, or several times a day—or at organizations like Amazon, several times per second.

How the heck can you have change control when you are rolling out changes every few seconds?

By taking the risk out of change up front, running every change through the same battery of tests and checks that we described earlier. And by optimizing for small, incremental changes.

While ITIL change management is designed to deal with infrequent, high-risk "big bang" changes, most changes by Agile and DevOps teams are small and low-risk, and can flow under the bar. They can be treated as standard or routine changes that have been preapproved by management, and that don't require a heavyweight change review meeting.

Many larger changes can also be made this way, using *dark launching*. This is a practice made famous at Flickr and Facebook, where changes to code are hidden behind a *feature flag*: a switch that will only be turned on after getting approval. In the meantime, the team can continue to make and test changes in incremental steps, releasing the code to production without impacting operations. This can, in some cases, involve running the new code in simulation mode to collect data on usage and performance, or deploying it to a small community of users for beta testing, until everyone is confident that the feature is ready.

The Dark Side of Dark Launching

Feature flags and dark launching carry some potential operational and security risks that you need to understand and consider:

- Although dark features are hidden to users while they are being rolled out, the code may still be accessible to attackers. Adding these features increases the attack surface of the application, which is especially a concern given that some of this code is still work in progress and is more likely to contain bugs which could be exploitable.

- While dark features are being rolled out, the code will be more complicated, harder to understand, more difficult to change, and more expensive to test because you need to cover more paths, and sometimes combinations of paths if multiple features overlap. Feature switches should be short-lived, to minimize these risks. Once the feature has been rolled out, the switch should be deprecated, and the code cleaned up and refactored.

Before turning on the feature, the team members could hold an operational readiness review, or "pre-mortem" review meeting to go over their preparedness, explore failure scenarios and their ability to respond to them, and ensure that everyone is informed of the change in advance.

The risk of change can also be minimized by automating the steps involved, ensuring that changes are tested and deployed consistently and repeatably. All changes—to code and to configuration—should be rolled out using your automated build and delivery pipelines, the same pipelines that you use for testing, to take advantage of the built-in controls, to make sure that the steps have been rehearsed and proven, and to provide full traceability and visibility. Everyone knows what changes were made, when, by who, how they were tested, and how and when they were deployed.

By the time that you're ready to deploy to production, you've already run the change through development, to acceptance testing, and staging, all using the same steps.

In this model, changes become constant, routine, and predictable.

Dealing with Separation of Duties

One concern that needs to be addressed in change management, especially in DevOps environments where engineers can push changes automatically into production using continuous deployment, is *separation of duties*.

Separation of duties ensures that no single person can have full control from start to end of a change, and that changes cannot be made without testing and approval. This is intended to prevent malicious insider attacks and fraud, and to prevent honest insiders from taking shortcuts and bypassing the checks and balances that are designed to protect the system and the organization from security risks and operational risks.

Separation of duties is spelled out as a practice in governance frameworks like ITIL and COBIT, and it's expected in other frameworks and regulations like ISO/IEC 27001, SOC 1 and SOC 2, SOX 404, PCI DSS, NIST 800-53, Reg SCI, and others. It ties into change control, as well as data privacy (by limiting the number of people who have access to production data).

Auditors are used to looking for evidence of separation of duties, such as network segmentation between development and production systems, and matrices clearly showing that developers, testers, operations, and support analysts are assigned to different roles, with access restrictions to the different systems and commands.

The most obvious implementation of this principle is the Waterfall/CMMI model which requires a series of documented handoffs between roles:

- Business analysts define requirements, and get approval from the business owner.
- Designers take the requirements and create specifications.
- Developers write code to implement the specifications, and then hand the code off for testing.
- Independent testers verify that the code meets the specifications.
- Operations packages the code into a release, and waits for a change manager to complete an impact analysis and risk assessment, and schedule the change to be deployed.
- All these steps are documented and tracked for management review and sign off.

Auditors like this a lot. Look at the clear, documented handoffs and reviews and approvals, the double checks and opportunities to catch mistakes and malfeasance.

But look at all the unnecessary delays and overhead costs, and the many chances for misunderstandings and miscommunication. This is why almost nobody builds and delivers systems this way any more.

The DevOps Audit Toolkit makes the argument that you don't need all of these hand-offs to prevent fraud and insider maliciousness, and to ensure that all changes are properly authorized, tested, and tracked. You can even empower developers to push changes directly to production, as long as they do the following:

- The team agrees and ensures that all changes meet the Definition of Done, which includes that all changes are tested against the acceptance criteria defined for each story, and successfully reviewed by the Product Owner, who represents the interests of the business and management

- Peer reviews (or pair programming) ensure that no engineer (dev or ops) can make a change without at least one other person in the organization being aware of it and understanding it. You could even insist that the team assign reviewers randomly to prevent collusion.

- Every change—to code or configuration—is made through automated build and deployment pipelines, which ensure that they are tested and tracked.

- Developers can be given read-only access to production system logs and monitors so that they can help in troubleshooting. But any fixes or patches need to be made through the automated build pipeline (fixing forward) or by automatically rolling changes back (again, through the same automated pipeline).

- All changes made through the pipeline are done in a transparent way, logged and published to dashboards, chat rooms, and so on.

- Production access logs are regularly reviewed by management or compliance.

- Access credentials are reviewed regularly: including access to different environments, access to repos, and access to the pipelines and configuration management tools.

- Automated detective change control tools (such as Tripwire, OSSEC, AIDE, and UpGuard) are used to alert on unauthorized changes to the build environment and to production systems. If you are deploying changes a few times per month or even several times per week, this is straightforward. If you are making changes multiple times a day, you need to be careful to filter out approved, automated changes to show the exceptions. It's also important that these alerts are sent to someone outside of the engineering team, to security or compliance or management for review, to ensure that there is no conflict of interest.

For an informed and balanced auditor's perspective on separation of duties in DevOps environments, see Douglas Barbin's article, "Auditing DevOps – Developers with Access to Production" (*https://www.schellmanco.com/blog/2012/12/auditing-devops-developers-with-access-to-production/*).

Building Compliance into Your Culture

Building compliance into your culture takes time and persistence. This is something that needs to be done from the top down, and from the bottom up.

Management needs to understand what is required for compliance purposes and communicate these requirements down to every team. They also need to show that they are serious about meeting compliance, in the way that they spend money, and the way that they make decisions about priorities.

For teams, compliance should—and has to—build on top of the team's commitment to doing things right and delivering working software. Teams that are already working toward zero defect tolerance, and teams that are following good technical practices, including continuous integration, should be more successful in meeting compliance.

The more that you can leverage from these practices, and especially from automation, the easier it will be to satisfy compliance. In the model that we've described here, many compliance requirements can be met by reinforcing good engineering practices that teams are already following, or should be following, and taking advantage of audit trails provided by automated tooling.

Even within a structured and prescriptive control framework like PCI, give engineering teams the opportunity to come up with their own ideas on how to meet requirements, the chance to automate as much work as possible, and a voice in what documentation needs to be done. Help them to understand where the lines are, how high the bar needs to be set, and where they could have some flexibility to meet a governance or compliance requirement.

These aren't problems to be avoided or evaded. They are problems that need to be solved in ways that are efficient, effective and, where possible, satisfying to the people who need to do the work. They should be treated in a Lean way: map the value stream, recognize and understand the constraints, identify the bottlenecks and inefficiencies, measure, learn, and improve.

All of this is a heavy lift for startups, or for teams that don't have strong leadership and management support. But it is achievable—and worth achieving.

Keeping Auditors Happy

To make auditors happy, you need to provide them with evidence that you've met specific compliance requirements, or evidence that proves compliance with defined outcomes.

Just as beauty is in the eye of the beholder, compliance is in the opinion of the auditor. Auditors might not understand the approach that you are taking at first, especially auditors who are accustomed to reviewing detailed policies and procedures, and making people fill out checklists and spreadsheets.

You will need to explain how your pipelines work, walk them through your controls, and through the code and repos and tests and audit logs, and show how it all ties together. But a good auditor should be able to appreciate what you are doing, and recognize how it is good for you, as well as for them.

If you follow the approach outlined here, using your automated build pipelines as a control plane for compliance, you can prove that you are regularly scanning and reviewing code and infrastructure for vulnerabilities, and you can track when vulnerabilities were found and fixed.

You can provide a complete audit trail for every change, from when the change was requested and why, who authorized the change, who made the change and what that person changed, who reviewed the change and what they found in the review, how and when the change was tested and what the results were, to when it was deployed:

- You can prove that changes were reviewed and tested, and prove that changes were all made in a standardized, repeatable way.

- You can show that compliance policies and checks were enforced in reviews, in testing, in scanning, and in release control.

- You can show that you've enforced separation of duties between development and operations.

- And, if you are following the controls consistently, you can prove that all of this was done for every change.

In the same way that frequently exercising build and deployment steps reduces operational risks, exercising compliance on every change, following the same standardized process and automated steps each time, minimizes the risks of compliance violations. You — and your auditors — can be confident that all changes are made the same way, that all code is run through the same tests and checks, and that everything is tracked the same way, from start to finish.

 As part of your evidence, be prepared to show auditors logs of test failures and build failures, and that these errors were subsequently remediated, to demonstrate that your controls are actually working and catching mistakes.

Auditors can verify that your control program is consistent, complete, repeatable, and auditable. We can see the smile on your auditor's face already.

Dealing with Auditors When They Aren't Happy

Your auditors won't always be happy, especially if they are coming in to investigate after a security breach.

Although many regulations lay out reporting requirements in the event of a breach, it's not always clear what your priorities should be, especially when you are in the middle of dealing with a security incident. There are a lot of factors to understand and consider.

How serious is the breach? Different agencies have different bars for what you need to report, and when. What if you fall under several different compliance and legal jurisdictions?

Who do you need to report to first? Legal counsel? Your Board? A forensics specialist? Law enforcement? Your partners and customers? Your insurance agent? The regulators? Government agencies? Who do you contact? What information do you need to provide, and how quickly?

You should have all of this worked out in advance as part of your incident response playbooks.

Once you've dealt with disclosure, you need to prepare for the follow-up analysis and audit(s) to understand what went wrong, how badly it went wrong, who will be held responsible or accountable, and how much it will cost to make up for what went wrong. If you experience a serious breach, and you work in a regulated environment, your organization will by definition be found noncompliant—after all, if you were 100% compliant, how could anything have possibly gone wrong? An investigation just has to prove this, and with the power of perfect hindsight, it will. After a breach or a serious compliance failure, everyone will be trying to find the smoking gun, and they will keep looking for mistakes and gaps and scapegoats until they have enough smoke to fill out their report.

Repeatable, automated workflows with built-in audit trails, and evidence checked into version control, will at least make this less painful and less expensive for you and for the investigators, and help to show that you were doing some (hopefully most) things right.

Certification and Attestation

Getting certified to a standard like ISO/IEC 27001, or an attestation that you've met the requirements of a SOC review, or a similar assessment can be an important goal in meeting your compliance requirements.

This paperwork helps you make a case to your auditors, as well as to your customers and your owners—and your competitors—that you've taken responsible and reasonable steps to protect your organization and your customers. Certification could also be used as safe harbor in defending legal actions in the event of a breach or some other failure.

Certification takes a lot of work. But it shows that your organization has reached a significant level of maturity, and it's an authentic validation of your commitment to do things right.

Continuous Compliance and Breaches

In compliance environments, we talk about certification and attestation as if they are the end goal of the compliance process. In some respects, however, they are just the beginning. The aim of compliance schemes is to ensure that the organization is continuously compliant. Each of the requirements (at least in prescriptive, rules-based regulations) are designed to be recurring and present in all day-to-day activities. This is why most certifications or attestation reviews are done across a period of time, such as a year, to verify that your controls were consistently applied.

This moves compliance from being a moment in time, auditable requirement to a continuous compliance need. By using the automation suggestions in this chapter, your team and organization can verify its continued compliance and identify issues early. While this may not prevent a compliance breach from happening, it will mean that if the auditors are sent to your door, you will have evidence of your processes and approaches up to and at the time of the breach, not just on your last attestation or certification audit.

Certification Doesn't Mean That You Are Secure

Certification or a successful attestation report does not mean that your organization is compliant. It means that you've satisfied a series of conditions that a regulator would reasonably expect, using a recognized and validated approach. A regulator could still find you in breach of compliance for some reason, although you've reduced your risk significantly.

Certification does not mean that you are secure. Several organizations that held certifications or passed all of their audits still suffered from high-profile breaches or serious operational failures. Just because you've met a certification qualification doesn't mean that you can stop looking, learning, and improving.

Key Takeaways

While compliance does not imply security for all systems, it is a requirement to operate for many organizations, and can play an important part in building your security approaches and culture.

- Compliance regulations lay out minimum requirements for security controls, reviews, and oversight. This can be done in two different ways: a detailed rules-based approach like PCI DSS, or an outcome-based model like SOX 404.

- Compliance will put constraints on an Agile team's freedom to "inspect and adapt" the way that it works, but the team can still have a voice (and choices) in how to meet compliance obligations.

- Instead of trying to enforce compliance through manual checklists and point-in-time audits, compliance rules can be built into engineering workflows and automation, to continuously enforce controls and record evidence for auditors in your build pipelines.

- Separation of duties between developers and operations presents concerns for regulators as responsibilities between these organizations blur, especially in DevOps environments. You will need to take careful steps and rely heavily on automation to manage these risks.

Compliance is everyone's responsibility, even if you are not cutting code every day, or if you are only playing a supporting role in the development life cycle. You can help protect the organization's systems and help meet compliance requirements through good information security practices like locking your devices whenever you step away; choosing strong, unique passwords for all your work systems; and not sharing your accounts or passwords with others.

And finally, be vigilant and speak up if something doesn't seem right. Everyone needs to do their part to detect and report any incidents or issues that could compromise compliance. If you spot something, please report it. Remember, compliance needs to be 24/7, and the consequences for a lapse can be serious. It's up to everyone to play their part.

CHAPTER 15

Security Culture

A lot of this book talks about tools and techniques, but it's critical to recognize that being Agile is about being people first. It's just as important to talk about the people side of security, and how to build on the Agile values of empathy, openness, transparency, and collaboration if you truly want to be able to develop an effective and forward-looking security program.

Focusing only on the technical aspects will inevitably mean that you fall short, and can in many ways be considered the main failure of the approaches taken to information security programs through the 1990s and early 2000s.

Every organization already has a security culture. The question really is whether you want to take ownership of yours and influence it, or whether you want it to be something that manifests unchecked and unsupported? This chapter can help you take an objective view of your security culture as it currently stands, as well as providing some practical steps to thinking about how to own your organization's security culture and continue to evolve it over time.

Building a meaningful security culture requires buy in from everyone, not just the security team, and if people outside of the security team have a better idea of some of the challenges discussed in this chapter then that will drive greater empathy and understanding. While it's true many of the practical aspects discussed are for the security team to implement (or take elements from), it's important for both Agile teams and the security team to read and understand the following sections.

The Importance of Security Culture

It can be easy to feel that the term *culture* has become both overloaded and overused in the engineering context, and as such we run the risk of ignoring the benefits that can arise from a clear and concise discussion of culture. Furthermore, the development of a thoughtful *security culture* within an organization is something that usually gets insufficient attention—in many cases this is isn't even something that a security team sees as being its responsibility. If however you understand that security is the intersection of technology and people, investing energy in developing a strong security culture is imperative for the overall success of a greater security program.

Defining "Culture"

In an effort to not over complicate the discussion here, when referring to *security culture*, the definition of culture given by Karl Wiegers in his book *Creating a Software Engineering Culture* (Dorset House) will be used as the basis from which to build:

> Culture includes a set of shared values, goals, and principles that guide the behaviors, activities, priorities, and decisions of a group of people working toward a common objective.

Building from this definition, when we talk about security culture, all we're really trying to achieve is for everyone in an organization to understand that security is a collective responsibility, and if it is to be successful, is not something that can be solely addressed by the security team. Building the principles and behaviors that allow members of an organization to buy in is the key to achieving this. Unfortunately, this has been something that has often been done quite poorly, the result often being people actively trying to avoid any involvement at all in the process of security. This can be seen as entirely rational with the burden and drag many of the traditional approaches to security place on the people they are trying to protect.

Push, Don't Pull

Developing a shared understanding between the security team and developers that everyone's individual actions directly contribute to the overall security posture of the organization is an important step in building a security culture. This encourages everyone to engage proactively with the security team, which can switch the way in which a security team works with the rest of the organization from a purely *push* based model to one that is at least partly *pull* based.

The less a security team has to push its way into a process, the less that team is viewed as being an obstacle by the others that are focused on nonsecurity tasks. The greater the degree of *pull* that is seen toward a security team, the greater it can be said that *security as part of the everyday* is being realized. Having an organization that actively reaches out to, and engages with, the security team contributes massively to building a sense that the security function is not there to block progress, but instead is there to support the innovation of others.

Building a Security Culture

Culture is not something that can be purchased off the shelf, or something that can be *fast tracked*. Every organization has its own culture that reflects its unique values and needs, and as such: any associated security culture must equally be tailored and developed to speak to those needs. Successful security cultures that work in one organization may not translate well to another; however, there may well be numerous elements that can be observed and then tailored to fit into the target organization. The things discussed in this chapter should be seen as inspiration or starting points for how you may want to further develop your own security culture, rather than *rules* that have to be followed.

It is also worth noting that the development of a security culture is not a task that can ever really be considered complete: it must be continually iterated on and refined as the organization in which it exists changes and evolves. Security cultures must also be outward looking to understand the overall technology and threat landscapes within which an organization operates, and ensure they stay apace of the changing ways in which technology is embraced and used by everyone in the organization.

The overall aim of a security culture is to change, or at least influence, both the engineering culture and overall culture of the organization to consider security requirements alongside other factors when making decisions. An important distinction to recognize is that a security culture is the set of practices undertaken to facilitate such changes, not the changes themselves.

This doesn't mean the goal is to develop an engineering culture in which security overrules all other considerations, but just that security will be taken into account alongside the other requirements and priorities during the development life cycle. While this may sound like a very obvious statement, in the experience of the authors of this book, security can often be treated very much as a second-class citizen that can be ignored or just has lip service paid to it.

Now that we have a handle on engineering and security culture in the abstract, what does it mean to take these ideals and make them into a reality at your organization? As already stated, there is no one-size-fits-all cultural recipe for security; every organization has its own unique norms, needs, and existing culture, and any security culture effort will need to fit in with those. This is not to say that the security culture may not seek to change existing organizational traits that manifest poor security practices, just that realism and pragmatism beat idealism when trying to establish any form of security culture at all.

Now let's look at a real-world example of a highly successful security culture, and how you can take ideas and lessons from this to build or strengthen your own security culture.

Thinking about your security culture, your approach to security, as a brand, can be helpful in giving you an external reference point from which to view your own work. A brand is promise to its customers: it articulates what they can expect from it and how it is different from its competitors. Similarly, a clearly defined security culture is a promise to the others in an organization about the kind of security experience you are pledging to them, the kind of support you are committed to provide to help solve problems rather than create them, and how you want the organization to perceive the security team. And as with brands, it can take a long time to build and a far shorter time to undermine.

Companies spend vast amounts of energy refining and protecting their brand as they understand its importance to their longer-term success. Invest in your security culture in a similarly committed way, and it will pay back dividends over time and equally help set up a future that is bright.

Principles of Effective Security

In terms of a small case study, we will look at the security team and program in place at Etsy. Far from being held as an ideal situation to mimic, it is a useful example to look at and learn from the efforts that have been tried and iterated upon over a number of years. Essentially, we may be able to make our own efforts show results in a shorter time frame from learning from the successes and mistakes Etsy has already undertaken.

At Etsy, the security culture is based on three core principles. The activities of the security program are then viewed and evaluated from the perspective of how well they uphold or further these principles. None are set in stone, and all are up for re-evaluation and refinement as Etsy continues to evolve as an organization and learn from outside influences.

Who Is Etsy and Why Should We Care?

Etsy (*https://www.etsy.com*) is the world's largest online marketplace for handcrafted goods, founded in 2005. After some early stumbles with its technology, Etsy made radical changes to how it built and delivered software, bringing in new leadership and a new way of working. Former CTO and now CEO, Chad Dickerson, and Etsy's current CTO, John Allspaw, both came from Flickr where they pioneered a highly collaborative approach in which developers and operations engineers worked closely together to deploy small changes to production every day. Allspaw's presentation at Velocity in 2009, "10+ Deploys per Day: Dev and Ops Cooperation at Flickr" (*https://www.youtube.com/watch?v=LdOe18KhtT4*), is regarded as one of the seminal moments in launching the DevOps movement.

Today, Etsy continues to be a DevOps leader, and like many other internet companies, is an engineering-led organization where technologists are intimately responsible for driving business results, including being responsible for supporting any changes that they make.

At the time of writing, Etsy has over 300 engineers pushing new code into production 50+ times a day, which means that the way that security is approached needs to be fundamentally different in order for it to be successful. In a similar way to the work done in the DevOps space, Etsy has become recognized as a pioneer in progressive approaches to security and security culture.

While Etsy evolved its security philosophy and practices to meet its own specific needs, many of the approaches can be just as helpful for companies that do not follow a continuous deployment development pattern. In this chapter we will look closer at the approaches developed by Etsy and its security teams and see how they contribute to building a positive security (and DevOps) culture.

Enable, Don't Block

If any of the security principles at Etsy can be considered the most important, it would be the principle of enablement.

> Effective security teams should measure themselves by what they enable, not by what they block.
>
> —Rich Smith

Many security programs, teams, and professionals measure their success in terms of what they have blocked: those vulnerabilities or activities that could have resulted in a negative impact to the organization that the security team managed to stop from happening. While on the surface this measure seems a reasonable one—that security is here to stop the bad things—an interesting effect of this mindset is the way that over a relatively short period it creates a negative spiral of involvement with a security team.

If other people across the organization become conditioned to think of a security team as being blockers, as being the ones who get in the way of getting *real work* done, then they will quickly learn to avoid them at all costs. The clear result of this is the creation and perpetuation of a diverging view between the real and perceived security posture of the organization. The security team has only a minimal view of the things occurring that could really benefit from its input as the rest of the organization spends energy actively avoiding the security team, being aware of what they are doing through fear of being derailed.

If the organization sees the security team as a blocker then they will try to route around the team regardless of whatever process and policies may be in place: the more you block, the less effective you become because more and more activities are hidden from you.

If, however, we turn the goal of the security team from a mindset of trying to prevent stupid teams of clueless engineers and product managers from making mistakes with their silly projects, to one of enabling innovation and findings ways to do even the craziest ideas securely, this begins to make a security team into an attractive resource to interact with and seek guidance from.

This switch in mindset from one which is measured on what it prevents into one that measures itself on what it facilitates is so fundamental to all that follows, that without fully embracing it, it may be difficult to truly consider that an organization *gets* what progressive security is all about.

This isn't to say that a security team is forbidden from ever saying no to something. What it is saying is that in many cases when "No" would be the de facto response, a "Yes, and" or a "Yes, but" may actually be the more long-term beneficial answer.

"Yes, and" leaves the door open to a security team to provide consultation, support to get the idea or project to a place where it can still achieve its goals, but without some (or all) of the aspects that created the security concerns.

"No" is a security team's ace and as such should be played sparingly: used too often or as the go-to response for any project that requires out-of-the-box thinking to come up with a meaningful compromise between the business and security goals means that the security teams blocks more than it enables. An unfortunate side effect of saying no is that it can often remove a security team from the decision-making and feedback loops. The development team stops working with the security team to solve problems and instead just puts up with it, or ignores and works around it. Such a breakdown in collaboration and consultation with a security team results in a huge loss to the organization in terms of creative problem-solving, and critically, value creation.

If members of the security team don't relish the prospect of solving new, difficult, and complex problems that have no black-or-white correct answer, then it's time to consider whether you have the wrong people dealing with your security. Lazy security teams default to "no" because it is a get out of jail free card for any future negative impact that may come from the project they opposed. Ineffective security teams want the risk profile of a company to stay the same so that they do not have to make hard choices between security and innovation. Nothing will get a security team bypassed quicker than the expectation by others in the organization that the brakes will get applied to their project because the security folks don't want any change to the risk profile.

It goes without saying that organizations with such teams create silos between the engineers in a company who are striving to drive the business forward, and the security experts who should be striving to help understand and balance the risks associated with either innovation or day-to-day tasks.

Unfortunately, security is rarely black and white in terms of solutions. There are many times that residual risks persist, and they should be balanced against the upsides of the project being supported to succeed. Mindful risk acceptance can be the correct approach as long as the risks and potential impacts are understood, acknowledged, and weighed against the upsides of the project continuing on still having them. Mindful risk acceptance always beats blind risk ignorance.

Understanding and assessing the risks associated with a project presents a perfect opportunity for creative dialog between the security team and the development team. This conversation is not only crucial in order to determine the acceptable level of risk, it also helps engender understanding on both sides, and can go a long way to reducing the level of stress that can often be felt by a development team when considering the security of its creation. Conversations around what level of risk is acceptable, and the benefits that can arise from allowing that risk to remain, demonstrate that everyone is on the same side and they are working together to get the best possible product released, with security being one element that helps define *best*.

Perfect security is often an illusion dependent on the associated threat model and should rarely be used as a reason to nix a project overall. *Pragmatic security* is a watchword that should be far more widely observed for most commercial security problems and solutions. Too often a security team can fall into the pattern of making everything a critical issue; this is akin to crying wolf and will be the fastest way to get a group of developers to devalue (or outright ignore) the input from a security team.

There are too many cases where bad judgment calls are made in this regard. Let's look at one example: an ill-fated attempt to halt the release of a marketing campaign site due to its lack of HTTPS. The site was hosted on both separate servers and a separate domain to the organization's main site and only contained static public data. While there was a violation of the organization's stated policy that all web properties must be only SSL, the actual risk presented was minimal aside from the potential reputational damage of having a non-HTTPS protected domain. The marketing team, who were the project owners, was best placed to determine the criticality of the risk. As with many marketing efforts, time was not running on the side of the project, and significant amounts of both social and security capital were cast to the wind by the security team in an effort to arbitrarily stand behind policy in the absence of risk, with the bid to stop the project ultimately failing and the site going live on schedule.

Be on the lookout for third parties such as penetration testers also making mountains out of molehills in terms of a finding's criticality and impact in an effort to demonstrate value from an engagement. All too often, findings will be presented from the perspective of ultimate security rather than pragmatic security, and it is the responsibility of the security team receiving an external assessment to temper and prioritize findings as appropriate, given the team's far greater contextual understanding of the organization's operations and risk tolerance.

You're only a blocker if you're the last to know. The security team needs to be included early on in the development life cycle and have its feedback incorporated into the development stories as they build. This isn't just a responsibility for developers, however—a security team also needs to encourage early and frequent engagement with developers. One important way in which this can be done is by ensuring that the appropriate urgency is assigned to any issues found, and only blocking progress when there are no reasonable alternatives to do so, rather than blocking being the default response to any and every security issue. Sometimes allowing a security issue to ship and getting a commitment from developers that it will be fixed at an agreed upon future date may be the best approach, at least for noncritical issues.

An ineffective security organization creates a haven for those who find excuses to avoid change at all cost in the hope that they can avoid blame for future new insecurities. An effective security organization, however, finds and removes that mindset and replaces it with a mindset that accepts that security issues may arise as a result of change, and relishes the prospect of tackling such problems head-on, recognizing and rewarding the enabling role played by a security team that helps support disruptive innovation take place as securely as possible.

Understanding whether the rest of the organization views you as enablers or as blockers is a good first exercise when you are getting serious about developing a progressive security culture.

Transparently Secure

> A security team who embraces openness about what it does and why, spreads understanding.
>
> —Rich Smith

People on security teams can often fall into the trap of playing *secret agent*. What is meant by this is that secrecy, segregation, and all sorts of other activities are undertaken in the name of security that oftentimes actually harm the goal of making an organization more secure because the security team wants to feel special or cool.

The principle of transparency in a security culture may at first seem counterintuitive; however, transparency is a principle that can take many forms, and it is really quite intuitive when you think about it in terms of spreading understanding and awareness about security to a larger group that is not security experts.

Examples of effective transparency can be as simple as explaining why a particular issue is of great concern to the security team, along with a clear and realistic explanation of the impact that could arise. Showing developers how unsanitized input may be misused in their application and the impact that this could have to the business is a far more transparent and valuable discussion of the concerns than pointing them to a coding best practices guide for the language in question and discussing the issue in the abstract. One drives empathy, understanding, and will help incrementally spread security knowledge. The other will more likely come across as an unhelpful edict.

Whenever there is an external security assessment (whether it is a penetration test or a continuous bug bounty) be sure to include the relevant development teams from scoping to completion, ultimately sharing the findings of any issues uncovered, and having the developers fully in the loop as mitigations and fixes are discussed and decided upon.

There is nothing more adversarial than a security team seeming to be working with an external party to pick holes in a system, and then have a series of changes and requirements appear from the process in a black-box fashion. The team whose project is being assessed rarely wants to have urgent requirements or shortcomings tossed over the wall to it, it wants to be engaged with to understand what the problems are that have been found, how they were found, and what the possible real-world impacts could be. Chapter 12 goes into this area in more detail and won't be repeated here; however, the cultural aspects of how to have supportive conversations when security issues are found during assessment is important to consider before the pen testers have even looked at the first line of code or have thrown the first packet.

A great deal of the value of an assessment comes from being as transparent as possible with the teams whose work is subject to review. It is not only a chance to find serious security bugs and flaws, but is also a highly engaging and impactful opportunity for developers to learn from a team of highly focused security specialists. Simple, but unfortunately rare, approaches such as sharing a repository of security findings from internal or external assessments with the developers directly helps engage and share everything in the full gory detail. This can often also result in the creation of a positive feedback loop where developers end up contributing to a repository of issues themselves when they are able to see the kind of things the security folks care about. It may be surprising the number of security relevant bugs that are often lying around within the collective knowledge of a development team.

Another way in which the transparency principle can be embraced is by becoming more inclusive and inviting developers to be part of the security team and jump into the trenches. This may be part of the onboarding or bootcamp process that new developers go through when joining an organization, or it may be part of some continuing training or periodic cross-team exchange: the important thing is that people from outside of the security team get a chance to see what the day-to-day looks like. Having developers see the grisly details of a security team's work will do more than anything else to drive empathy and understanding. Oftentimes it will result in the seeding of people across an organization who are not formally on the security team, but who remain closely in touch with them and continue to facilitate visibility to the development process while continuing to learn more about security. At Etsy these are called "security champions" and are a key component to the security team being able to stay available to as many other teams as possible.

A security team that can default to openness and only restrict as the exception will do a far better job at spreading knowledge about what it does, and most importantly, why it is doing it.

Don't Play the Blame Game

> Security failures will happen, only without blame will you be able to understand the true causes, learn from them, and improve.
>
> —Rich Smith

As much as it may be uncomfortable to admit, in a sufficiently complex system nothing that any security team does will ever be able to eliminate all possible causes of insecurity. Worse still, the same mistakes may happen again at some point in future.

Being blameless as one of the core tenets of your approach to security may seem like a slightly strange thing to have as one of a list of the three most important principles—surely part of keeping an organization secure means finding the problems that cause insecurity, and in turn making things more secure by finding what (or who) caused those problems, right?

Wrong!

Anyone working in a modern organization knows how complex things get, and how the complexity of the environment seems to continue to increase more than it simplifies. When technology and software are added to this mix, a point can be reached quite quickly where no single person is able to describe the intricacies of the system top to tail. Now, when that grand system is declared as something that needs to be secured, the difficulty of the task at hand can become so immense that shortcuts and corner-cutting exercises inevitably need to be found, as without them no forward progress could be made within the time frames required.

One such shortcut that has been used so pervasively that it regularly goes unquestioned is blame. Finding who is to blame is often the main focus of the activity that follows the discovery of an issue—but that misses the point. It is imperative to understand that building a security culture based around the belief that finding who to blame for a security issue will result in a more secure future is fundamentally flawed.

Many security issues may seemingly arise as a result of a decision or action an individual did, or didn't, take. When such situations arise—and they will—a common next thought is how the person who seems at fault, the human who made the error, should be held accountable for his lapse in judgment. He caused a security event to occur, which may have caused the security team or possibly the wider organization to have a day from hell, and he should have the blame for doing so placed squarely at his feet.

Public shaming, restriction from touching that system again, demotion, or even being fired could be the order of the day. This, the blameful mindset will tell us, also has the added benefit of making everyone else pay attention and be sure they don't make the same mistake lest they also suffer the same fate.

If we continue on this path of blaming, then we end up succumbing to a culture in which fear and deterrence is the way in which security improves, as people are just too scared of the consequences to make mistakes.

It would be fair to say that software engineering has much to learn from other engineering disciplines when thinking about blame, and in a wider sense, safety. A notable thinker in the space of safety engineering is Erik Hollnagel, who has applied his approaches across a variety of disciplines, including aviation, healthcare, and nuclear safety—and luckily for us, also in the space of software engineering safety. Hollnagel's perspective is that the approach of identifying a root cause and then removing that error in an effort to fix things, and therefore make the system safer, works well for machines, but that the approach does not work well for people.

In fact, Hollnagel argues that the focus on finding the cause and then eliminating it has influenced the approach taken to risk assessment so completely that root causes are oftentimes retrospectively created by those investigating rather than being truly found. When human factors are considered in accidents, Hollnagel asserts that the inevitable variability of the performance of the human part of the system needs to be accounted for in the design of the system itself if it is to have a reduction in risk. A quote attributed to Hollnagel that summarizes his views of accidents involving humans well is:

> We must strive to understand that accidents don't happen because people gamble and lose.
>
> Accidents happen because the person believes that:
>
> ...what is about to happen is not possible,
>
> ...or what is about to happen has no connection to what they are doing,
>
> ...or that the possibility of getting the intended outcome is well worth whatever risk there is.

Unless there is compelling evidence that someone in the organization is deliberately trying to cause a security event, the cause of the incident should not just be neatly explained away as human error and then quickly step into applying the appropriate blame. It is key to a progressive security culture to have a shared understanding that the people working in your organization are not trying to create a security event, but instead are trying to get their work done in a way that they believe would have a desirable outcome; however, something either unexpected or out of their control occurred, resulting in the incident. Rather than spending energy searching for the root cause as being who to blame, efforts should be taken to understand the reasons that underly why the person made the decisions she did, and what about the system within which she was working could be improved in order for her to detect things were about to go badly wrong.

If the focus is on assigning blame and delivering a level of retribution to the people perceived as the cause, then it follows that the people with the most knowledge about the event will not be forthcoming with a truthful perspective on everything they know, as they fear the consequences that may follow. If, however, the people closest to the security event are safe in the belief that they can be 100% honest in what they did, and why, and that that information will be used to improve the system itself, then you are far more likely to get insights to critical shortcomings of the system and potentially develop modifications to it to make the future use of it safer.

A mechanism that has been developed to help with this approach of finding the reasoning behind a decision, and then improving the system to ensure more informed decisions are made in future, is the blameless postmortem.

When considering blameless postmortems, it is important to go into the process understanding that the issues you are about to investigate may very well happen again. Preventing the future is not the goal—learning is, and to that end, learning needs to be the focus of the postmortem itself. Participants must consciously counter the basic human urge to find a single explanation and single fix for the incident. This is often helped by having a postmortem facilitator who gives a brief introduction reminding participants what they are all there for: a semi-structured group interview. Nothing more.

While this perspective sounds great on paper, how does it work in reality? From one of the author's experiences at Etsy, security postmortems were some of the best attended meetings at the company and provided a regular opportunity to investigate root causes that resulted in significant improvements to the security of the systems. Postmortems empower engineers to do what they do best, to solve problems in innovative ways, as well as establish trust between engineers and a security team. The well attended meetings also provided a powerful opportunity to deliver security education and awareness to a large and diverse group of people from across the organization. Who doesn't want to attend a meeting that's digging into the details of high-impact security events and listen to experts from across the organization collaborate and problem-solve in realtime in front of them?

Finally, it is worth explicitly noting that postmortems can be a valuable way to create and share a knowledge base of issues across teams. By tackling root causes and reoccurring patterns holistically rather than on a case by case basis, solutions are devised scalably and systemically.

As we touched on in Chapter 13, the important takeaway is that while much of what has been discussed regarding blameless postmortems in the software engineering space has been written from an ops perspective, the lessons learned apply just as much to security, and there are many lessons that can be learned from the last near decade of DevOps development. For further reading on blameless postmortems, see the following:

- "What Etsy Does When Things Go Wrong: A 7-Step Guide" (*http://bit.ly/etsy-7-step-guide*)
- "Blameless PostMortems and a Just Culture" (*http://bit.ly/blameless-postmortems-just/*)
- "Etsy's Debriefing Facilitation Guide for Blameless Postmortems" (*http://bit.ly/etsy-debrief-guide*)
- "To Err Is Human: The ETTO Principle" (*http://bit.ly/etto-principle*)

A Beautifully Succinct Example: The Secure Engineer's Manifesto

While the three principles of effective security are a wordy way of covering many things that an organization may want to consider in terms of its security culture, a beautifully succinct example of embodying many of them in an easy to understand and culturally resonating way came to one of the author's attention during a presentation by Chris Hymes discussing the security approach built up at Riot Games. It went:

The Secure Engineer's Manifesto

1. I will panic correctly.
2. I understand laptops can ruin everything.
3. I will resist the urge to create terrible passwords.
4. YOLO is not a motto for engineers.

While deliberately lighthearted, it is a great example of supporting and empowering a larger engineering populace to be responsible for their security, while at the same time getting some important and meaningful security advice across in a way that is not dictatorial.

Chris freely admits his manifesto list builds off of and riffs upon other practitioners' advice and perspective, most notably a fantastic blog post by Ryan McGeehan, titled "An Information Security Policy for the Startup" (*http://bit.ly/isp-for-startup*).

As you consider the security culture you are establishing at your organization, pulling together, and tweaking to fit your needs, a manifesto that your teams can rally around can be a powerful way of getting buy in to your security vision.

Scale Security, Empower the Edges

A practical approach to progressive security that embodies many of the principles described is actively including those outside of the security team in the security decision-making process itself, rather than excluding them and having security as something that happens to them. In many scenarios, the users themselves will have far more context about what may be going on that the security team will; including them in the security decision and resolution process helps ensure that responses to security events are proportional and prioritized.

Including everyone in security decision and resolution loops can be realized in a variety of ways and is something that should be fine-tuned for a particular organization's needs. Examples of including everyone in the security decision-making process would be the following:

- Alert users over the internal chat system in the event of noncritical security events such as failed logins, logins from unfamiliar IPs, or traffic to an internal server they don't normally access, and asking them to provide quick context on what's going on. In many cases the explanation will be an innocuous one, and no further action will be required. In the event that the user does not know what has happened or does not respond within a time frame, the security team can step in and investigate further. A great discussion of this is "Distributed Security Alerting" (*http://bit.ly/distributed-security-alerting*) by Slack's Ryan Huber.

- Notify users at login time if their OS/browser/plug-ins are out of date, giving them the option to update immediately (ideally with one click, if possible), but also, and most importantly, allowing them to defer the update to a future point in time. The number of deferrals allowed before the only option is to update, as well as the versions of the software that can have updates deferred on, is down to the security team, but the important thing is to provide the user some shades of gray rather than just black and white. For example, if a user's browser is only slightly out of date, it may be an acceptable trade-off to let him log in to get the action he needs to do complete and update later on, rather than blocking his access completely and forcing a browser restart at a incredibly inconvenient moment for him.

- Ask a user over email or chat if she has just installed some new software or has been manually editing her configuration as a change has been seen on her system such as a new kernel module being loaded, her shell history file got deleted, or a ramdisk was mounted, for example. While suspicious and possibly indicative of malicious activity, in an engineering environment there are many reasons a developer would be making lower-level changes to her setup.

- In internal phishing exercises, have the main metric being focused on as not the click-through rate on the phishing emails, but the report rate of users who let the security team know they received something strange. A commonly misplaced intention of phishing awareness programs is the aspiration to get the click-through rate down to zero. As the authors of this book can attest to only too well from across a multitude of organizations, while the goal of *everyone* in an organization doing the right thing and not clicking on the phish *every* time is laudible, it is wholly unrealistic. If the win condition is that all people have to do the right thing every time, then you're probably playing the wrong game as you will rarely win. If your focus is on trying to ensure that one person needs to do the right thing, that being notifying the security team he received a phish, then that is a game you are far more likely to win.

These are just a few examples among many possibilities, but they all succeed at pulling the user and her specific context into the decision loop, which contributes to a security team that can better prioritize its work, and a user base that does not feel that security is a stick that is always being used to hit them. Additionally these kinds of interactions provide excellent points at which tiny snippets of security education can be delivered, and starts to build up a workforce that feels connected and responsible for the security decisions being made. Eventually this will result in the creation of positive feedback loops where users are actively engaging with a security team in the truest sense of *see something, say something*, or proactively giving security a heads-up that they are about to do something that may set off some alerts.

The Who Is Just as Important as the How

If this all makes sense in terms of what the mission of an effective security team should be, then the next step is actually executing on this mission. A great culture needs great people, and too often members of a security team are hired based on their technical skills alone, with little consideration for their soft skills. If it is believed that people are just as important as technology to having an effective security program, then we need to hire security practitioners with that in mind.

One reason why many security teams are actively avoided in their organization is that the personalities and attitudes of the members of the security team are actively working against the wider goal of making security approachable and understandable by the wider organization. Too often security practitioners can be patronizing or condescending in their interactions with the people they are there to support, some seemingly even taking delight in the security issues encountered by their coworkers.

While this is not a book about people management, it's worth noting that the manager responsible for a security program has a special responsibility to be on the lookout for behavior and attitudes from the security team that are not conducive to the wider security goals, and to put a stop to it if and when it is found. The cardinal rule of thumb that should be front of mind when thinking about security team hiring is one that seems obvious, but historically seems to have been too often not followed:

> Don't hire assholes.

Closely followed by:

> If you inadvertently do, or you inherit one, get rid of them ASAP.

A single abrasive member of a security team can do more to undermine the efforts made in the implementation of a progressive security program than almost anything else, as they are the face of that program that others in an organization have to interact with on a daily basis.

A great book that discuses this in much greater detail is *The No Asshole Rule: Building a Civilized Workplace and Surviving One That Isn't* (Business Plus) by Robert I. Sutton. In the opinion of the authors, this should be required reading for every security manager, and should be kept close at hand and visible in case its valuable lessons start to be forgotten.

Security Outreach

Cory Doctorow has a fantastic passage in his 2014 book, *Information Doesn't Want to Be Free* (McSweeney's), that sums up the aims of security outreach very succinctly:

> Sociable conversation is the inevitable product of socializing. Sociable conversation is the way in which human beings established trusted relationships among themselves.

Security outreach is not buying pizza as a bribe for people to sit through a Power-Point presentation about how to validate input. It is a genuine investment in social situations that will drive conversations between people on a security team and those outside of a security team. These conversations inevitably form the basis of trusted relationships, which in turn drive greater empathy around security for all involved.

And let's be clear, this empathy goes both ways, this isn't purely a drive for others in a company to understand how hard the job of the security team can be; it is equally to drive understanding for those on the security team as to some of the daily struggles and annoyances faced by their nonsecurity coworkers who just want to get their job done. Creating circumstances in which the real people behind the usernames or email addresses can get to know one another is key to avoiding situations where assumptions are made of the others.

Security outreach gives the security team the chance to not fall victim to the temptation that developers are lazy or just don't care about security, and it gives developers to opportunity to sidestep the assumption that the security team takes a special delight in causing them extra work that slows them down. Security outreach helps everyone assume best intent from their colleagues, which is something that will not only benefit security at an organization, but many other aspects of it as well.

Examples of security outreach events that are distinct from security education are things like the following:

- A movie night showing a a sci-fi or *hacker* movie. Bonus points if those attending wear rollerblades and dress up!
- A trophy or award that the security team gives out with much fanfare on a periodic basis for some worthy achievement. Examples could be the most phishing emails reported or the most security bugs squashed.
- A bug hunt afternoon where the security team sits in a shared space and hacks on a new product or feature that has reached a milestone, looking for bugs, demonstrating their findings on a big screen, and being available to talk to people about what they are doing and what it's all about.
- Just as simple as inviting others from the company to the bar near the office for a few drinks on the security team's dime.

Again, every situation is different so you should tailor appropriate activities to your organization and the people that make it up.

Ensure there is management buy in to the concept of security outreach, and assign budget to it. It really will be some of the best ROI that your security program will see.

Securgonomics

Much of the discussion so far has been about the theoretical aspects of how a security culture can be established and nurtured; however, as culture is central to how people work with one another and act as a collective, the real-life aspects shouldn't be ignored. *Securgonomics* is a completely made-up term created by one of this book's authors (okay, it was Rich) as part of some presentation slideware: a portmanteau of *security* and *ergonomics*.

If the definition of ergonomics is:

> er·go·nom·ics \ˌər-gə-ˈnä-miks\
>
> noun
>
> the study of people's efficiency in their working environment

then the definition of securgonomics (if it were, in fact, a real word!) would be:

> se.cure·go·nom·ics \si-ˈkyu̇r-gə-ˈnä-miks\
>
> noun
>
> the study of people's efficiency of security interactions in their working environment

While a made-up term, it captures the very real observation that security teams can often fall into the trap of separating themselves from the people they are there to support. An Agile approach aims to break down silos because they inhibit easy communication and collaboration, and this needs to extend into the real-world space inhabited by security teams and others in an organization. The goal of all of this is to lower the barriers to interacting with the security team.

The use and design of the physical office space needs to help make the security team visible, easy to approach, and therefore easy to interact with. Too often a security team will lock itself behind doors and walls, which creates a very real *us* and *them* segregation. While it is true that security teams may be dealing with sensitive data as part of its daily role, it is also true that for much of the time its activities are not any more sensitive than the work being done by its coworkers.

Security teams can too often fall into the stereotypical trope of being *secret squirrels* working on things that couldn't possibly be shared outside of the group. While occasionally this may be true, much of the time this perspective is falsely (and unnecessarily) created by the members of the security team themselves. A team that locks itself away from the rest of the organization will be at a significant disadvantage if it is trying to be a team of transparent enablers that help security become a responsibility that is genuinely shared by people across the organization.

Look at where your security team(s) are physically located, and ask yourself questions like these:

- Does this help or hinder others to be able to easily come over and interact with team members?
- Do people see the team as part of their daily routine, or do they have to go out of their way to speak to team members in person?
- Do new hires see the security team's location on their first-day office tour?
- Is the security team near the teams that it works with most closely and frequently?
- Can others see when the security team is in the office? Can they see when team members are busy?

Where possible, having the security team in a location that has a lot of footfall enables easy interaction with them in a low-lift way. If others wander by the security team on the way to the coffee station or on their way in and out of the office, then micro-interactions will inevitably occur. Not requiring people to make a special journey to the security team will mean that more ad hoc conversations will happen more regularly. This has benefits to everyone, not the least of which is building up trusted relationships between the security team and everyone else.

Where the security folk sit is important; but even if they are in a prime spot where they are easily accessible to all, it doesn't mean they should rest on their laurels: they need to also work to incentivize other people in the organization to interact with them. This doesn't need to be overthought and can be as simple as having a sticker exchange, a lending library for security books, or some jars of candy. At Etsy, security candy became a phenomenon all of its own, whereby others across the organization took part in choosing which sweets would be in the next batch of candy to be ordered ,and where the current inventory could be queried through the company-wide chatbot, *irccat*.

There was even a hack-week project that set up an IP camera over the candy jars to allow remote viewing of what was currently up for grabs. While a fun and silly endeavor, the ROI seen from such a simple act of sharing candy with others in the office incentivized engagement and interaction with the security team in a way that vastly outweighed the monetary cost involved.

Having said all that about the physical location of the security team(s), the final piece of advice would be to not tether the team members to their desks. Having a security team whose method of work enables team members to be mobile around the office and to go and sit with the people they are working with where possible is equally important.

Set the expectation across the organization that a security engineer will go and sit alongside the developer with whom they are diagnosing an issue or explaining how to address a vulnerability. This simple act is a very visible embodiment of the principle of being a supportive and enabling team that wants to understand the other people in an organization, and that they are there to help others succeed on their missions in a secure way.

Dashboards

Lots of teams have dashboards displayed on big screens in their working environment to keep a high-level overview of trends and events that are occurring, and obviously security is no different. However, it is worth pointing out the cultural relevance that dashboards can hold and the dual purposes of the dashboards that may be on display. Having a better understanding of the different objectives that dashboards can help achieve will hopefully empower better decisions about which dashboards make the most sense for your environment.

We can roughly group workplace dashboards into four types:

1. Situational-awareness dashboards
2. Summary dashboards
3. *Vanity* dashboards
4. Intervention dashboards

Situational awareness dashboards are dashboards that display data that is of most use by a security team itself. The data displayed shows the current state of an environment or system, along with as much historic or contextual data as possible so as to allow team members to make a determination as to whether something may be wrong or not. The primary objective of a situational dashboard is for a security team to at a glance have a sense of whether everything is as expected for a given system. It is worth noting that situational dashboards only indicate that something is amiss and needs investigating, rather than telling you exactly what is taking place attack-wise. They provide easy ways of seeing symptoms. It is for the team then to jump in and determine the cause.

Examples of situational awareness dashboards are displays of data such as "successful versus unsuccessful login attempts over time" (Figure 15-1), "number of 2FA SMS, call and push codes sent over time," and "number of detected XSS attempts over time" (Figure 15-2). The cultural benefits of situational awareness dashboards really center around them acting as a source of reassurance for people to see that the security of systems is being monitored and acted upon when needed. They can also be a source of engagement with the security team, especially if time-series graphs are being displayed and big changes are relevant. If people see graphs going crazy, they are often curious as to what caused the change and what is being done in response.

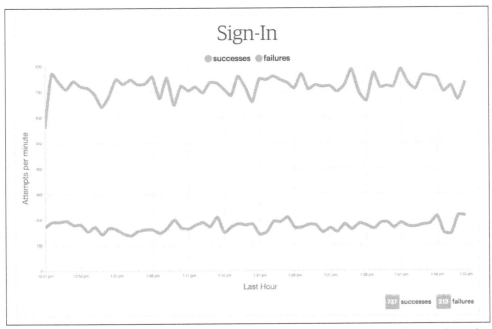

Figure 15-1. An example of a situational-awareness dashboard showing the number of successful logins to a web application versus the number of failed login attempts. Patterns between these two metrics can indicate different situations that warrant follow-up by the security team; for example, a rise in failed logins versus successful logins would be indicative of a password-guessing attack taking place. A drop in successful logins could indicate a problem with the authentication system, with legitimate users being denied access.

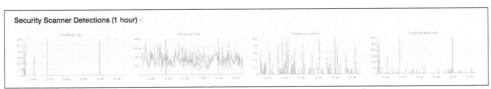

Figure 15-2. Another example of a situational awareness dashboard, this time showing a number of different types of attack/scanner detections. Spikes and extended shifts in behavior should prompt the security team to follow up to investigate the cause.

If a situational dashboard is dealing with user identifying information, such as a username, then care should be taken to pseudonymize that information to avoid creating a display that feels implicitly blameful or that becomes a source of embarrassment.

An example where such obfuscation of data could well be prudent would be dashboards showing the recent VPN logins of users and the location from which the login originated. A pseudonymized identifier for the user is still useful for a security team to see events that team members may want to follow up on without displaying the real names associated with any such events. Then as part of the team's follow-up, the pseudonymized identifier can be reversed back to a real user ID, which will be used to track down what may be happening.

Summary dashboards are really just a dashboard representation of periodic data roll-ups or executive summaries. Examples of summary dashboards would be displays of data like "total number of reported phishing emails in the last four weeks," "dollars paid out in bug bounty this year," or "external ports shown as open in the last portscan." They present historic data summaries, often with minimal or no trend data, such as the week-over-week change.

Of the four dashboard categories, it can be argued that summary dashboards are the least useful for security teams, as they do not give information on the current state of security for a system or environment and so do not prompt responses or actions from a security team. They also have minimal value in terms of eliciting engagement from others. Summary dashboards don't really provide much more information besides, *Look! We've been doing things*. Most of the information they show is better provided in rollup emails or executive summaries sent to those who need to know on a periodic basis. If space is at a premium, then look to your summary dashboards as the first to drop.

The mixture of the types of dashboards that make most sense for your organization is something that only you can determine; but collecting analytics on the interactions they prompt, anecdotal or otherwise, of the different mixtures of dashboards would be encouraged. If the dashboards displayed on big screens are also made available on the intranet for people to view in their browsers' tracking hits can also be a useful proxy metric for the level of interest different dashboards create.

Vanity dashboards cover those dashboards that display data or visualizations that actually have minimal direct value to the security team's day-to-day work. Instead, their purpose is to look cool and cause passersby to pause and watch, and hopefully, ask a question about what the cool stuff is.

Vanity dashboards often are the least data-dense of any of the dashboard categories, and value looking cool over actually showing data that can be acted upon. Common examples are animated spinning 3D globes showing the geographic sources of incoming attacks, or current top malware being detected/blocked in email. Many security vendors make such animated dashboards freely available on their websites, in the hope that animations that look like they are in Swordfish will convince you to buy their wares. Still, they can be a great source of vanity dashboards for minimal effort. If you would like to build your very own PewPew map (with sound!), there is an open source project called pewpew (*https://github.com/hrbrmstr/pewpew*) that will get you started and has lots of options for you to tweak and enhance (see Figure 15-3). Creating fun and ever-changing maps can be a lighthearted way to build a positive security culture for both the security team and the people that will get to view the results.

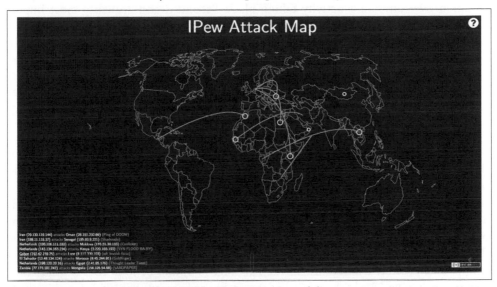

Figure 15-3. An example of a PewPew map, courtesy of the pewpew opensource project (https://github.com/hrbrmstr/pewpew).

Despite the flashy appearance and low informational value of vanity dashboards, they can carry with them some of the highest cultural impact, as they play on the interest many people across an organization have about security (or *hacking*). They also create great opportunities for people to engage with the security team to talk about what all the laser shots coming from Eastern Europe to the data center actually mean. They are also the ones that people will often pause for a few seconds to watch, which presents an opportunity for security team members to chat with someone about that low-priority alert associated with their IP that came through earlier on.

Of the four types of dashboards, vanity dashboards are those that you should look to switch up periodically to keep them fresh and to continue to illicit engagement from the organization.

Intervention dashboards are possibly the simplest of all the dashboards, as well as being the ones that are (hopefully) seen least often. The sole purpose of intervention dashboards is to alert a security team to a critical situation requiring immediate attention; they are triggered by some pre-configured event and should interrupt the display any of the other types of dashboards. Examples of intervention dashboards would be events such as a critical credential has been detected as being leaked to GitHub, or that an internal honeypot is being interacted with.

Intervention dashboards have a couple of specific benefits beyond other types of alerts and notifications that a security team will likely already be using. Firstly they are a public collective alert. When an intervention dashboard is triggered, the entire security team is made aware at the same time and can prioritize the response to the situation over any other activity taking place. Secondly, and arguably most importantly, intervention dashboards allow others within an organization to see that a serious event is in flight and that the security team is working on understanding and/or responding to the situation. While this second point may self-obvious or self-evident, the value of people outside of a security team being aware that something security related is underway not only facilitates greater empathy for the work of a security team, but also results in future opportunities to engage and educate when people enquire about what is happening.

Some rules of thumb for intervention dashboards are that they should be reserved for the most critical security events that are being monitored, and the frequency of them being displayed should be low and result in an all-hands-on-deck response from the security team. The subject of any intervention dashboard should also be readily actionable, ideally having a dedicated runbook associated with them that drives the initial response and information gathering activity. The data density of intervention dashboards should be low, with a clear description of the triggering event, a timestamp, and possibly a reference to the runbook or initial actions that should come first in a response. The look and feel of the dashboard screen that is triggered is pretty much a free-for-all as long as it is immediately noticeable and stands out from the other dashboards in the rotation; for example, a plain red screen with flashing white Arial text, or a gif of an angry honey badger could both serve this purpose equally well (angry honey badgers are way cooler though).

For any of the dashboards to be available and useful, the correct monitoring and data collection needs to be in place. Approaches to security relevant monitoring are covered in Chapter 8, *Threat Assessments and Understanding Attacks*.

Key Takeaways

So we made it through our cultural journey! Here are some key things to be thinking about in terms of developing a progressive security culture:

- You have a security culture whether you know it or not; the question is whether you want to take ownership of it.
- People are just as important as technology when thinking about security, but have been underserved in many of the traditional approaches to security. An effective security culture puts people at the center when thinking about solutions.
- Your security culture will be unique to you. There isn't a cookie-cutter approach.

- Enabling, transparent, and blameless are the core principles of Etsy's security culture that provide the foundations upon which everything else is built.
- Treat your security culture as a brand, take it seriously, and recognize that it is hard-fought and easily lost.

CHAPTER 16

What Does Agile Security Mean?

Agile, and Agile security, mean different things to different people and can be done in different ways.

Each of us has had very different experiences with Agile security, and different stories to tell. We've encountered different problems and have come up with different solutions. And we would like to share some of this with you.

Laura's Story

My pathway to getting here has been wobbly, a career made largely of serendipity and asking people, "But what if?" at the worst possible moments.

My friends and security community in New Zealand know me as a security cat herder, and a chaotic force (hopefully for good), but not someone that people really understand to begin with.

I've skipped a bit though. Let me show you how I got here (please stay with me; it's relevant, I promise).

Not an Engineer but a Hacker

I'm from a family of people who get stuff done. We build things: bridges, helicopters, biochemical things. It's in our blood. We are a group of people who don't so much like the rules and formalities of our fields, but each of us is excellent at asking, "How can I do x?" and just doing it anyway. We are scrappy fighters who love to build things and make them better, faster, and stronger.

In my family, this was called hacking, and I never questioned it.

For various reasons, my childhood dream of being Sculley from the X-Files never happened, and I found myself employed as an apprentice software developer (in COBOL) at 17. This was 2001.

Suddenly, the family skills I had acquired for building gadgets and fixing things turned into code. I was able to build systems and stick my tinkerer's fingers into taxation systems and banks. I was in my element.

Years passed, and I studied for a degree and graduated while accumulating a string of interesting software development jobs. I'd spent time at CERN in Switzerland, UK government agencies, and even a strange summer as a web developer. I'd written production code in multiple languages, created safety-critical systems and robots. It had been quite the adventure.

The trouble was, I was still the same scrappy hacker underneath it all, and this gave me a super power. I was really good at finding bugs in software, particularly security-related ones. I was able to see the many ways a workflow would go wrong, or strange edge cases that weren't considered.

Rather than this making me a useful member of the team, this made me trouble. Where I touched, delays and complications would follow. This was not the skillset of a software engineer.

Your Baby Is Ugly and You Should Feel Bad

So when you find that you are more adept at breaking software than at building elegant engineered designs, you need to find a niche that suits you.

For me, that became Red Teaming and penetration testing.

I spent seven years breaking software around the world and telling hardworking developers that their new baby was ugly and they should feel bad. I also learned to do the same with human systems, through social engineering and manipulation.

While this was fun to begin with, I had moved away from my roots. I was no longer building things and solving problems. I was breaking things.

The worst part of it was that I understood how the mistakes were made. I'd been a developer for long enough by then that I had empathy and full understanding for the circumstances that led to insecure code. Slowly, as the same issues cropped up again and again, I realized that breaking systems wasn't going to change things alone. We had to start changing the way software was built to begin with.

Speak Little, Listen Much

In 2013, I began researching. I needed to understand why so many developers around me were writing vulnerable code and why so few teams were working with security. I spent six months buying developers and managers tea and cake, and asking them the same question.

How does security work in your world?

The answers were depressing.

Time after time, the message was clear. The understanding was there. We knew that we should care about security, but the help and techniques that were offered didn't work. They were patronizing or inappropriate, judgmental and slow.

I was meeting a community of people who wanted to do their jobs well, who wanted to build amazing products; and to them, my community (the security world) were the people who turned up uninvited, were rude, and caused them pain.

Something had to change.

Let's Go Faster

In 2014, I started SafeStack. My aim was to help companies go really fast while staying secure. I started out in August and gave myself until December to find a customer. If it didn't work out, I would get a real job.

The old-school governance and gate-driven approaches of my past were cast out (they hadn't worked for 15 years anyway), and we started with a blank slate.

Step one was build for survival, focusing our efforts on responding to incidents and knowing there were issues.

From then on, we took each of the normal controls we would recommend in a governance approach. We broke them down into their actual objectives (what they were trying to achieve) and found the simplest ways we could to automate or implement them. We liked to call this minimum viable security.

It was a rough-and-ready, low-documentation, hands-on approach relying on pragmatism and the idea that we could incrementally improve security over time rather than try and conquer it all at once.

I was back to my roots. I was hacking in the way that my family had taught me, but with the intention of making people safer. I was never going to build my own digital cathedral. I'm not wired for that. I was going to help dozens of others build their amazing creations and help protect them as they do.

Trouble was, I was just one person. By December 2014, I was working with 11 organizations and more were on their way.

To get this working, I had to get help. I built a team around me, and we rallied the developers and engineers to help us solve problems. After all, this was their world, and they are born problem solvers.

Creating Fans and Friends

Fundamental in all of this was the idea that we (the security team) were no longer allowed to be special-power-wielding distractions. We had to become a much-loved supporting cast. We needed to build a network of fans, friends, and evangelists to become our eyes and ears inside the teams, to help scale.

This should all seem familiar. Everything I have helped share in this book comes from these experiences.

We Are Small, but We Are Many

Since 2014, I have helped over 60 organizations in 7 countries with this mission, from tiny 4-person teams to giant corporations and government departments.

For some, resources were plenty; for others, we had nothing but what we could script and knock together ourselves. In many cases these organizations had no security team, no CISO, and nobody on the ground with a dedicated security focus.

This is my happy place. This is where I herd my cats.

Security doesn't have to be something you do once you are rich or well resourced. Security is about collaborative survival. Once you have a team working alongside you as allies, you can achieve great, secure things and go fast regardless of your circumstances.

Jim's Story

Most of my experience has been in development, operations, and program management. I've never worked as a pen tester or a security hacker. I've always been on the other side of the field, playing defense, building things rather than breaking them. For the last 20 years or so, I've worked in financial markets, putting in electronic trading and clearing platforms in stock exchanges and banks around the world. In these systems, security—confidentiality and integrity of data, service availability, and compliance—is as important as speed, scalability, and feature set.

But the way that we think about security, and the way that we work, has changed a lot over that time. I used to manage large programs that could take several years to complete. Lots of detailed requirements specification and planning at the beginning, and lots of testing and stress at the end.

Security was more of a data center design and network architecture problem. If you set up your closed environment correctly, bad guys couldn't get in; and if they did, your surveillance and fraud analysis systems would catch them.

The internet, and the cloud, changed all of this of course. And so did Agile development, and now DevOps.

Today we're pushing out changes much, much faster. Release cycles are measured in days at most, instead of months or years. And security is as much of a problem for developers as it is for system engineering and for the network team and data center providers. It's no longer a thing that developers can leave to somebody else. We think about security all the time: in requirements, design, coding, testing, and implementation.

These are some of the important things that I've learned about security in an Agile world.

You Can Build Your Own Security Experts

We talk a lot in this book about building an Agile security team, and how the security team needs to work with engineering. But you can build a secure system and an effective security program without a dedicated security team.

At the organization that I help lead now, we don't have an independent security team. I own the security program, but responsibility for implementing it is shared between different engineering groups. I've found that if you take security out of a legal and compliance frame and make it a set of technical problems that need to be solved, your best technical people will rise to the challenge.

To make this work, you'll need to give people enough time to learn and enough time to do a good job. Get them good help early, tools, and training. But most important, you need to make security an engineering priority, and you need to walk the talk. If you compromise on security and try to cut corners to hit deadlines or to keep down costs, you'll lose their commitment, and kill your security program.

This isn't a one-time commitment from you or from your team. You'll need to be patient and relentless, reinforcing how important security is. You'll need to make it safe for people to treat failures as learning opportunities. And you'll need to reinforce successes.

When engineers and team leads stop thinking about pen tests and audits as nonsense compliance and see them as important opportunities to learn and improve, as challenges to their competence, then you know you're making real progress.

Not everybody will "get security," but not everybody has to. Sure you need to train everyone on the basics so they know what not to do and to make compliance happy. A few hours here or there, broken into little bite-size pieces, should be enough—and is probably all that they will put up with. Because most engineers really just need to know what frameworks or templates to use, to keep their eyes open for sensitive data, and learn to rely on their tools.

The people who select or build those frameworks and templates, the people who build or implement the tools, are the ones who need to understand security at a deeper technical level. These are the people you need to get engaged in your security program. These are the people you need to send to OWASP meetings and to advanced training. These are the people you need to get working with pen testers and auditors and other security experts, to challenge them and to be challenged by them. These are the people who can provide technical leadership to the rest of the team, who can reinforce good practices, and ensure that the team makes sound technical decisions.

You won't be able to do all this without leaning on someone who eats and breathes security, at least in the beginning. Get a security expert to help on early design and platform decisions to make sure that the team understands security threats and risks and the right ways to deal with them from the start. And as we've talked about in this book, you'll probably need to go outside for security check-ups and tune-ups along the way to make sure that you're staying on track and keeping up with new threats.

The best way that I've seen this implemented is Adobe's security "karate belt" program (*http://www.adobe.com/content/dam/Adobe/en/security/pdfs/adb_security-culture-wp.pdf*). Everyone on each engineering team should have at least a white belt —or better, a green belt—enough training to help them stay out of trouble. Someone on the team needs to be a brown belt, with the the skills to defend against real attacks. And teams should have access to a black belt, a master whom they can ask for advice and guidance when they aren't sure what to do, or who can come in and get them out of a really bad situation.

This is truly scalable down to small teams and up to the biggest organizations. It's probably the only way to scale security for Agile teams.

Choose People over Tools

You can't move safely at speed without automation. But be careful, different tools work better for different projects and platforms. One size doesn't fit all.

When it comes to tools, simpler is usually better. You can take tools that solve specific problems and chain them together in your build pipelines. Tools that are easy to install and use, that run fast, and that can be managed through APIs are more useful than standardized enterprise platforms with management dashboards and built-in compliance reporting.

Security tools have improved a lot over the last 10 years, they are more accurate, easier to integrate, easier to understand, faster, and more reliable. But tools can only take you so far, as we've seen in this book. People (the right people) make an important difference.

Smart people making good decisions up front, asking the right questions, and thinking about security in requirements and design, will solve a lot of important security problems for the team. Dangerous vulnerabilities like SQL injection and CSRF and

XSS, and access control violations can be prevented by building protection into frameworks and templates, and making sure that everyone knows how to use them properly. Make it easy for engineers to write secure code and you'll get secure code.

You need to take advantage of automated scanning and continuous testing to keep up. But there's still an important role for manual reviews: reviewing requirements, as well as design and code to catch mistakes in understanding and in implementation. And for manual testing too. Good exploratory testing, running through real-world scenarios, and hunting for bugs can find problems that automated testing can't, and will tell you where you have important gaps in your reviews and suites.

Learn to lean on your tools. But depend on your people to keep you out of trouble.

Security Has to Start with Quality

A lot of security isn't black magic. It's just about being careful and thoughtful, about thinking through requirements and writing good, clean code.

Vulnerabilities are bugs. The more bugs in your code, the more vulnerabilities. Go back and look at some of the high-severity security bugs that we've talked about in this book, like Heartbleed and Apple's Goto Fail. They were caused by bad coding, or inadequate testing, or both. Mistakes that teams who aren't forced to work under unfair conditions could catch in code reviews or testing, or prevent by following good coding guidelines and disciplined refactoring.

Thinking defensively and preparing for the unexpected, protecting your code from other people's mistakes (and your own mistakes), checking for bad data, and making sure that you can handle exceptions properly, will make your system more reliable and more resilient to runtime failures, and it will also make it more secure.

Like a lot of software engineering, this isn't that hard to understand, but it is hard to get right. It takes discipline, care, and time. But it will take you a long way to better, and safer code.

You Can Make Compliance an Everyday Thing

Compliance is an unavoidable yet necessary evil in industries like the financial markets or health care. But you can find ways to do this on your terms. To do this, you have to get things out of legal policies and generic compliance guidelines and into concrete requirements and asserts, problems that engineering people can understand and solve, and tests that need to be added.

The DevOps Audit Defense Toolkit that we walked through in the compliance chapter is something that more people need to know about. Using it as a guide will help you to understand how to get compliance into code, out of documents and spreadsheets and into your build pipelines and regular operations workflows. Writing security and compliance policies directly into code, and automating the tests and scans to make sure that they are enforced will take time, but you can leverage a lot of the automation that Agile and DevOps teams are already using, and again, the tools keep getting better.

Once you have this in place, it changes everything. You know (and you can prove) that every change is handled in the same way, every time. You know (and you can prove) what tests and checks were done, every time. You get full auditability and traceability built in: you can tell what was changed, by who, and when it was changed, every time. Compliance becomes another part of what people do, and how they work.

Sure, auditors still want to see policy documents. But rules automatically enforced in tests, rules and checks that you can prove you are following every day? Priceless.

Michael's Story

Like my coauthors, it is a bit of a mystery to me how I got here. I've stood on stage in front of hundreds of people, explaining how to do security well, and thought to myself, "How have I got any right to tell anyone this?"

I've worked in a variety of industries, worked with hardware designers and people who programmed Z80 microprocessors in early 2003, with a financial startup writing low-latency web servers, and a games company writing networking code for XBoxes, Playstations and PSPs. Eventually I managed to settle into *The Guardian* newspaper just as they were embarking on one of the biggest and newest Agile technology programs.

I'd been following the Agile world for most of my career, and I'd been doing test-driven development in C++ back in the Bingo world, and the financial startup had been doing early Scrum by the book (30-day sprints, immutable backlogs—the entire shebang).

Now I was joining a team delivering using XP, with some of the smartest Agile thinkers from Thoughtworks.

The *Guardian* project started as a typical XP project, but we started to tinker. We built information radiators and looked at the value of build systems. I worked equally with developers and systems administrators, working to see how we could automate every step of our manual systems where possible. I probably spent more time dealing with the frameworks around writing code than I did writing code.

Over seven years, we took that team on a helter-skelter ride, from an organization that developed the code by SSH'ing onto the development server, writing the code in VIM, and deploying by using FTP to copy the code repository into production, into an organization that used distributed version control, AWS cloud services, and deployed into production automatically hundreds of times per day.

We made each of the steps because we needed to fix an internal problem, and we had a great mix of skills in the team that could take a step back and instead of creating a small iterative improvement, ask whether we could make a more fundamental change that would help more.

From there I went to the UK's Government Digital Service. It was always intended that I was joining government as a technical and Agile expert. I knew how to build highly scalable systems on the cloud, and I knew how to build teams that not just followed the Agile process, but could actively adopt and use it effectively.

I had forgotten my teenage love affair with security, but if there's one thing there's a lot of in government, it's security.

Every team in government was wrestling with the same problems. They wanted to start building software, delivering it fast, but the government security machinery was opaque and difficult to deal with. I found teams that were informed that the IP addresses of their live systems were classified information which they weren't allowed to know. I found teams that were being told that a government security manual (which was classified so they couldn't read it) said that they were only allowed to deploy software by burning the software onto CD. I found security teams that insisted that the only valid language the development team could use was C or C++ because of, you guessed it, a classified government security manual.

I had two secret weapons in my arsenal here. I had a sufficiently high clearance that I could go and find these manuals and read them, and GDS had started to build up a relationship with people from GCHQ who had written these manuals.

We discovered that much of this advice was outdated, was contextual (C and C++ are recommended languages if you are building cryptographic operations in embedded hardware devices—the manual was never intended for people writing web applications!), and was being misunderstood and misused.

So I set about fixing this. One step at a time, I went to almost every government department, I met their security teams, and I realized that over the years, departments had been systematically de-skilled security. Very rarely did I meet a technologist who could understand government security, or a security person who understood modern technology.

In my time as a developer, the industry had shifted from Waterfall to Agile, from packaged software to continual releases, and from single monolithic systems to vast interconnected networks of systems. Very few security people in government had the time or inclination to keep up with these changes.

I resolved to be the change, to try to be the person who understood both security and technology! I'd had enough of a misspent childhood to understand hacking, and I'd spent far too long in development teams; I knew the technology and the way things were moving.

I've come to the conclusion that we are on the precipice of a startlingly dangerous moment in computer history. The uptake of computer systems is far higher than at any time in history, and it will only continue. We are going to see dramatic changes in the number and scale of systems that are connected to one another, and the way that this will change the systems is almost unknowable. Connected cars and cities, the Internet of Things, and computer-powered healthcare are just the tip of iceberg.

Knowledge of security hasn't kept up. While some of the brightest minds in security are looking at these problems, the vast majority of security people are worrying about computing problems from the early 90s. We're still blaming users for clicking phishing emails, we're still demanding passwords with unmemorable characteristics, and we are still demanding paper accreditations that cover computer security principles from the 60s (Bell & LePadula say hi).

There are four main principles at work here.

Security Skills Are Unevenly Distributed

Top developers are still writing code that contains the simplest class of security problem. From SQL injection attacks to buffer overflows, the level of security knowledge given to junior and beginning developers is woefully inadequate.

Furthermore, languages and frameworks tend to push the cognitive load up to the developer, when the developer is clearly uninterested or incapable of making the appropriate choices. Major cryptographic libraries allow the developer to make deliberate choices that are insecure, or worse, come with defaults or sample code that is insecure.

We could insist that all developers are security experts, but that's not feasible. Security isn't terribly interesting or fun to most people, and like many things, it takes a lot of effort to get beyond the apprentice level of blindly doing as you are told to start to see and understand the patterns and reapply them in novel situations.

Instead, we need to ensure that secure is the default operation for tools, languages, and frameworks. We need our best security people to be focused on building tools that are secure and usable, and we need to ensure that it's much easier to use things correctly and securely.

Security Practitioners Need to Get a Tech Refresh

I've sat in meetings with expert security people, with self-proclaimed decades of experience in security, who have told me that I need to pass every JSON message in an internal microservices architecture through an antivirus sheep dip.

These people have technical skills that are woefully out of date, and they cannot possibly begin to understand the problems that they are causing by insisting on applying patterns they don't understand to technological contexts that they don't understand.

If a security person is working with modern technology systems, he needs to understand what a cloud architecture looks like. He needs to understand the difference between user-based uploads and machine-generated messages. He needs to understand how fast deployments and changes can happen and how code is reused in the modern era.

Given how hard it has been to educate some of these people on how differently you manage servers in a Cattle-based IaaS, then trying to explain or understand the security implications of a PaaS like Kubernates, or even worse a Function As A Service like AWS Lambda feels impossible.

While these security people cannot understand the technologies they are securing, they cannot hope to be helpful to the organization in enabling change and enabling the business to achieve its goals.

Accreditation and Assurance Are Dying

The old-school world of built packages and systems produced to specification is ideally suited to accreditation and assurance mindsets. If you can compare the intended behavior to the actual behavior, you can build confidence in how the system is going to perform.

As technology creates increasing levels of abstraction, and technical teams use ever more complex tools and platforms, the ability to provide assurance is rapidly reduced.

We need a replacement for these capabilities. We need to understand what value they are intended to deliver, and how they change to fit a new set of practices.

There will always be some area of software development that will use these mechanisms. I don't for one moment expect that the flight controllers on a fighter jet be updated over the air several times per hour!

But knowing the context and usability of these techniques matters, and we need to be able to pick and choose from a variety of options to get the level of confidence in the systems that we use.

Security Is an Enabler

I feel like this will be the epitaph on my gravestone. If security exists for any reason, it is as an enabling function to enable the rest of the organization to deliver on its mission as fast and safely as possible.

While anybody considers security to get in the way, it will be worked around, ignored, or paid lip service. We cannot simply force the business to bend to the will of security and attempts to try won't work.

Risk management should be about enabling the organization to take appropriate risks, not about preventing the organization from taking risks. Building a security team that can do this requires combining technologists and security people into a single, working team and ensuring that everyone understands their role in helping the organization.

Rich's Story

As with all the authors who contributed to this book, my journey to getting here is not one that has too much overlap with anyone else's. More luck than judgment was involved with me ending up in the security field, with more than a few detours on the way.

What follows is the somewhat potted history of how I ended up in the position of being invited to write a book about security, and is actually the first time I have ever gone through the process of actually writing down my security history. In doing so I gained a much better understanding of myself in terms of how my perspectives on security have developed over time, and how I have arrived at where I currently am on my security journey. I hope that some of the steps along my pathway will resonate with you as you read, and if not, will at least be an entertaining anti-pattern of how not to go about getting into the security industry!

The First Time Is Free

I was a geek from a young age, writing my first programs in BASIC on an Acorn Electron around the age of 7 or 8. While I will spare the reader from the variety of fun games and misdeeds that got me to a place where I was able to earn a legitimate living from security, I will share what I am pretty sure was the first hack I successfully pulled off.

I'm not sure of my exact age, but best guess I was 8 or 9, and the target was my older brother who was 14 or 15 at the time. We shared use of the Acorn computer, and in typical sibling fashion he wanted to keep his little brother from playing with his toys, in this case by password-protecting the floppy disks that held the games he had copied from friends at school. I wanted to play those games pretty badly, and this gave me the motivation to work out how to bypass the protection he had placed onto the disks.

The attack was far from complex. The lightly obfuscated password was hardcoded into the BASIC source that was on the disk, and a few advanced disc filing system

(ADFS) commands allowed me to interrupt the code from being interpreted when the disk was loaded, list the source, and unscramble the password.

While very simplistic, I distinctly remember feeling on top of the world at getting at the games my brother had worked to keep from me, and I still get the same feeling even now when I successfully circumvent something that has been put there to stop me.

A few years later I was given an old modem by a generous coworker of my father and was able to access BBSs on the local provider, Diamond Cable, and from there I was pretty much hooked. A lot of "learning by doing" took place to satisfy innocent curiosities, and as I grew into my teenage years, the internet happened, and I became more explicitly interested in "hacking."

What I lacked in any formal computer or programming training, I was lucky enough to make up for in acquaintances (both online and IRL) who were generous with their knowledge and were patient with helping me understand. I have often wondered what this stage of my journey would have been like if the security industry was already a thing at that time and there was money to be made. Would people have been less willing to share? I would like to think not, but I worry that the genuine sense of exploration and desire to understand how things work would have been lost to the goal of making money and far stricter computer misuse laws. While there is more information about hacking and security more freely available today than ever before, I am convinced that the then relative scarcity of available information made the whole endeavor more satisfying and community oriented. I consider myself lucky to have been growing up and learning about security as BBSs gave way to the internet and all that followed. If I were starting out now I'm not sure I would have been half as successful as I was back then.

This Can Be More Than a Hobby?

With that as my start, my background in professional security was, for a very long time, solely offensive. Vulnerability research, exploit and attack tool development, along with a heavy helping of pen-testing, Red Teaming, and consulting across a number of companies and countries. This eventually culminated in building up a small company of old-skool hackers, called Syndis, performing made to order goal-oriented attack engagements from Reykjavík, Iceland.

For me, security directly related to finding new ways to break into systems, and I cared little for how to look for systemic solutions to the issues I found; it was the issues alone I found motivating. I was in the church of problem worship. Looking back at the earlier stages of my career, I am certain that I demonstrated many of the less than desirable characteristics of the stereotypical security asshole that I have warned you away from in these very pages. I suppose it takes one to know one.

A Little Light Bulb

It was really only after starting up Syndis that my interest moved beyond the purely technical joy of breaking and circumvention, and into the challenges that came with trying to build defensive solutions that had a realistic understanding of the way an attacker actually approached and compromised systems. While I was leading some security consulting engagements at Etsy, I observed that the security team's approaches of *attack-driven defense* dovetailed nicely with *Goal-oriented attack* methodologies . With the benefit of hindsight I can see they were flip sides of the same coin, but this was not something I was particularly aware of (or cared about) at the time.

Then something really weird happened—it became less about the technical problems and trying to measure my worth by how low of a level of understanding I had of a particular esoteric system or technology, and more about the intersection of technology and people. A little light bulb went off for me that while I could be considered to have been relatively successful in my chosen field, I had unknowingly only actually been recognizing and addressing half of the problem. The user, that soft underbelly that social engineering or a spear-phishing attack would so readily expose, became ever clearer as the key to actually being able to make any meaningful progress of making things better. Security is a human problem, despite how hard the industry has been working to convince itself otherwise and make things all about the technology.

By this point I had conducted hundreds of attack service engagements, resulting in the compromise of tens of thousands of systems, across a wide range of industry verticals, in many countries, and the results were always the same—I won. Given enough motivation and time, the attack goals were achieved, and the customer got a detailed report of just how their complex systems were turned against them. In well over a decade dedicated to this work, there was no feeling that the task of compromise was getting harder. If anything, quite the opposite—successful compromise increasingly seemed a given, it just became a series of footnotes as to how it was achieved on that particular engagement.

Computers Are Hard, People Are Harder

So now that the light bulb had gone off, what changed? Most concretely, I became far more aware of the challenges associated with having a human-centric view of security, and the importance of having a strong culture around security and its recognition. It also became far more readily apparent that the function of security experts was to support getting things done rather than acting as a blocking function: a small cognitive shift, but one that turns head over heels the way that one goes about security and possibly more importantly how others perceive security and those who practice. Together, along with innumerable smaller revelations that I continue to recognize, the foundations have been laid for my next phase of learning about how to make systems, and by extension, people, more secure. While I still get an incredible amount of exhilaration from finding security issues and exploiting them, I get fulfillment from trying to address the challenge of solutions that have people and usability at their core.

And Now, We're Here

So it's taken a while to get here, but if you ask me what Agile security means to me, it's the clear articulation that people are just as crucial to a secure solution as any technology or math. It's the progressive mindset taken to the problem of keeping people secure that also recognizes it's carrots, not sticks, that result in meaningful change. It's the admission that the security industry has up until shockingly recently tasked itself with selling expensive sticks with which to beat users while conveniently not measuring the effectiveness of those sticks but claiming success anyway. It's the understanding that focusing on half the problem will never get you a full solution, as you are just as clueless as you are informed. To me Agile security has little to do with Scrum or Lean or continuous deployment beyond the reasons they were conceived, and that is to put people at the center of the development process and to enable effective communication and collaboration.

This book caused me to pause and pull together much of what I learned on my security journey. During the crazy process of writing a book, I have learned a great deal from Jim, Laura, and Michael as well. I really hope it has been useful to you, and contributes in at least a small way to your own security journey. Thanks for inadvertently being part of mine.

Index

About the Authors

Laura Bell is the founder and lead consultant for SafeStack, a security training, development, and consultancy firm. Laura is a software developer and penetration tester specializing in the management of information and application security risk within startup and Agile organizations. Over the past decade she has held a range of security and development roles, and experienced firsthand the challenges of developing performant, scalable, and secure systems. Historically, the security function of an organization has been separate from the technical innovators; however, Laura educates clients and audiences that this no longer works in modern business because developers and implementers want to be empowered to understand their own security risk and address it.

Michael Brunton-Spall is the lead security architect for Government Technology, Government Digital Service, a service in the Cabinet Office of the UK government. He helps set and assess security standards, and advises on building secure services within government. He works as a consulting architect with a variety of government departments, helping them understand and implement Agile, DevOps, service operation, and modern web architectures. Previously, Michael has worked in the news industry, the gaming industry, the finance industry, and the gambling industry.

Rich Smith is the director of R&D for Duo Labs, supporting the advanced security research agenda for Duo Security. Prior to joining Duo, Rich was Director of Security at Etsy, cofounder of Icelandic red team startup, Syndis, and has held various roles on security teams at Immunity, Kyrus, Morgan Stanley, and HP Labs. Rich has worked professionally in the security space since the late 1990s covering a range of activities including building security organizations, security consulting, penetration testing, red teaming, offensive research, and developing exploits and attack tooling. He has worked in both the public and private sectors in the US, Europe, and Scandinavia, and currently spends most of his time bouncing between Detroit, Reykjavik, and NYC.

Jim Bird is a CTO, software development manager, and project manager with more than 20 years of experience in financial services technology. He has worked with stock exchanges, central banks, clearinghouses, securities regulators, and trading firms in more than 30 countries. He is currently the CTO of a major US-based institutional alternative trading system.

Jim has been working in Agile and DevOps environments in financial services for several years. His first experience with incremental and iterative ("step-by-step") development was back in the early 1990s, when he worked at a West Coast tech firm that developed, tested, and shipped software in monthly releases to customers around the world—he didn't realize how unique that was at the time. Jim is active in the

DevOps and AppSec communities, is a contributor to the Open Web Application Security Project (OWASP), and helps out as an analyst for the SANS Institute.

Colophon

The animal on the cover of *Agile Application Security* is an Egyptian yellow-billed kite (*Milvus aegyptius*). In Latin, Milvus means "kite" and aegyptius means "of Egypt," thus a kite from Egypt. Accurate enough, although the bird is found throughout most of Africa.

As suggested by its common name, it is easily recognized by its yellow bill. Its plumage is brown and its legs and feet are unfeathered, revealing skin as yellow as its beak. It measures about 55 cm (22 in.) in length and its wingspan is between 160–180 cm (5 ft., 3 in.–5 ft., 11 in.). The yellow-billed kite has a slow-sailing flight with a widespread tail and pinions that appear motionless. The rudder-like tail enables it to turn with ease. It is graceful in flight, and capable of bursts of surprising speed.

Like many other raptors, it relies on termites as a major food source. It grabs the termites with its talons and eats them in flight. The yellow-billed kite also frequents the quieter stretches of road where it forages for carrion. Urban areas suit this bird well, as it is not uncommon for the kite to swoop down and steal food from humans or other birds.

The yellow-billed kites are monogamous during the breeding season. If the male brings sufficient food, the female may not hunt during the entire breeding attempt. The kite builds a bowl-shaped nest of sticks in the canopy of a suitable tree, lining it with bits of soft material that can be found. The female lays a clutch of two or three white eggs that hatch after an incubation period of about 35 days. Chicks leave the nest after 42–56 days, but will depend on both parents for another 15–50 days.

Many of the animals on O'Reilly covers are endangered; all of them are important to the world. To learn more about how you can help, go to *animals.oreilly.com*.

The cover image is from *Lydekker's Royal Natural History*. The cover fonts are URW Typewriter and Guardian Sans. The text font is Adobe Minion Pro; the heading font is Adobe Myriad Condensed; and the code font is Dalton Maag's Ubuntu Mono.

Learn from experts.
Find the answers you need.

Sign up for a **10-day free trial** to get **unlimited access** to all of the content on Safari, including Learning Paths, interactive tutorials, and curated playlists that draw from thousands of ebooks and training videos on a wide range of topics, including data, design, DevOps, management, business—and much more.

Start your free trial at:

oreilly.com/safari

(No credit card required.)

Milton Keynes UK
Ingram Content Group UK Ltd.
UKHW051538210924
448609UK00002B/9